THE BEDFORD BIBLIOGRAPHY
for
TEACHERS OF
WRITING
Fourth Edition

THE BEDFORD BIBLIOGRAPHY *for* TEACHERS OF WRITING

Fourth Edition

Patricia Bizzell
College of the Holy Cross

Bruce Herzberg
Bentley College

Bedford Books *of* St. Martin's Press
BOSTON

For Bedford Books
President and Publisher: Charles H. Christensen
General Manager and Associate Publisher: Joan E. Feinberg
Managing Editor: Elizabeth M. Schaaf
Developmental Editor: Laura Arcari
Editorial Assistant: Miranda Pinckert
Assistant Managing Editor: John Amburg
Production Assistant: Stasia Zomkowski
Copyeditors: Sunny Salibian & Ara Salibian
Cover Design: Hannus Design Associates

Manufactured in the United States of America.

0 9 8 7 6
f e d c b a

For information, write: St. Martin's Press, Inc.
175 Fifth Avenue, New York, NY 10010

Editorial Offices: Bedford Books *of* St. Martin's Press
75 Arlington Street, Boston, MA 02116

ISBN: 0-312-11556-3

Preface

In the opening sentence of the preface to the first edition of *The Bedford Bibliography* in 1984, we stated that "The study of composition is well established as a specialization in English, a serious discipline worthy of advanced graduate work." The former claim we based on the growing quantity and sophistication of scholarship in the field, on the rising numbers of composition specialists being hired and tenured, and on the appearance of more and more courses on composition theory and pedagogy in graduate-school offerings. Still, our claim that the field was "well established" may have been just a little tendentious—a statement of confidence and hope rather than a clear fact. Today, though, despite continuing problems of acceptance by literary traditionalists in some English departments, the study of composition seems unequivocally well established. The latter claim in our opening sentence, that the discipline was worthy of graduate work, was true then as now. Then, however, we had vanishingly few colleagues with degrees in composition, whereas now we are blessed with many.

More scholars means more scholarship: extraordinary growth in the quantity of scholarship in the discipline has been particularly evident to us in the time since the third edition of the *Bibliography* in 1991. Most notable is the proliferation of books, both edited collections and monographs. Relatively few books appeared in the 1984 edition—a half dozen collections of previously published articles and a couple of pedagogical books by single authors. In subsequent editions of the *Bibliography*, those numbers increased, to be sure, but preparing for the current edition, we faced unprecedented hundreds of books in history, theory, and every branch of pedagogy. In addition, new journals have arisen and established ones have flourished. Each year since the late 1980s, the comprehensive *CCCC Bibliography* has recorded between sixteen hundred and two thousand items. To add to the volume of scholarship to be considered for this edition of *The Bedford Bibliography*, we decided to include works on technical and business writing, English as a second language, and advanced composition, and to make separate categories for literacy studies, audience, and literature and composition.

Reviewing and selecting from this mass of material would have been impossible for the two of us alone. For past editions, we asked some colleagues for suggestions in their areas of expertise and benefited from suggestions offered by readers and reviewers, but for the current edition we formally enlisted a dozen consultants (identified and thanked in the Acknowledgments below) to sift through the materials in particular categories and suggest which books and essays should be considered for inclusion in the *Bibliography*. This task was not easy for any of us. Making selections has been very difficult.

Which books and essays should, indeed, go into the *Bedford Bibliography*? Since the first edition, we have described the *Bibliography*'s purpose this way:

> The materials available for study in this discipline are extensive and include not only the traditional works of rhetoric dating back over two

thousand years to ancient Greece but also a flood of research on writing produced in our own time. Dealing with this growing mass of material presents a serious challenge to both experienced and inexperienced teachers of writing, many of whom were trained exclusively in literary studies before composition was included in the graduate curriculum. *The Bedford Bibliography for Teachers of Writing* is intended as a guide for those who wish to extend their knowledge in this prospering discipline, knowledge that is essential for teaching English in colleges today. . . . In selecting works for the *Bibliography,* we have tried to represent the theoretical and pedagogical concerns in composition studies today. At the same time, we have tried to choose materials that will be useful to the working teacher of composition. We have thus omitted some works important for graduate study in the field but not immediately applicable to classroom practice.

For the most part, we have attempted to adhere to the same guidelines in the fourth edition. We recognize, however, that the *Bibliography* has been used in graduate courses in composition and that there are now many teachers who are specialists in the field. Although we continue to believe that the job of the *Bibliography* is to introduce the wide range of valuable scholarship in the field to the many writing teachers who are not specialists, we have indeed included citations for works of history, theory, and research that are not, strictly speaking, "immediately applicable to classroom practice" but which engage pressing issues for the discipline. We have had nonetheless to make some uncomfortable decisions about what theoretical issues, scholarly disputes, and research findings might or might not be of interest to this audience and about which of the older pedagogical materials included in past editions of the *Bibliography* have retained or lost their usefulness. Some pieces that should be on the reading lists of courses in composition theory or cited as milestones in the development of the field will thus not be found here.

In this fourth edition of the *Bibliography,* we have grouped the 455 entries under five major headings and twenty-six subheadings (see the table of contents). This attempt to organize the interests and concerns of the field reflects not only the great proliferation of scholarship since we prepared the last edition but also the inclusion of some new areas of study and the deletion of the "Related Fields" section, which appeared in previous editions.

First, under the heading "Resources," we have placed information on basic tools for research in the field, in the sections "Periodicals" and "General Bibliographies." (Bibliographies on specific topics appear in the appropriate sections.) Under the second major heading, "History and Theory," we have three subheads. "The Rhetorical Tradition" cites primary texts from classical to modern times. "History of Rhetoric and Education" consists of selected secondary texts covering the same period. "Rhetoric and Composition Theory" is a collection of important work done in recent years on discourse, argument, ideology, cultural studies, approaches to composition pedagogy and research, and other theoretical concerns.

The third major heading, "Composing Processes," is divided into sections roughly following the classical model of the composing process. Research on composing and theories of process, including work that discusses composing in social contexts, can be found in the first section under this heading, also called "Composing Processes." Next, "Invention: Heuristics and Pre-Writing" cites works about finding or developing ideas, corresponding to "invention" in classical rhetoric. These works deal with methods of exploring a subject and beginning to develop ideas through writing. "Arrangement and Argument" corresponds to "arrangement" in classical theory. Works cited here feature systems for classifying the structures of paragraphs and essays, structures that can be used to teach patterns for composing. Other works treat forms of argumentation, such as the enthymeme or the Toulmin model. "Audience," the next section, groups works defining audience and its uses in teaching writing. The next section, "Revision," includes works on the place of revision in the composing process, especially as a way of developing ideas. Under "Style, Grammar, and Usage" we have grouped works on sentence combining, other methods of increasing syntactic fluency in student writing, and prose style; we have also placed here works on teaching Standard English usage and grammar. "Response and Evaluation" includes works on responding to student writing, conference teaching, grading, portfolios, and assessment. The final section, "Literacy," is made up of works on literacy theory, cultural literacy, literacy programs, diversity, and teaching issues associated with these concerns.

The fourth major heading, "Curriculum Development," begins with a section, "Course Development," that includes works on writing-course design, innovations such as service learning, and teaching. Then special topics are addressed: "Collaborative Learning," works on the theory and practice of writing groups and peer response; "Essay and Personal Writing," works on the genre of the essay, on "voice" in writing, and on pedagogical techniques for helping students write more honestly and less pompously; "Literature and Composition," works on the theoretical connections between the two and on the use of literature in composition classes; "Basic Writing," works that help teachers to understand the circumstances of underprepared writers, the conditions of multicultural basic-writing classrooms, the kinds of errors beginning college writers make, and the effects on their writing of cultural and political considerations; and "Gender and Writing," works that address the influence of socially constructed gender roles and sexual orientation on writing, and techniques for feminist teaching. Three categories are new to this edition: "Advanced Composition," with works on history and theory as well as pedagogical techniques for teaching advanced writing courses; "English as a Second Language," with works analyzing the special problems of college writing for students whose first language is not English; and "Writing in the Workplace," which includes works on history, theory, research, and teaching in business and technical communication.

The fifth major heading, "Writing Programs," provides introductory material on administrative concerns. "Writing Program Administration" addresses program design and evaluation, teacher training, and working conditions; "Writing Centers" cites theoretical and practical works on setting up and managing tutorial workshops, including tutor training; "Writing across the Curriculum" provides material on cross-disciplinary course design and on faculty development in interdisciplinary writing programs; "Computers and Composition" cites recent work on using computers, hypertext, and networks in writing instruction.

In the annotations of articles and single-author books we attempt to summarize the thesis and main points of the work. In annotations of edited collections, of which there are now a great many, we characterize the central theme of the collection and then list several of the authors and essays included, choosing titles that give a sense of the contents of the collection. In collections of previously published articles we include cross-references if the article has been cited separately. For edited collections of new essays, however, we have, as a matter of policy, not cited articles separately when the entire collection is cited. We have been partial to edited collections whose themes are carefully articulated and whose contributors have adhered to the volume's stated purpose. We believe that these collections are a valuable contribution to the field.

The entries in the *Bedford Bibliography* are numbered consecutively. Numbers in brackets, used for citations in "A Brief History of Rhetoric and Composition" and for cross-references in the bibliographic listings, refer to these entry numbers and can also be used to locate items in the index.

In selecting works for the *Bedford Bibliography,* our chief concern has been to provide access to materials that would be helpful to practicing writing teachers. Even so, we have undoubtedly left out much that is important, despite our efforts—and the efforts of our consultants—to be fair, if not exhaustive. We welcome, as always, suggestions for revision.

Acknowledgments

We are grateful to the forty-six readers who generously answered our questionnaire about the *Bibliography*, providing us with detailed responses, suggesting changes, and commenting on the new format. We are particularly indebted to our consultants, without whom a daunting task would have been inconceivable. Thanks to David Bleich, University of Rochester; Beth Daniell, Clemson University; Lester Faigley, University of Texas at Austin; Linda Flower, Carnegie Mellon University; Elizabeth Flynn, Michigan Technological University; Janice Forman, UCLA; S. Michael Halloran, Rensselaer Polytechnic Institute; Muriel Harris, Purdue University; Deborah Holdstein, Governors State University; David Jolliffe, DePaul University; Kate Mangelsdorf, University of Texas at El Paso; Carolyn Miller, North Carolina State University; Joan Mullin, University of Toledo; Gary Olson, University of South Florida; Mike Rose, UCLA; John Schilb, University of Maryland; Kurt Spellmeyer, Rutgers University; Lad Tobin, Boston College; Myron Tuman, University of Alabama; and Vivian Zamel, University of Massachusetts, Boston. Thanks also to Laura Arcari, who worked with us on the project until, to our great regret, she left Bedford Books, and Miranda Pinckert, who saw the project through to completion. We can never forget that *The Bedford Bibliography* was the brainchild of Chuck Christensen, the guiding force behind all of Bedford's work. Finally, we warmly thank those who have used the *Bibliography* and told us that they found it helpful. They have made the project worthwhile.

Contents

CURRICULUM DEVELOPMENT   87

WRITING PROGRAMS   129

INDEX OF AUTHORS CITED   145

A Brief History of Rhetoric and Composition

Classical Rhetoric: Stages of Composing, Functions of Discourse

The formal study of rhetoric in the West began in Greece in the fifth century B.C.E. with the Sophists [40], followed by Isocrates [41], Plato [42], and Aristotle [43]. The main line of Greek rhetoric was extended by Roman rhetoricians, notably Cicero [44, 46] and Quintilian [48, 49]. Classical rhetoric, although concerned with oratory, still influences writing instruction. For example, by Roman times a five-stage model of the process of composing a speech had evolved. Three of these stages—invention, or discovering ideas; arrangement, or organizing ideas; and style, or putting ideas into words—have been modified into elements in modern models of writing processes. Memory and delivery, the last two classical stages, dwindled in postclassical times into mechanical techniques before being revived for serious study in modern departments of speech.

Scholars traditionally regarded classical rhetoric as a system with the built-in assumption that one first finds knowledge and then puts it into words. In our own day, in the context of a renewed interest in the Sophists, this view has been challenged by a number of historians of rhetoric, who argued that knowledge is actually created by words (see Jarratt [88] and Swearingen [106]). But the strongest influence on rhetoric has undoubtedly been the Aristotelian model. Aristotle described a number of *topoi,* or topics, for discovering ideas and arguments. These topics—ways of analyzing, evaluating, and extending virtually any subject—constitute a heuristic, or method of systematic inquiry.

Scholars have also emphasized classical rhetoric's sorting of discourse forms according to social function. Many classical rhetorics divide oratory into three categories. Deliberative speeches, primarily devoted to political purposes, aim to persuade hearers to choose or avoid some future course of action. Forensic speeches, used primarily in legal situations, aim to accuse or defend someone involved in a disputed past action. Epideictic speeches, produced in classical times on ceremonial occasions, aim to help hearers see some present event or person as worthy of praise or blame. Epideictic orations may make more use than others of literary ornaments and vocal pyrotechnics.

Although these classical categories for oral discourse have been reshaped by later rhetoricians, the premise that discourse can be classified according to social function has been persistently influential. In eighteenth-century American colleges, for example, discourse was classified according to its use by clergymen, lawyers, or politicians. Contemporary composition scholars have redirected the interest in social function to analyses of the ways in which audience or social context affects the interpretation of written text.

Medieval and Renaissance Rhetoric

We often think of the Middle Ages as a time when many classical sources were not accessible: Quintilian and much of Cicero, for example, were lost until the Renaissance. But it is more accurate to see medieval rhetoricians selecting and reshaping the classical heritage in light of Augustine's reinterpretation of rhetoric to suit Christian purposes [50]. One important emphasis in medieval rhetoric following Augustine was the redirection of deliberative discourse from political to religious ends. The goal became saving souls, not leading the state. Another important emphasis was the desire to codify authoritative classical precepts on good composition. Classical rhetoric texts had often been prescriptive, providing rules for achieving effective speeches. In the Middle Ages, this prescriptive impulse so intensified that many medieval rhetoric texts consist entirely of lists of rules and examples illustrating them.

Medieval university students studied grammar, rhetoric, and dialectic—the "trivium." As exemplified in the popular classical textbooks of Donatus, grammar means not simply the study of correct constructions but also the analysis of style. The study of grammar thereby shaded over into the medieval study of rhetoric, which emphasized style. Grammar and rhetoric merely prepared the beginning student for the serious business of the university, the study of dialectic, which offered practice in oral argumentation on historical, religious, or legal issues. Bishop Isidore of Seville wrote an important summary of the arts of grammar, rhetoric, and dialectic.

Dialectic was regarded as a preparation for logic, the oral arguments of which became opportunities for stylistic display, but the subject was still not considered closely allied with rhetoric. The study of rhetoric was manifested, however, in techniques for adult practitioners, for example, in *ars dictaminis*, the art of composing official letters through which church and state business was conducted, and *ars praedicandi*, the art of preaching. Medieval theorists of poetry also drew on rhetorical studies of style.

In the early Renaissance, major texts by Cicero and Quintilian were recovered. In the sixteenth century, a proliferation of rhetorics following classical models but written in the vernacular appeared, such as those in English by Leonard Cox, Richard Sherry, Thomas Wilson, and George Puttenham. Most of these rhetoricians emphasized the study of style, sometimes linking their practice explicitly with poetic. The generally acknowledged master of stylistic rhetoric in the Renaissance was Erasmus, whose *Copia* (1512) [52] was originally conceived as a textbook.

Another source of change for Renaissance rhetoric was the influential work of Peter Ramus (Pierre de la Ramée) [53], whose ideas were recorded in *Institutiones Oratoriae* (1545) by his colleague Talaeus (Omer Talon). Ramus wished to reform the medieval trivium by reemphasizing the classical division of the stages of composing. Ramist rhetoric intensifies the separation between these stages and the importance of their sequence, at the same time divorcing invention and arrangement from rhetoric and assigning them to logic. Ramists hoped to define a logical, scientific discourse, untainted by nonlogical appeals, that would win assent from the rational audience by virtue of rationality alone. Ramus's fellow Puritans widely adopted this plain style for all serious matters.

Rhetoric under the Ramist scheme is left to deal only with style, memory, and delivery. Memory had figured importantly in some early Renaissance hermetic precursors of modern science, and delivery would give rise in the eighteenth century to elaborate elocutionary techniques for public speakers and actors. Still, memory and delivery tended to continue their decline in importance as the Renaissance dissemination of printing made written texts ever more important to academic, religious, and political life. Rhetoricians, then, came increasingly to focus upon the study of language as the dress of ideas that were generated elsewhere. The goal of rhetorical study was to clothe one's ideas in the most elegant dress possible, and rhetoric thus came to be seen as the finishing refinement of an upper-class education.

Rhetoric in the Eighteenth Century: The Scottish Influence

Seeing rhetoric as the study of the dress of thought rather than the study of thought itself threatened to trivialize it. Rhetoricians from the University of Edinburgh sought to stop this trend by arguing that the study of correct and persuasive style produced not only competent public speakers but virtuous people. This was a strong defense, for the study of rhetoric in American colleges focused on oratory that would be useful to clergy, lawyers, and politicians. In addition, the Edinburgh rhetoricians connected the study of persuasion with the more prestigious scientific discipline of psychology. And these rhetoricians adapted ornamentation from Cicero to correct the emphasis on plain style that the Puritans had kept alive from Ramism.

Perhaps the most influential book to come from Edinburgh to America was Hugh Blair's *Lectures on Rhetoric and Belles-Lettres* [56], published in 1783 and adopted as the standard text at Yale in 1785 and Harvard in 1788. Blair's text was widely used in American colleges and secondary schools until the end of the nineteenth century. Americans found Blair's emphasis on the moral qualities of belletristic taste particularly important, since his approach justified the social leadership of the well-trained orator.

Less popular in the schools but perhaps more important for modern rhetoric was another Scottish rhetorician, George Campbell, whose *Philosophy of Rhetoric* (1776) [55] professes to validate its principles by relating them to the working of the human mind. More innovative than his contemporaries, Campbell extended the purpose of rhetoric beyond persuasion, defining eloquence as the "art or talent by which discourse is adapted to its end."

A later rhetorician in the Scottish tradition was Alexander Bain, who showed the importance of psychology for achieving goals of persuasion in *English Composition and Rhetoric: A Manual* (1866) [60]. Bain argued that persuasive discourse is organized by associating ideas in a way that produces the desired emotion in the audience. From Bain's work comes the now familiar taxonomy of essay structures, or modes of discourse: narration, description, exposition, and argumentation.

In America, the Scottish revision of classical rhetoric had special significance. A nascent democracy, so the argument went, needed people of refinement who could direct the vulgar taste into virtuous channels; the psychology of persuasion could help these leaders consolidate their control. Hence, the study of rhetoric both conferred and garnered prestige. Long before American colleges had English departments, they had distinguished professors of rhetoric.

Rhetoric in Nineteenth-Century America: The Harvard Influence

In 1806 Harvard College established the Boylston Professorship of Rhetoric and Oratory and became, thereafter, the dominant influence on the development of rhetoric at other American colleges. Edward T. Channing, who held the chair for thirty-two years (1819–1851), continued the Scottish emphasis on belletristic taste and the psychology of persuasion but shifted the emphasis in practice from speaking to writing and increased attention to literary exempla. From the literary models, Channing derived rules for correct grammar, style, and organization, which were taught more and more prescriptively as the century went on.

Francis J. Child, who held the Boylston Professorship after Channing (1851–1876), had studied philology at a German university before taking the chair and came to Harvard determined to turn the study of English from rhetoric to literature. Child bitterly resented the time he had to spend correcting student compositions. He delegated as much of this work as he could to faculty underlings and concentrated on enlarging Harvard's offerings in literature. In 1876, to keep Child from moving to Johns Hopkins (the first American university to be organized in departments on the German model), Harvard created the first Professorship of English for him, and Child spent the next twenty years developing the English literature curriculum. His successor in the Boylston Professorship, A. S. Hill, continued the rule-bound focus on written composition begun by Channing, but it was now clear that composition was a second-class subject and that rhetoric was hardly mentioned in the English department.

These changes are neatly encapsulated in Harvard's 1874 entrance requirement in English composition:

> Each candidate will be required to write a short English composition, correct in spelling, punctuation, grammar, and expression, the subject to be taken from such works of standard authors as shall be announced from time to time. The subject for 1874 will be taken from one of the following works: Shakespeare's *Tempest, Julius Caesar,* and *Merchant of Venice;* Goldsmith's *Vicar of Wakefield;* Scott's *Ivanhoe* and *Lay of the Last Minstrel.*

The Harvard model of freshman composition began to spread, particularly with the publication in 1890 of Harvard Professor Barrett Wendell's *English Composition: Eight Lectures*. Blair and Bain had used literary exempla to illustrate rhetorical principles. In the Harvard course, this belletristic tradition culminated in rules derived from the exempla and rigidly applied to student essays. Furthermore, the works of literature to be studied were strictly specified in lists of standard authors, such as the one given in the entrance requirements. These lists soon came to dictate secondary-school curricula, since one needed to know the listed works to perform well on admissions tests at prestigious colleges. And the prestige of those colleges that regulated their admissions according to the lists made it hard for other colleges to avoid similar requirements.

Progressive Education in Twentieth-Century America

In the early twentieth century, more and more secondary-school and college teachers came to oppose the domination of college admissions by the standard lists of works generated at Harvard and other elite Eastern schools. The National Council of Teachers of English (NCTE) was formed in 1911 largely to consolidate resistance to the lists and to the conception of English studies they represented. To further this cause, the NCTE began to publish *English Journal* in 1912 [8]. The first president of the NCTE was Fred Newton Scott of the University of Michigan. A past president of the Modern Language Association (MLA), Scott possessed impeccable credentials in literary scholarship; nevertheless, he deplored the demotion of rhetoric and promoted an understanding of writing that reemphasized self-expression and the adaptation of prose to its social purposes.

At the same time, departments of speech were growing more numerous in American colleges, taking over the study of historical rhetoric and many of its traditional concerns, such as response to audience. Speech teachers broke away from the NCTE in 1914 to form their own professional organization, the National Association for Academic Teachers of Public Speaking—now the Speech Communication Association.

English teachers' dissatisfaction with the reading lists soon became caught up in the larger progressive reform movement, which directly challenged the idea that the goal of higher education in America should be to empower an elite. The progressives believed that the purpose of education is to integrate a diverse population into a community of productive citizens. Progressive education sought to equip students with intellectual and social skills they would need as adults and to give attention to the needs of each individual student. John Dewey was an important leader of this movement. He became chair in 1894 of the Department of Philosophy, Psychology, and Pedagogy at the University of Chicago, and his *School and Society* was published in 1899.

Progressive education sought to free writing instruction from the service of canonical literary study. Correctness remained a goal of writing instruction, justified not by some authoritative set of rules but by its usefulness in the world beyond school. While respectful of the diverse cultural backgrounds of a school population that included record numbers of immigrants, progressive education stressed the communicative function of writing to help draw diverse groups together and integrate them into the mainstream of American society. A class writing project, for example, might collect data about some local social problem and prepare a report to be sent to the appropriate public official.

The progressives were not very often successful, at least on the college level, in separating composition and literature. In progressive hands, however, writing about literature became a way to understand one's own responses to the text. Such an approach can be found in Louise Rosenblatt's *Literature as Exploration* (1938) and in early issues of *College English,* which the NCTE began to publish in 1939 [4]. As progressive education moved into the 1930s and 1940s, its social agenda became more modest, but the main goal was still life adjustment—helping adolescents pass through their difficult developmental period and emerge as productive citizens.

Progressive education was also innovative in its interest in the social sciences as a source of information for English studies. Of course, progressives were not the first to look in this direction; rhetoric in the eighteenth and nineteenth centuries had incorporated some study of psychology. But with the demotion of rhetoric in the late nineteenth century, contacts between English and the social sciences were downplayed. Progressive education, in contrast, aimed to study students' abilities, needs, and achievements scientifically and to redesign curricula accordingly. These efforts had very little effect on college writing instruction, however.

Freshman English courses were rarely devoted only to writing instruction. Their main goal was to introduce students to literary study and in the process to correct the writing in students' literary essays according to long-established standards of grammatical, stylistic, and formal correctness. Where writing courses did exist, they usually patterned their syllabi after Bain's modes of discourse and justified their existence with arguments similar to Blair's for the good writer as a virtuous person. Widespread changes did not begin to occur until after World War II.

Beginnings of Modern Composition Studies: New Criticism

In the 1930s, New Criticism began to supplant biographical and philological criticism as the dominant mode of academic literary study. New Criticism put its emphasis on the close analysis of literary texts and appeared to have no common ground with the current forms of rhetorical study or composition pedagogy. By the 1940s, at any rate, the separation in English departments between literary study and the teaching of writing was so complete that academics committed to literary study could easily ignore the writing program.

New Criticism ultimately had a profound effect on writing instruction, however, because it approached literary texts as complex structures of meaning.

In its view, changing a word in a poem changed the poem's meaning—it did not simply select an alternative dress for an idea that remained unchanged. New Criticism therefore made it possible to see the relation between thought and language as fundamental rather than superficial. The freshman English course patterned on a nineteenth-century model (the current-traditional model, as Daniel Fogarty called it [137]) treated the relation between thought and language too mechanically. What could be taken for granted in the writing class quickly became problematic.

Recognizing the need for serious reconsideration of the freshman writing course, the NCTE mandated the Conference on College Composition and Communication (CCCC) in 1949. The journal *College Composition and Communication* appeared in 1950 [3]. In the 1950s, the CCCC did much to lay the foundations for the modern discipline of composition studies. On the practical side, the CCCC worked to improve conditions for the graduate assistants who taught almost all college writing courses and to exchange ideas among college writing-program administrators. The conference also championed the cause of semanticists and linguists looking for a home in college English departments and urged that the Ph.D. in English literature include coursework in linguistics as preparation for teaching writing.

Reinforcing these efforts pertaining to college composition was the post-Sputnik concern in the early 1960s to encourage excellence in all areas of American education. To make the college writing course more rigorous, ways were sought to expand its focus beyond socialization or linguistics to the full traditional range of rhetorical concerns. Distinguished literary critics such as Wayne Booth began to write on rhetoric. In 1963, the NCTE published a survey of research to date in composition, compiled by Richard Braddock, Richard Lloyd-Jones, and Lowell Schoer. Little valuable work was found, but the study itself encouraged high standards for new research in the field. To give such research an outlet, the NCTE began publishing the journal *Research in the Teaching of English* in 1967 [20].

The 1960s: Classical Rhetoric, Writing Processes, and Authentic Voice

With the encouragement of the CCCC in the early 1960s, composition specialists looked to the classical texts that had rarely been studied in English departments (although speech departments had preserved an interest in them) and to transformations of the classical heritage by later rhetoricians. Several important collections of premodern documents on rhetoric and discussions of classical rhetoric's value to the modern student were published. This renewed attention to classical sources helped to foster an increased interest in stages of the writing process and in style as an expression of personal ethos.

The classical model is a five-stage process, consisting of invention, arrangement, style, memory, and delivery. After the Ramists excluded invention and arrangement, and memory and delivery dwindled into elocution, American writing courses, in their focus on one stage, style, had lost a sense of writing as a process. Now writing as a process was reemphasized in the study of what Gordon Rohman called the pre-writing stages, those that precede production of a finished piece of work. Invention and arrangement began to be reclaimed for composition studies as preliminary stages in the writing process. Style, too, was seen as a process of developing ideas by recasting sentences, not merely pouring ideas into preset sentence forms.

Interest in the writing process and in writing as self-expression prompted the MLA and the NCTE to sponsor the 1966 conference at Dartmouth College on the teaching of English (see John Dixon [282]). Attended by American and British educators from the elementary, secondary, and college levels, the conference helped spread the conviction that writing instruction should emphasize self-expressive uses of language and assist students in shaping their ideas through writing. Unlike the Harvard-model course, which imposed standards on passive students, the new Dartmouth-model writing course encouraged more interaction among teacher and students, more dramatic and collaborative activities. One influential process-oriented pedagogy appeared in James Moffett's *Teaching the Universe of Discourse* (1968) [291].

The Dartmouth Conference called for writing instruction that takes more notice of students' needs for self-expression as opposed to their adjustment to social demands. Now composition studies searched for a pedagogy to help students find personal writing styles that were honest and unconstrained by conventions. Such a style came to be termed the writer's authentic voice—an important concept in the work of Ken Macrorie [319] and Peter Elbow [307, 316]. The need for such pedagogy seemed especially poignant in the late 1960s and early 1970s, when many writing teachers sought some critical response to the opaque, impersonal prose that dominates politics. Authentic-voice pedagogy contributed techniques, such as Elbow's freewriting, that became part of every writing teacher's repertoire.

The 1970s: Cognitive Processes, Basic Writing, and Writing across the Curriculum

In the 1970s, interest in the writing process prompted inquiry into what cognitive psychology and psycholinguistics might discover about it. Composition scholars began to refer not to the "writing" process but to the "composing" process, as in the pioneering work of Janet Emig [135, 168]. The significance of this shift in terminology was its emphasis on the cognitive activities involved in writing. "Composing," in other words, is what goes on in the writer's head and is then recorded in writing. This interest in composing processes first focused on what had been the initial stages in the classical process, invention and arrangement. Theorists developed structured invention techniques that would guide the student through an optimal composing process. The particle-wave-field heuristic devised by Richard Young, Alton Becker, and Kenneth Pike was one influential modern invention technique [188].

Progressive educators before World War II had urged researchers to use social-scientific methods for investigating students' real needs. These urgings were rarely heeded in college English departments. Now empirical studies based on observations of working writers began, such as those of Nancy Sommers [211] and Sondra Perl [176]. The whole composing process came under study. Research indicated that there might be more than one successful composing process. Furthermore, the process no longer seemed to be neatly linear, as described in the classical model, but appeared recursive and hierarchical, as developed in the model of Linda Flower and cognitive psychologist John R. Hayes [172].

In comprehensive theoretical works, the philosophical and psychological bases for the study of composing were explored. Frank D'Angelo argued that the forms of discourse are structurally similar to the forms of cognitive processes and perhaps even to the brain itself [192]. To teach the forms of discourse, then, is not merely to teach conventional modes of arrangement but to provide students with models of actual cognitive processes. If the forms of discourse parallel cognitive processes, they should be equally accessible to every student, regardless of cultural background.

In the 1970s, the increasing number of college freshmen whose home language was not Standard English severely tested the applicability of cognitive theories of writing. The work of William Labov [343] and other sociolinguists on dialectal variation helped writing teachers see that this new classroom population, in need of so much help with the requirements of academic writing, was not cognitively deficient but, rather, linguistically and culturally diverse. One immediate result of this new understanding was a 1974 resolution by the CCCC on students' right to their own languages. This resolution argued that students would learn Standard English more easily if they were allowed to write some school assignments in their home languages, whether or not these were Standard. The document also called for teacher education to include work in dialectal variation.

Later in the decade, studies of basic writing explored the pedagogical problems posed by dialectal variation in the classroom. Mina Shaughnessy's important work, *Errors and Expectations* (1977) [354], argues for respect for students' home languages but also advises teachers on how to help these students become more comfortable with academic writing. Many student errors with Standard forms are actually regular, if not rule-governed, attempts to achieve academic correctness. A student whose home language is Black English, for example, might write her school papers in neither Black English nor Standard English but in an idiosyncratic blend of the two. Furthermore, socialization to school is a problem for many basic writers. If students' home cultures place little value on the intellectual abstractions of academic work, for example, a typical research paper assignment might seem pointless. The study of error, therefore, as Shaughnessy argues, must consider students' cultural background and how this may affect their relation to the social contexts of school as well as what appears on the page when they write.

With so many students seeming to need extra help in mastering college-level writing, many composition scholars came to feel that professors in all disciplines must be enlisted in the effort of teaching writing or, rather, helped to see that they were already contributing to students' introduction to academic discourse. They could learn to make this contribution in better ways, which would improve both students' writing and their learning of disciplinary content. To address these needs, cross-disciplinary writing programs, or programs in "writing across the curriculum," to use James Britton's phrase, began to develop. The first American writing-across-the-curriculum program was started at Carleton College in Minnesota in 1974, and Elaine Maimon directed an influential program at Beaver College in Pennsylvania [446, 447].

These programs typically attempt to educate students and faculty from all disciplines about the conventions of academic discourse and about the range of activities that constitute mature composing processes. Maimon argues that the literary training most composition scholars have received makes them uniquely suited to analyze the conventions of discourse for writers who are not aware of the conventions' function in the generation of knowledge [446]. Toby Fulwiler stresses the importance of journal keeping in the composing processes of all academic disciplines. Fulwiler finds that writing-across-the-curriculum programs encourage students and teachers alike to become more confident writers and eager collaborators in a literate community of scholars [441]. James Kinneavy suggests that a further outcome may be wider participation in a literate community beyond the academy, in which important public issues can be discussed [444].

The 1980s: Social and Historical Approaches to Rhetoric

In the 1980s, composition scholars focused on the social nature of writing, building upon previous work in both basic writing and writing across the curriculum. Research into the cognitive processes of writers continued, but it was informed by new interest in how these processes are conditioned by social circumstances. For example, Mike Rose shows that writer's block may be as much a result of bad writing instruction as of individual cognitive disabilities [177]. Moreover, ethnographic studies, such as that by Shirley Brice Heath [262], which focus on writers at various school levels and beyond school, became increasingly important.

James Kinneavy's early work on the modes of discourse (1971) [146] returned to Aristotle for a revitalized sense of the decisive role of social function in determining the form of discourse. Kinneavy classifies rhetorical situations according to their emphasis on the writer (expressive), audience (persuasive), subject matter (referential), or verbal medium (aesthetic). Kinneavy's theory allows for the literary analysis of a wide variety of texts, thus laying the groundwork for studies in writing across the curriculum. His work became more influential in the 1980s as these studies proliferated.

The search for a social theory of writing became broadly interdisciplinary. Composition scholars studied not only writing but all aspects of language use, which they regarded as actually creating knowledge, not merely disseminating it. These interests have been shared with scholars in history, literary criticism, philosophy, psychology, sociology, and speech communication. Scholars in all these fields sought an account of discourse—language in use—that acknowledges the power of rhetoric to help create a community's worldview, knowledge, and interpretive practices.

If rhetoric is epistemic, then there can be no language that does not require interpretation. As Richard Rorty shows, modern philosophers have failed to define a value-neutral language in which purely objective and rational arguments can be conducted (see [155]). Chaim Perelman describes the ways a community united by discourse establishes its interpretive practices [157, 158]. His "universal audience" is the audience that is presumed to adhere perfectly to a given community's interpretive practices and hence to serve as that community's standard of the purely objective and rational audience. Different communities can be expected to hold different conceptions of their universal audience.

Literary-critical theories of the role of the reader in making meaning also discuss the establishment of interpretive practices. Stanley Fish describes readers as participants in interpretive communities, which are defined by their agreement on the conventions of discourse. Fish's work suggests a method for analyzing the conventions a writer must learn to enter the academic discourse community. No taxonomy of such conventions has appeared, although studies of a number of fields have exposed much about disciplinary conventions. More recently, studies of writing in various disciplines have revealed and analyzed the social creation of disciplinary knowledge through discourse.

Historical studies of rhetoric have been another resource for a social theory of discourse. Andrea Lunsford and Lisa Ede drew on Aristotle for a theory of argument that legitimates ethical and pathetic as well as logical appeals. This theory supports the idea that cultural assumptions have more to do with persuasion than the "universal" rationality of a proposition [147]. S. Michael Halloran shows that when the classical emphasis on socially rooted appeals disappeared from nineteenth-century colleges, public debate on important national issues diminished [68, 82]. James Berlin describes the reduction of rhetoric to stylistic prescriptions [62]. He suggests that the roots of a more socially responsive rhetoric may be found in Emersonian romanticism.

The field of composition studies grew in professional respectability during the 1980s. By the end of the decade, graduate degrees in composition and rhetoric—not simply one introductory survey or teaching practicum—had come to be offered by departments of English in many prestigious universities. Under the auspices of the NCTE, the CCCC began publishing comprehensive bibliographies in the field [36]. The U.S. Department of Education funded an empirical research institute, the Center for the Study of Writing, at the University of California at Berkeley and Carnegie-Mellon University. Series of bibliographic anthologies, collections, reprints, and monographs began to appear regularly from a number of research and university presses.

Part of the field's coming-of-age process was increased interest in the history of rhetoric and composition, now an extensive area of scholarly work and a regular curricular offering. Composition work was not to be seen as a temporary response to unusual gaps in college-bound students' preparation. Rather, writing teachers and researchers came to view themselves as the most recent generation of serious thinkers about language in use, heirs of the rhetorical tradition. Many of our classroom practices were recast in light of historical traditions. For example, personal writing was connected with the genre of the personal essay stretching back at least to the Renaissance, as traced variously by William Covino [74] and Kurt Spellmeyer [320].

Although historical studies of rhetoric and poetic suggested theoretical bases for the location of composition studies in English departments, the relationship between composition studies and literary studies was (and is still to some extent) uneasy. Some composition scholars called for the formation of departments of composition and rhetoric, separate from departments of English. Some worked to redress the professional inequities that prompted the impulse to separate through, for example, the Wyoming Resolution and ensuing professional policy work by both the CCCC and the MLA [417]. Greatly increased self-consciousness about the institutional structures in which we work gave rise not only to more scholarship on writing-program administration but also to more ideologically sensitive criticism of our institutional functions, for example, in James Berlin's work on the history of twentieth-century writing [62, 113].

Analyses of the political problems within the profession extended to efforts to connect our profession with political problems in society at large, to a degree not seen, perhaps, since the late 1960s. An important intersection of personal work life and national political life emerged in the analyses of inequity and redress offered by feminist critics within composition studies. In 1988, Elizabeth Flynn [361] could lament that issues of feminism were rarely raised at our annual conventions, but this situation changed dramatically the very next year.

The late 1980s also saw a rise in awareness of the degree to which race and social class affect the situation of basic writers. Linda Brodkey analyzes teacher-student class differences in "he Literacy Letters" [333], and Mike Rose provides an autobiographical account of how such barriers may be negotiated in *Lives on the Boundary* [349]. "Politics" became a key concept for understanding the educational difficulties of all writers: witness Richard Bullock and John Trimbur's collection, *The Politics of Writing Instruction* [127]. Composition scholars gave increased attention to pedagogical innovations with an explicitly liberatory political agenda, drawing once again on the work of Brazilian literacy educator Paulo Freire [257] (see Cooper and Holzman [335]) and learning from education theorists like Henry Giroux [140]. The desire to trace the influences of class, race, and gender to their roots also seemed to generate a great deal of attention among college-level writing teachers to work in the acquisition of literacy and its cognitive and cultural implications, as the works in the "Literacy" section of the *Bibliography* attest.

By the end of the 1980s, seeing writing in social and cultural contexts was the prevailing tendency in the field. Concern for writing in communal contexts appeared in the work of many theorists. Linda Flower, in a variation on the theme, argued for a sociocognitive theory of writing, according to which, writer, text, and context are mutually constitutive [171]. Studying writing in context means more than assessing the immediate audience. Rather, as Marilyn Cooper argues, we must consider a complex "ecology of writing" that comprises not only immediate personal relationships and social purposes but also larger generic and cultural constraints on composing [167]. To study this rich network, we need to look not only at the individual writer but at the collaborative situation of his or her classroom, personal and institutional histories, and writers' and teachers' political hopes.

Rhetoric and Composition Studies in the 1990s: The Challenge of Diversity

The powerful themes of the 1980s—social construction, politics, literacy, and gender issues—have extended into the 1990s to work that relates composition to postmodernism, cultural studies, and multiculturalism. Social construction has been widely accepted as a theoretical basis for understanding language use, as can be seen in the research directions of technical and business communication, English as a second language (ESL), and writing centers. The history of composition, too, has received generous and fruitful attention.

The connections among social construction, postmodernism, politics, and cultural studies and their implications for composition have been explored by a number of scholars. James Berlin, for example, argues that the postmodern critiques of unified consciousness and master narratives confirm the social view of knowledge-creation as well as the necessity of seeing texts as ideological [112]. Similar connections are drawn by Lester Faigley, who shows in addition how computer networks feed into postmodern consciousness [136]. The contributors to Patricia Harkin and John Schilb's *Contending with Words* explore the sources of postmodern ideas in the works of influential theorists and discuss the implications of theory for the writing classroom [142].

Perhaps the greatest challenge in college education in recent years has been the growing cultural diversity of the student body, reflecting at last the diversity of America as well as growing global interconnections. In 1991, Mary Louise Pratt called upon educators to think of the curriculum and the classroom as "contact zones" in which cultural groups of unequal power can interact under conditions that enable sharing and understanding [159]. Composition teachers and scholars have been quick to respond to Pratt's challenge (see, e.g., Bizzell [121]). Teaching a diverse student body is, of course, the responsibility of teachers who must help students negotiate cultural crossings but, at the same time, check their own tendencies to make blanket assumptions about other cultures. We are aided in these efforts by powerful accounts like Keith Gilyard's [341] and Victor Villanueva's [279] of composition scholars who themselves crossed cultural boundaries.

To what extent are multicultural students isolated in English-as-a-second-language courses? Guadalupe Valdes shows that it is difficult and often damaging to make distinctions among students on the basis of culture-based linguistic usages [388]. The distinctions between ESL students and basic writers are even more difficult to make, but cultural diversity should be embraced, for it can enrich our classrooms and our teaching. We must expect and prepare for ESL students in all classrooms, as Amy Tucker explains: composition teachers must become students of culture [387]. The enormous contribution of ESL scholars in the study of diversity has marked this edition of *The Bedford Bibliography* and will be evident not only in the new section on teaching English as a second language, but in a number of other sections as well.

Diversity is a dominant note in literacy studies in the 1990s as well. The meaning of literacy for linguistic and cultural minorities in a multiethnic context is the concern of the contributors to Ferdman, Weber, and Ramirez's *Literacy across Languages and Cultures* [381], Beverly Moss's *Literacy across Communities* [269], and Brian Street's *Cross-Cultural Approaches to Literacy* [275]. Seeing the problem as one of redefining *cultural* literacy is the focus of yet another collection, Denise Murray's *Diversity as Resource* [270]. Extending the work of Labov and Heath in sociolinguistic and anthropological studies of literacy outside the academy, these scholars help composition teachers to understand the cultural histories and languages from which our students increasingly come.

Composition teachers and scholars have not been slow to come up with innovative pedagogies that truly use diversity as a resource. Akua Duku Anokye, for example, describes exercises for a widely diverse basic-writing class that use personal narratives not only as arts of the contact zone but as part of a move toward academic discourse [329]. Writing centers, similarly, are responding to the challenge of diversity. Anne DiPardo, for example, connects the difficulties of center clients from diverse cultures to campus tensions aroused by diversity and shows how tutors can help [419].

Feminist teaching, the place of women in the history of the field, and gender issues in the classroom have continued to be important scholarly concerns in rhetoric and composition in the 1990s. An excellent collection edited by Andrea Lunsford, *Reclaiming Rhetorica*, reveals and explores the contributions of women to rhetorical theory through the ages [95]. Such work begins to fill in disturbing gaps in our understanding of the history of rhetoric. In the classroom, gender bias continues to be a concern addressed by composition scholars. For example, Harriet Malinowitz casts light on the writing problems of gay and lesbian students [369]. A variety of other women's concerns are reflected in studies of autobiographical writing (Hollis [318]), of academic women's sense of authority (Kirsch [365]), and the history of gender-coded texts (Brody [359]).

Reclaiming Rhetorica represents not only some of the gender concerns of the discipline in the 1990s but also its movement toward greater refinement in the study of history. A number of scholars have shed light on the teaching of rhetoric in nineteenth-century American colleges, finding there the stories of how the field of composition was positioned—and in some ways compromised—for the century to come. In 1990, Alfred Kitzhaber's 1953 dissertation on *Rhetoric in American Colleges, 1850 to 1900*—long a standard work on the subject—was finally published. John Brereton traces the history of composition instruction during the formative years 1875 to 1925 through original documents, providing a striking direct look at our professional ancestors [65]. And David Russell's much admired history of writing in the academic disciplines tells the rather grim story of how writing has been treated outside of composition courses since 1870 [105].

The 1990s appear to be a time for stocktaking in the discipline, a trend perhaps related to the impulse to write the field's history. The best example is a series of collections of "landmark" essays on the writing process [176], invention [189], voice [316], writing centers [430], and writing across the curriculum [437] published by Hermagoras Press. Relatively little new work has appeared in the 1990s on the writing process and its elements (prewriting, invention, revision), on argument, on academic discourse, or on writing across the curriculum. Forging ahead into new frontiers, though, compositionists have embraced networking and hypertext. In his historically contextualized exposition of the achievement and promise of hypertext, David Bolter explains how electronic text radically changes the relationship between writer and reader and revives features of oral literature [451]. Several new collections of essays provide advice on using computers and analyze their effects on pedagogy [452, 453], explore the wonders of on-line writing centers [423], and warn of the implications of computers for literacy and culture [454, 455].

Scholarship in composition and rhetoric continues to be richly interdisciplinary; however, according to the contributors to Ann Gere's collection *Into the Field*, that interdisciplinarity should not be construed as simply borrowing [139]. It is, rather, a matter of positioning on disciplinary boundaries that need to be crossed or erased. When discourse and language analysis have become powerful tools for understanding all disciplines, when the composition classroom has become a critical crossroads of culture in American higher education, and when technology impinges on literacy, the need to be creatively open to new knowledge is essential. This is a challenge that the field of composition is accepting with characteristic energy and high regard for students and their best interests.

Bibliography

Resources

Periodicals

1   *ADE Bulletin.* New York: Association of Departments of English. Three times a year, beginning 1964. Subscriptions and submissions: Stephen Olsen, MLA, 10 Astor Pl., New York, NY 10003-6981.

    The journal of the Association of Departments of English. Articles on writing program and English department administration and the relationships between composition and literature. Ed. Stephen Olsen.

2   *The CEA Forum.* Lewisburg, Pa.: The College English Association. Quarterly, beginning 1970. Subscriptions and submissions: Dept. of English, Youngstown State Univ., Youngstown, OH 44555.

    The journal of the College English Association. Most articles concern the teaching of literature and composition. Ed. Barbara Brothers and Bege Bowers.

3   *College Composition and Communication.* Urbana, Ill.: NCTE/CCCC. Quarterly, beginning 1950. Subscriptions: 1111 Kenyon Rd., Urbana, IL 61801. Submissions: Joseph Harris, CCC Editor, English Dept. 501 CL, University of Pittsburgh, Pittsburgh, PA 15260.

CCC   The principal journal of the Conference of College Composition and Communication. Most articles explore pedagogical applications of composition theory and research. Ed. Joseph Harris.

4   *College English.* Urbana, Ill.: NCTE College Section. Eight times a year, beginning 1939. Subscriptions: 1111 Kenyon Rd., Urbana, IL 61801. Submissions: *College English,* UMass–Boston, Boston, MA 02125.

CE   The principal journal of the NCTE College Section. Articles on teaching literature, literary theory, the history of the discipline, and teaching writing. Ed. Louise Z. Smith.

5   *Composition Studies* (formerly *Freshman English News*). Fort Worth: Texas Christian Univ. Three times a year, beginning 1972. Subscriptions and submissions: Christina Murphy, Writing Center, Box 32875, Texas Christian Univ., Fort Worth, TX 76129.

    Short articles on the theory and practice of teaching and writing and, occasionally, longer theoretical essays. Ed. Christina Murphy.

6   *Computers and Composition.* Norwood, N.J.: Ablex Publishing Co. Three times a year, beginning 1984. Subscriptions: Ablex Publishing Co., 355 Chestnut Street, Norwood, NJ 07648. Submissions: Humanities Dept., Michigan Technological Univ., 1400 Townsend Dr., Houghton, MI 49931.

Articles on the uses of computers in teaching writing. Eds. Cynthia Selfe and Gail Hawisher.

7 *English for Specific Purposes: An International Journal.* Oxford, England: Elsevier Science Ltd. Three times a year, beginning 1982. Subscriptions: Elsevier Science Ltd., 660 White Plains Road, Tarrytown, NY 10591. Submissions: Tony Dudley-Evans, University of Birmingham; or Peter Master, San Jose State University; or Liz Hamp-Lyons, University of Colorado at Boulder.
Articles analyze the discourse conventions of writing in particular professions and disciplines. Ed. Tony Dudley-Evans, Peter Master, and Liz Hamp-Lyons.

8 *English Journal.* Urbana, Ill.: NCTE Secondary Section. Eight times a year, beginning 1912. Subscriptions: 1111 Kenyon Rd., Urbana, IL 61801. Submissions: Leila Christenbury, School of Education, Virginia Commonwealth University, P.O. Box 842020, Richmond, VA 23284-2020.
The principal journal of the NCTE Secondary Section. Articles on teaching literature and writing and on pedagogical research in the secondary schools. Ed. Leila Christenbury.

9 *Focuses.* Boone, N.C.: Appalachian State University. Twice a year, beginning 1988. Subscriptions and submissions: William Wolff, Department of English, Appalachian State University, Boone, NC 28608. Articles on writing centers, composition programs, and writing as a discipline. Ed. William Wolff.

10 *Journal of Advanced Composition.* Ames, Iowa: Association of Teachers of Technical Writing, with support from Iowa State Univ., Univ. of South Florida, and Ithaca College. Annually, beginning 1980; twice a year, beginning 1990. Subscriptions and submissions: Thomas Kent, English Department, Iowa State University, Ames, IA 50011.
Articles on rhetorical theory, interviews with scholars, and pedagogical articles on expository, technical, creative, and other advanced writing courses.

11 *Journal of Basic Writing.* New York: City Univ. of New York Instructional Resource Center. Twice a year, beginning 1978. Subscriptions and submissions: Instructional Resource Center, City Univ. of New York, 535 East 80th St., New York, NY 10021.
From the Instructional Resource Center, previously directed by Mina Shaughnessy. Articles on literacy, teaching grammar and basic writing, English as a second language (ESL), and theoretical issues in basic writing. Ed. Karen Greenberg and Trudy Smoke.

12 *Journal of Business and Technical Communication.* Ames: Iowa State University. Four times a year, beginning 1987. Subscriptions: Sage Periodicals Press, 2455 Teller Road, Thousand Oaks, CA 91320. Submissions: Charles Kostelnick, 203 Ross Hall, Iowa State University, Ames, IA 50011.

Articles on business and technical writing practice and teaching. Ed. Charles Kostelnick.

13 *Journal of Second Language Writing.* Norwood, N.J.: Ablex Publishing Co. Three times a year, beginning 1992. Subscriptions: 355 Chestnut Street, Norwood, NJ 07648-9975. Submissions: Ilona Leki, Department of English, Univ. of Tennessee, Knoxville, TN 37996-0430.
    Full-length articles on theories of ESL composition. Selected bibliographies of recent scholarship. Ed. Ilona Leki and Tony Silva.

14 *Journal of Teaching Writing.* Indianapolis: Indiana Teachers of Writing and Indiana Univ./Purdue Univ. at Indianapolis. Twice a year, beginning 1981. Subscriptions and submissions: Barbara Cambridge, IUPUI, 425 University Blvd., Indianapolis, IN 46202.
    Articles cover composition theory and the relation of composition to other fields, as well as pedagogical concerns. Ed. Barbara Cambridge.

15 *Journal of Technical Writing and Communication.* Amityville, N.Y.: Baywood Publications. Four times a year, beginning 1971. Subscriptions: 26 Austin Place, Amityville, NY 11701. Submissions: Charles H. Sides, Fitchburg State College, Fitchburg, MA 01420-2697.
    Articles on research and teaching in technical and professional writing. Ed. Charles H. Sides.

16 *Philosophy and Rhetoric.* State College: Pennsylvania State Univ. Press. Quarterly, beginning 1968. Subscriptions: Pennsylvania State Univ. Press, 820 N. University Dr., University Park, PA 16802. Submissions: Dept. of Philosophy, Pennsylvania State Univ., 240 Sparks Bldg., University Park, PA 16802.
    Articles on classical rhetoric, rhetorical theory, and language theory from the perspectives of English, speech, and philosophy. Ed. Henry Johnstone.

17 *PRE/TEXT.* Arlington: Univ. of Texas. Quarterly, beginning 1979. Subscriptions and submissions: English Dept., Box 19035, Univ. of Texas, Arlington, TX 76019-0035.
    Long essays on rhetorical theory and pedagogical philosophy. Ed. Victor Vitanza.

18 *Quarterly Journal of Speech.* Annandale, Va.: Speech Communication Association of America. Quarterly, beginning 1915. Subscriptions: 5105 Backlick Rd., Annandale, VA 22003. Submissions: Barbara Warnick, Dept. of Speech Communication, DL-15, University of Washington, Seattle, WA 98195.
    The principal theoretical journal of the Speech Communication Association. Articles on rhetorical theory and the history of rhetoric, and analyses of texts and speeches. Contributors from English and philosophy as well as speech. Ed. Martha Solomon.

19 *Radical Teacher*. Cambridge, Mass.: Boston Women's Teachers Group, Inc. Three times a year, beginning 1975. Subscriptions and submissions: P.O. Box 102, Kendall Square Post Office, Cambridge, MA 02142.
Articles on the political concerns of teachers and students; perspectives on progressive pedagogy, feminism, and Marxism in teaching in all disciplines.

20 *Research in the Teaching of English*. Urbana, Ill.: NCTE. Four times a year, beginning 1967. Subscriptions: 1111 Kenyon Rd., Urbana, IL 61801. Submissions: Editor, RTE, Harvard University Graduate School of Education, Larsen Hall, Appian Way, Cambridge, MA 01238.
Research reports on teaching English at all school levels, cognitive development and language skills, and the composing process. Editor: Sandra Stotsky.

21 *Rhetoric Review*. Tucson, Ariz.: Rhetoric Review Association of America. Twice a year, beginning 1982. Subscriptions and submissions: Theresa Enos, Dept. of English, Univ. of Arizona, Tucson, AZ 85721.
Both theoretical and practical articles emphasizing the importance of rhetoric to composition instruction. Ed. Theresa Enos.

22 *Rhetoric Society Quarterly*. St. Cloud, Minn.: Rhetoric Society of America. Quarterly, beginning 1968. Subscriptions: Rhetoric Society of America, Department of Philosophy, St. Cloud State Univ., 720 Fourth Avenue South, St. Cloud, MN 56301. Submissions: Jeffery Walker, 1194 Westerly Parkway, Pennsylvania State Univ., State College, PA 16801.
Articles on rhetorical theory, history, and professional concerns. Contributors from both English and speech. Ed. Phil Keith and Eugene Garber.

23 *Rhetorica*. Berkeley: Univ. of California Press, International Society for the History of Rhetoric. Twice a year, beginning 1983. Subscriptions: Univ. of California Press, Journals Dept., 2120 Berkeley Way, Berkeley, CA 94720. Submissions: Craig Kallendorf, Dept. of English, Texas A&M University, College Station, TX 77843.
The journal of the International Society for the History of Rhetoric. Articles on premodern rhetoric by contributors from English, speech, philosophy, and history. Ed. Craig Kallendorf.

24 *TESOL Quarterly*. Alexandria, Va.: TESOL. Four times a year, beginning 1967. Subscriptions: TESOL Publications, 1600 Cameron Street, Suite 300, Alexandria, VA 22314-2751. Submissions: Sandra McKay, Dept. of English, San Francisco State Univ., San Francisco, CA 94132.
Articles on teaching and research in English as a second language. Ed. Sandra McKay.

25 *Teaching English in the Two-Year College.* Urbana, Ill.: NCTE. Quarterly, beginning 1974. Subscriptions: 1111 Kenyon Rd., Urbana, IL 61801. Submissions: Mark Reynolds, P.O. Box 250, Brewton, AL 36427.
Summaries and reviews of composition theory, as well as teaching suggestions for teachers of freshman and sophomore writing courses. Ed. Mark Reynolds.

26 *The Writing Center Journal.* Logan, Utah: National Writing Centers Association. Twice a year, beginning 1980. Bethlehem, Pa.: National Writing Centers Association. Subscriptions and submissions: Nancy Grimm, Editor, Michigan Technological University, 1400 Townsend Drive, Houghton, MI 49931.
Full-length articles on writing center administration and practices. Ed. Diana George, Nancy Grimm, and Edward Lotto.

27 *The Writing Instructor.* Los Angeles: Univ. of Southern California. Quarterly, beginning 1981. Subscriptions and submissions: P. Kevin Parker, University of Southern California, THH440-MC0354, Los Angeles, CA 90089-0354.
A journal from the University of Southern California Freshman Writing Program. Articles on teaching college writing, writing program administration, and curriculum development. Ed. P. Kevin Parker.

28 *Writing Lab Newsletter.* West Lafayette, Ind.: National Writing Centers Association of the NCTE. Ten times a year, beginning 1976. Subscriptions and submissions: Muriel Harris, Writing Lab, Heavilon Hall, Purdue Univ., West Lafayette, IN 47907-1356.
Short articles by lab directors and tutors, including student tutors, on writing-lab theory, problems, and techniques. Ed. Muriel Harris.

29 *Writing on the Edge.* Campus Writing Center, Univ. of California at Davis. Twice a year, beginning 1989. Subscriptions and submissions: John Boe, Campus Writing Center, Univ. of California, Davis, CA 95616.
Shorter articles on all facets of composition and rhetoric: history, theory, pedagogy, writing centers, and politics. Ed.: John Boe.

30 *Written Communication.* Beverly Hills, Calif.: Sage Publications. Quarterly, beginning 1984. Subscriptions: Customer Service, Sage Publications, 2455 Teller Rd., Thousand Oaks, CA 91320. Submissions: Debra Brandt and Mary Nystrand, Dept. of English, University of Wisconsin at Madison, 500 Lincoln Drive, Madison, WI 53706.
Research reports on social and cognitive factors in discourse production for young and adult writers. Ed. Debra Brandt and Mary Nystrand.

31 *WPA: Writing Program Administration.* Normal: Illinois State Univ., Council of Writing Program Administrators. Twice a year, beginning 1979. Subscriptions: Jeffrey Sommers, Dept. of English, Miami Univ., Oxford, OH 45056. Submissions: Douglas Hesse,

Dept. of English, Illinois State Univ., Normal, IL 61790-4240.
Articles on writing program administration and writing instruction; textbook bibliographies. Ed. Douglas Hesse.

General Bibliographies

32   "Annotated Bibliography of Research in the Teaching of English." *Research in the Teaching of English* (Spring and Fall 1967–present). Items focusing on empirical work are divided into sections on literature, humanities, and media; written and oral communication; language and verbal learning; bilingual and dialectal programs; and general English curriculum. Subdivided by educational level. Items are annotated beginning Spring 1973.

33   ERIC: Educational Resources Information Center. Operated by the National Institute of Education, U.S. Department of Education.
There are sixteen ERIC clearinghouses, each responsible for a particular area of education. ERIC/RCS, the Clearinghouse on Reading and Communication Skills, is sponsored by the NCTE. Abstracts of articles available through ERIC are published in *Resources in Education.* Microfiche and paper copies may be ordered through the ERIC Document Reproduction Service, Box 190, Arlington, VA 22210. ERIC materials since 1982 are available on CD-ROM; materials since 1966 are on OCLC.

34   Hillocks, George, Jr. *Research on Written Composition.* Urbana, Ill.: NCTE, 1986.
The National Conference on Research in English and ERIC/RCS have sponsored this comprehensive review of composition research since 1963. In bibliographic-essay format, Hillocks surveys work at all grade levels in seven areas: the composing process, the writer's repertoire, modes of instruction, grammar, criteria for better writing, invention, and meta-analyses comparing results in several areas. Hillocks evaluates many studies, sometimes in light of earlier research, and summarizes what is now known in each of the areas he surveys. In the last chapter, he draws implications for teaching from each area. He also recommends topics for further research and ways to improve the rigor of research design. Includes a 102-page bibliography.

See: Theresa Enos, *Encyclopedia of Rhetoric and Composition* [77].

35   Lindemann, Erika. *Longman Bibliography of Composition and Rhetoric: 1984–1985* (1987), and *1986* (1988), New York: Longman.
The 1984–85 volume contains 3,853 entries; the 1986 volume contains 2,724. Nearly all the entries have twenty-five- to fifty-word descriptive annotations. Includes journals, books, dissertations, textbooks, ERIC entries, and computer programs in the following categories: theory and research (in rhetoric, history of rhetoric, types of rhetoric, reading, linguistics, education, and psychology), teacher education and administration, curriculum (preschool through college, business and

technical writing, adult education, and ESL), textbooks and instructional materials, and testing and evaluation.

36   Lindemann, Erika. *CCCC Bibliography of Composition and Rhetoric, 1987.* Carbondale: Southern Illinois Univ. Press, 1990. Succeeding editions: *1988* (1991), *1989* (1992), *1990* (1993).

Hawisher, Gail E., and Cynthia L. Selfe. *CCCC Bibliography of Composition and Rhetoric, 1991.* Carbondale: Southern Illinois Univ. Press, 1993. Succeeding editions: *1992* (1994), *1993* (1995).
Successor to the *Longman Bibliography of Composition and Rhetoric* [35], which covers elementary and secondary as well as college materials, the *CCCC Bibliography* focuses on work related to college and university teaching and research. Categories are Bibliographies and Checklists; Theory and Research (in fourteen subcategories); Teacher Education, Administration, and Social Roles (four subcategories); Curriculum (thirteen subcategories); and Testing, Measurement, and Evaluation (four subcategories). Each item is briefly annotated.

37   Moran, Michael G., and Ronald F. Lunsford, eds. *Research in Composition and Rhetoric: A Bibliographic Sourcebook.* Westport, Conn., and London: Greenwood Press, 1984.
Sixteen bibliographic essays relate composition to other disciplines and provide pedagogical references, drawing upon research at all school levels. Essays include Louise Wetherbee Phelps, "Cross-Sections in an Emerging Psychology of Composition"; John C. Briggs, "Philosophy and Rhetoric"; Glynda A. Hull and David Bartholomae, "Basic Writing"; Mary Hurley Moran, "Vocabulary Development"; Frank J. D'Angelo, "The Sentence"; and Marvin K. L. Ching, "Usage." Also includes appendices on evaluating usage manuals, by Ching, and on writing textbooks, by Donald C. Stewart.

38   Tate, Gary, ed. *Teaching Composition: Twelve Bibliographic Essays.* Fort Worth: Texas Christian Univ. Press, 1987.
A substantially revised and enlarged edition of the important *Teaching Composition: Ten Bibliographic Essays* (1976). Includes Richard E. Young on invention (supplements the 1976 essay); Richard L. Larson on nonnarrative prose (summarizes and updates the 1976 essay); Edward P. J. Corbett on style (1976 essay reprinted with an update) [215]; Frank J. D'Angelo on the modes of discourse (substantially revised and updated); Richard Lloyd-Jones on testing (new essay); Mina P. Shaughnessy, "Basic Writing" [353]; Andrea A. Lunsford, "Basic Writing Update"; Jenefer M. Giannasi on language varieties (substantially revised) [340]; W. Ross Winterowd, "Literacy, Linguistics, and Rhetoric" (substantially revised and updated) [165]; Joseph Comprone, "Literary Theory and Composition" (new essay); Jim Corder, "Studying Rhetoric and Literature" (substantially revised); James L. Kinneavy on writing across the curriculum (new essay—surveys textbooks and programs as well as scholarship); and Hugh Burns on computers and composition (new essay). The essays on media (by Comprone) and "Composition and Related Fields" (by James L. Kinneavy and C. Robert Kline) are not in the new edition.

History and Theory

The Rhetorical Tradition

Listed in chronological order by date of composition.

39　Bizzell, Patricia, and Bruce Herzberg. *The Rhetorical Tradition: Readings from Classical Times to the Present.* Boston: Bedford Books, 1990.

Substantial excerpts and some complete works from classical rhetoric (Gorgias, Isocrates, Plato, Aristotle, Cicero, Quintilian, *Rhetorica ad Herennium*); medieval rhetoric (Augustine, Boethius, and others); Renaissance rhetoric (Christine de Pisan, Laura Cereta, Erasmus, Ramus, Wilson, Bacon); Enlightenment rhetoric (Margaret Fell, Sarah Grimké, Vico, Campbell, Blair, Whately, Sheridan, Nietzsche, and early compositionists); twentieth-century rhetoric (Bakhtin, Richards, Burke, Weaver, Perelman, Toulmin, Foucault, Derrida, Cixous, Kristeva, Gates). Includes period and author introductions and annotated bibliographies.

40　Sprague, Rosamond Kent. *The Older Sophists.* Columbia: Univ. of South Carolina Press, 1972 (new printing, 1990).

41　Isocrates. *Against the Sophists and Antidosis.* In *Isocrates*, II. Ed. and trans. George Norlin. Loeb Classical Library, Cambridge: Harvard Univ. Press, 1982.

42　Plato. *Apology, Menexenus, Gorgias, Protagoras, Phaedrus, Symposium, Republic* (ca. 370 B.C.E.). In *The Collected Dialogues of Plato.* Ed. Edith Hamilton and Huntington Cairns. Princeton: Princeton Univ. Press, 1961.

43　Aristotle. *Aristotle on Civic Discourse* (ca. 333 B.C.E.). Ed. and trans. George A. Kennedy. New York: Oxford Univ. Press, 1990.

44　Cicero. *De Inventione* (ca. 88 B.C.E.). Trans. H. M. Hubbell. Cambridge: Harvard Univ. Press, 1949.

45　*Rhetorica ad Herennium* (ca. 86 B.C.E.). Trans. Harry Caplan. Cambridge: Harvard Univ. Press, 1954.

46　Cicero. *De Oratore* (55 B.C.E.). *Books I–II.* Trans. E. W. Sutton and H. Rackham. Cambridge: Harvard Univ. Press, 1942. *Book III.* Trans. H. Rackham. Cambridge: Harvard Univ. Press, 1942.

47　Longinus. *On the Sublime* (ca. 40 C.E.). In *Aristotle, The Poetics, and Longinus, On the Sublime.* Trans. W. Hamilton Fyfe. Includes *Demetrius, On Style.* Trans. W. Rhys Roberts, Cambridge: Harvard Univ. Press, 1932.

48   Quintilian. *Institutio Oratoria* (ca. 88 C.E.) Trans. H. E. Butler. 4 vols. Cambridge: Harvard Univ. Press, 1922.

49   Murphy, James J., ed. *Quintilian on the Teaching of Speaking and Writing: Translations from Books One, Two and Ten of the Institutio Oratoria.* Trans. J. S. Watson; rev. by J. J. Murphy. Carbondale: Southern Illinois Univ. Press, 1987.
These selections from the *Institutio* concern Quintilian's ideas about child development and the relationships among reading, writing, and speaking. Murphy's helpful introduction sets Quintilian's life and work in the context of Roman times and traces the reception of his ideas through the Renaissance and to the present.

50   Augustine. *On Christian Doctrine* (426 C.E.). Trans. D. W. Robertson. New York: Library of Liberal Arts, 1958.

51   Murphy, James J. *Three Medieval Rhetorical Arts*. Berkeley: Univ. of California Press, 1971.
Contains medieval manuals on letter writing and on preaching, excerpts from textbooks on Aristotelian dialectic, and Geoffrey of Vinsauf's *Poetria Nova.*

52   Erasmus, Desiderius. *Copia: Foundations of the Abundant Style* (1512). Trans. Betty I. Knott, in *Collected Works of Erasmus,* ed. Craig R. Thompson, 42 vols. Toronto: Univ. of Toronto Press, 1978.

53   Ramus, Peter. *Arguments in Rhetoric against Quintilian* (1549). Trans. Carole Newlands and James J. Murphy. De Kalb: Univ. of Northern Illinois Press, 1983.

54   Burke, Edmund. *A Philosophical Enquiry into the Origin of Our Ideas of the Sublime and the Beautiful.* Ed. James T. Boulton. 1757. Rpt. Notre Dame: Univ. of Notre Dame Press, 1968.

55   Campbell, George. *The Philosophy of Rhetoric.* Ed. Lloyd Bitzer. 1776. Rpt. Carbondale: Southern Illinois Univ. Press, 1963.

56   Blair, Hugh. *Lectures on Rhetoric and Belles-Lettres.* Ed. Harold Harding. 1783. Rpt. Carbondale: Southern Illinois Univ. Press, 1966.

57   Witherspoon, John. *The Selected Writings of John Witherspoon.* Ed. Thomas Miller. 1810. Rpt. Carbondale: Southern Illinois Univ. Press, 1990.

58   Golden, James L., and Edward P. J. Corbett, eds. *The Rhetoric of Blair, Campbell, and Whately.* 1968. Rpt. New York: Holt, Rinehart and Winston, 1980.

59   Whately, Richard. *Elements of Rhetoric.* Ed. Douglas Ehninger. 1828. Rpt. Carbondale: Southern Illinois Univ. Press, 1963.

60   Bain, Alexander. *English Composition and Rhetoric: A Manual.*
1866; American ed., rev. 1888. Rpt. New York: Appleton, 1980.

History of Rhetoric and Education

61   Applebee, Arthur N. *Tradition and Reform in the Teaching of
English: A History.* Urbana, Ill.: NCTE, 1974.

Since the 1600s, English curriculum design in America has reflected a
struggle between traditional goals of preserving high literary culture and
a standard language and progressive goals of democratic social reform.
European cultural and institutional models dominated the curriculum
until the late 1800s, when the first English departments appeared in
American colleges. Applebee discusses English studies, in both literature and language arts, at the elementary, high school, and college
levels. He also discusses the work of professional organizations in
shaping curriculum. An excellent short history of American English
education.

62   Berlin, James A. *Rhetoric and Reality: Writing Instruction in
American Colleges, 1900–1985.* Carbondale: Southern Illinois Univ.
Press, 1987.

Discussions of writing pedagogy in textbooks and essays during the
twentieth century can be divided into three groups, based on their theoretical assumptions about the nature of reality and the purpose of
rhetoric. Objective theories regard external reality as empirically knowable and treat rhetoric as the medium (ideally transparent) for conveying
this knowledge. Subjective theories regard truth as attainable only
through inner vision and value a rhetoric that uses emotionally charged
language to stimulate subjective knowing as well as to communicate
one's vision to others. Transactional theories see truth as at least partly
provisional, arrived at by argument and interpretation. Transactional
theories, then, see rhetoric as a means of persuasion and of negotiating
different interpretations of reality. Objective theories dominated writing
instruction in the early years of the century, challenged only by progressive education and the communications movement. In recent years,
though, subjective and transactional theories have increased in importance. See Berlin [63].

63   Berlin, James A. *Writing Instruction in Nineteenth-Century
American Colleges.* Carbondale: Southern Illinois Univ. Press,
1984.

Three rhetorics shaped nineteenth-century writing instruction. The first,
classical rhetoric, was concerned with conveying universal truths to rational beings with the aid of emotional and ethical appeals. Early in the
nineteenth century, classical rhetoric was replaced by the rhetoric of the
eighteenth-century Scottish Common Sense philosophers, which emphasized conveying facts derived from sensory experience to beings
possessing normal faculties of perception, with the aid of forms of discourse suited to divergent kinds of experience. This rhetoric dominated
nineteenth-century writing instruction and remains influential in the
form of so-called current-traditional rhetoric. A third rhetoric, derived

from Emersonian romanticism, emphasized the individual writer's vision, which creates knowledge of reality by an interpretive insight into its underlying ideal structure, and which evokes a similarly holistic response from the audience. Romantic rhetoric did not challenge eighteenth-century rhetoric's dominance until the end of the nineteenth century, but it has recently inspired some of the most cogent critiques of curent-traditional rhetoric.

See: James A. Berlin and Robert P. Inkster, "Current-Traditional Rhetoric: Paradigm and Practice" [114].

64   Bolgar, R. R. *The Classical Heritage and Its Beneficiaries.* Cambridge: Cambridge Univ. Press, 1958.

A history of education from late Roman times to the fourteenth century in Byzantium, early medieval education in Ireland and England and in France under Charlemagne, Scholasticism, and classical education in the Renaissance. Bolgar points out the ways scholars selected and interpreted classical texts and analyzes the political motives for their choices and views.

65   Brereton, John C., ed. *The Origins of Composition Studies in the American College, 1875–1925: A Documentary History.* Pittsburgh: Univ. of Pittsburgh Press, 1995.

A number of histories of composition have focused on the formative years of the discipline, around the turn of the twentieth century. The major original documents from this critical period have, however, been difficult to access. Having many of them together in this volume makes it possible to see their self-consciousness about theoretical choices, their rhetorical sophistication, and their diversity. The documents are in five sets: Harvard's program from 1870–1900, with course descriptions, reports from the composition committee, and reflections by Adams Sherman Hill and Barrett Wendell; the new writing curriculum from 1895–1915, with essays by John Genung, program descriptions from a dozen representative institutions, and reports from the MLA's pedagogical section; the attack on Harvard, with essays on teaching composition by Gertrude Buck, Lane Cooper, Thomas Lounsbury, and others; textbooks, with excerpts from sixteen texts by Hill, Genung, Wendell, Scott, Cooper, Strunk, and others; and essay writing, with a wide selection of articles, textbook extracts, sample admission essays, and course materials. Includes a substantial introductory history by Brereton and, as a concluding chapter, Warner Taylor's *National Survey of Conditions in Freshman English* of 1929.

66   Brereton, John, ed. *Traditions of Inquiry.* New York: Oxford Univ. Press, 1985.

Eight essays assess the contributions of important teachers of writing: Wallace Douglas, "Barrett Wendell"; Donald C. Stewart, "Fred Newton Scott"; Ann E. Berthoff, "I. A. Richards"; John Brereton, "Sterling Andrus Leonard"; William F. Irmscher, "Kenneth Burke"; Walker Gibson, "Theodore Baird"; Richard Lloyd-Jones, "Richard Braddock"; Robert Lyons, "Mina Shaughnessy."

67   Bridenthal, Renate, Claudia Koonz, and Susan Stuard, eds. *Becoming Visible: Women in European History.* 2nd ed. Boston: Houghton Mifflin, 1987.

Twenty essays debunk myths about women's nonparticipation in history and consider how these myths arose and shaped European culture. An excellent introduction to women's history and education from the times of European tribal peoples, ancient Egypt, Greece, and Rome to the present day.

68   Clark, Gregory, and S. Michael Halloran, eds. *Oratorical Culture in Nineteenth-Century America: Transformations in the Theory and Practice of Rhetoric.* Carbondale: Southern Illinois Univ. Press, 1993.

Eleven original essays trace and analyze the development of American rhetoric from neoclassical oratorical forms that focused on civic matters to rhetorics that reflected a growing individualism and professionalism. Essays include an introduction by Clark and Halloran; Ronald F. Reid on Edward Everett and neoclassical oratory; Gregory Clark on Timothy Dwight; P. Joy Rouse on Margaret Fuller; Nan Johnson on elocution and the private learner; Nicole Tonkovich on *Godey's Lady's Book*; and Catherine Peaden on Jane Addams.

69   Conley, Thomas M. *Rhetoric in the European Tradition.* New York: Longman, 1990.

Rhetoric has been defined somewhat differently in different ages, reflecting the needs—and particularly the crises—of the times. Greek notions of rhetoric reflect several different views of nature and beliefs about the ends of rhetoric. The four basic Greek models, which see rhetoric as variously manipulative or consensus seeking (the Sophistic versions) or dialectical (in Plato) or problematic (in Aristotle) persist throughout the history of rhetoric, one or another dominating at different times. Conley traces the dominant theories from Greek to modern times, focusing on schools and individual rhetorical theorists, giving most attention to those who exerted the greatest influence on their own contemporaries and on later thinkers, and setting each in the historical and political context that seems to account for the nature of the rhetorical model. Conley's purpose is to provide the background material needed to comprehend the major texts themselves, as well as to reorder our idea of which texts and figures are truly the major ones.

70   Connors, Robert J. "The Rise and Fall of the Modes of Discourse." *CCC,* 32 (December 1981), 444–63.

This survey of the most popular rhetoric textbooks used in American colleges since the early 1800s shows that, until the 1950s, the dominant method of writing instruction was imitation of models of the modes of discourse—narration, description, exposition, and argument. In the 1950s, self-expression and audience models challenged the older method. Connors traces the influence of Bain, Hill, Scott, Genung, the CCCC, and others. Braddock Award winner.

71   Connors, Robert J., Lisa S. Ede, and Andrea A. Lunsford, eds. *Essays on Classical Rhetoric and Modern Discourse.* Carbondale and Edwardsville: Southern Illinois Univ. Press, 1984.

In this festschrift for Edward P. J. Corbett, seventeen contributors discuss the importance of classical rhetoric to modern composition studies. Essays include Robert J. Connors, Lisa S. Ede, and Andrea A. Lunsford, "The Revival of Rhetoric in America"; James L. Golden, "Plato Revisited: A Theory of Discourse for All Seasons"; James L. Kinneavy, "Translating Theory into Practice in Teaching Composition: A Historical View and a Contemporary View"; James C. Raymond, "Enthymemes, Examples, and Rhetorical Method"; John T. Gage, "An Adequate Epistemology for Composition: Classical and Modern Perspectives"; and S. Michael Halloran and Annette Norris Bradford, "Figures of Speech in the Rhetoric of Science and Technology." Also includes a bibliography of works by Corbett. Mina P. Shaughnessy Prize co-winner.

72 Corbett, Edward P. J. *Classical Rhetoric for the Modern Student.* 1965; 3rd ed. New York: Oxford Univ. Press, 1990.

Training in classical rhetoric can help modern students understand public persuasive discourse while they discover the educational tradition that has shaped Western culture for two thousand years. Chapters on discovery of arguments, arrangement of material, and style explain logic, the types of appeal, the topics, resources for invention, types of refutation, schemes, and tropes, illustrated by modern essays and speeches. The final chapter is a brief history of rhetoric. A comprehensive introduction to classical rhetorical theory and practice.

73 Corbett, Edward P. J., James L. Golden, and Goodwin F. Berquist, eds. *Essays on the Rhetoric of the Western World.* Dubuque, Iowa: Kendall/Hunt, 1990.

Twenty-four previously published essays, exemplars of twentieth-century scholarship in the history of rhetoric, including Hoyt Hudson, "The Field of Rhetoric" (1923); Everett Lee Hunt, "Plato and Aristotle on Rhetoric and Rhetoricians" (1925); Charles S. Baldwin, "St. Augustine on Preaching" (1928); William G. Crane, "English Rhetoric of the Sixteenth Century" (1937); Werner Jaeger, "The Rhetoric of Isocrates and Its Cultural Ideal" (1944); Marie Hochmuth Nichols, "Kenneth Burke and the 'New Rhetoric'" (1952); Donald Bryant, "Rhetoric: Its Function and Scope" (1953); Richard L. Johannesen et al., "Richard M. Weaver on the Nature of Rhetoric" (1970); and Wilbur S. Howell, "Renaissance Rhetoric and Modern Rhetoric: A Study in Change" (1975).

74 Covino, William A. *The Art of Wondering: A Revisionist Return to the History of Rhetoric.* Portsmouth, N.H.: Heinemann, Boynton/Cook, 1988.

Conventional histories of rhetoric depict its major texts as sets of prescriptions for constructing sentences, organizing speeches, and (amorally) manipulating audiences. In contrast, a revisionist history could see Plato, Aristotle, and Cicero as describing and performing a rhetoric that explores ambiguities. From this perspective, an alternative tradition might be traced through Montaigne, Vico, Hume, Byron, and De Quincey, a tradition of rhetoric used to inquire into uncertain questions from multiple viewpoints while remaining open to any stylistic innovations that facilitate such explorations. This rhetoric, an "art of wondering," is particularly appropriate to the postmodern epistemological orientation of Burke, Derrida, Feyerabend, and Geertz. It fosters tolerance and interdependence by keeping the exploratory conversation going.

75 Covino, William A., and David A. Joliffe. *Rhetoric: Concepts, Definitions, Boundaries.* Boston: Allyn and Bacon, 1995.

An anthology offering information and selections in nearly every area of rhetoric. "Part I: An Introduction to Rhetoric" defines the field in a few brief chapters. "Part II: Glossary of Major Concepts, Historical Periods, and Rhetors" is a small encyclopedia with sixty-eight one-page entries. "Part III: Perspectives on the History and Theory of Rhetoric" is an anthology of fifteen essays by well-known scholars chiefly on major themes in the history of the field. "Part IV: The Contents of Rhetoric" is an anthology of essays by authors in a wide range of fields, with three to five essays in each of the following categories: Rhetoric and Cultural Studies; Rhetoric and Non-Western Culture; Rhetoric, Feminism, and Gender Studies; Rhetoric and Philosophy; Rhetoric and the Arts; Rhetoric and Literary Criticism; Rhetoric and Science; Rhetoric and Linguistics; Rhetoric and Education; Rhetoric and Literacy; Rhetoric and Composition; Rhetoric and Technology; and Rhetoric and Oratory. Includes an index.

76 Crowley, Sharon. *The Methodical Memory: Invention in Current-Traditional Rhetoric.* Carbondale: Southern Illinois Univ. Press, 1990.

Current-traditional rhetoric, until recently the dominant approach in American schools, developed in the late eighteenth and nineteenth centuries when rhetoricians like George Campbell and Richard Whately rejected classical rhetoric's invention schemes. To discover arguments, they claimed, the writer had merely to investigate the workings of his or her own mind, for all minds worked alike. In this model of invention, the individual authorial mind was privileged over community wisdom, and the written text was regarded as a record of the mind's operations. Clarity and logic were the goal. Pedagogy based on this model emphasized the formal features of texts—correctness and logical organization, for example—that presumably reflected the well-ordered mind at work. The metaphysical principles, supposedly universal, on which this pedagogy is based make it inherently conservative and insensitive to cultural difference. A preferable rhetoric and pedagogy is one that values difference and the diversity of communal treasures as archives for invention.

77 Enos, Theresa, ed. *Encyclopedia of Rhetoric and Composition: Communication from Ancient Times to the Information Age.* New York: Garland, 1995.

Four hundred and sixty-seven entries by 288 scholars of rhetoric, composition, speech communication, and philosophy, covering the history, theory, concepts, and major figures in the field of rhetoric. Entries are arranged alphabetically and range from brief identifications of terms and minor figures to essays on major figures and topics. A selected bibliography follows each entry. Includes an index.

78 Enos, Theresa, and Stuart C. Brown. *Defining the New Rhetorics.* Newbury Park, Calif.: Sage Publications, 1993.

This collection of fifteen essays characterizes twentieth-century rhetoric as pluralistic. Essays include: Richard Leo Enos, "Viewing the Dawns of Our Past Days Again: Classical Rhetoric as Reconstructive Literacy"; Carolyn Miller, "Rhetoric and Community: The Problem of the

One and the Many"; S. Michael Halloran, "Further Thoughts on the End of Rhetoric"; Robert Scott, "Rhetoric is Epistemic: What Difference Does That Make?"; James Berlin, "Poststructuralism, Semiotics, and Social-Epistemic Rhetoric: Convergence Agendas"; Christopher Burnham, "Expressive Rhetoric: A Source Study"; Linda Flower, "Cognitive Rhetoric: Inquiry into the Art of Inquiry"; and James Porter, "Developing a Postmodern Ethics of Rhetoric and Composition."

79   Enos, Theresa, and Stuart C. Brown. *Professing the New Rhetorics.* Englewood Cliffs, N.J.: Blair Press, 1994.

Fourteen selections from major figures in the development of twentieth-century rhetorical theories, followed by thirteen essays of "commentary and application" by scholars in composition and speech communication. Theorists represented are Ferdinand de Saussure, I. A. Richards, Kenneth Burke, Mikhail Bakhtin, Richard Weaver, Ernesto Grassi, Stephen Toulmin, Richard McKeon, Chaïm Perelman, Michel Foucault, Michael Polanyi, Jürgen Habermas, Roland Barthes, and Wayne Booth. Scholars are Donald Bryant; Richard Ohmann; Robert Scott; Douglas Ehninger; S. Michael Halloran; Terry Eagleton; E. D. Hirsch, Jr.; Walter Fisher; Andrea Lunsford and Lisa Ede; Jim Corder; Paulo Freire and Donaldo Macedo; Particia Bizzell; and James Berlin.

80   Foss, Sonja K., Karen A. Foss, and Robert Trapp. *Contemporary Perspectives on Rhetoric.* 2nd ed. Prospect Heights, Ill.: Waveland Press, 1991.

The diversity of contemporary rhetoric is demonstrated by the work of eight thinkers: I. A. Richards, Richard Weaver, Stephen Toulmin, Chaïm Perelman, Ernesto Grassi, Kenneth Burke, Michel Foucault, and Jürgen Habermas. These theorists engage rhetoric as a study of language, as an expression of values, or as a form of knowledge. Following a brief history of rhetoric are chapters on each of the figures, providing biographical information and an overview of their contributions to rhetorical thought. Two concluding chapters briefly examine challenges to the rhetorical tradition (feminist, Afrocentric, Asian) and other current perspectives on rhetoric (fantasy-theme, performance, narrative, etc.).

81   Glenn, Cheryl. "sex, lies, and manuscript: Refiguring Aspasia in the History of Rhetoric." *CCC*, 45 (May 1994), 180–199.

Aspasia of Miletus, one of the few free, educated women of fifth-century B.C.E. Greece, left no writings and is known from secondary sources that refer to her as a rhetorician and philosopher courted by Pericles and consulted by Socrates. Many sources refer to Aspasia's influence: she is credited with contributing to—or even composing—many of Pericles' speeches and with influencing Socrates, Plato, and Xenophon. Her participation in the public life of Athens is extraordinary, for women there were relegated to domestic invisibility. For venturing into the public arena, Aspasia was characterized as licentious and immoral. History has figured her as apocryphal, and her work has been attributed to men. Few historians of rhetoric have treated her seriously; hence, she represents the general disappearance of women from the rhetorical tradition. Refiguring Aspasia is part of the larger project of recovering the contributions of women to rhetoric. Braddock Award winner.

82 Halloran, S. Michael. "Rhetoric in the American College Curriculum: The Decline of Public Discourse." *PRE/TEXT,* 3 (Fall 1983). Rpt. in Vitanza [163].

Classical rhetoric emphasizes effective communication about public problems. Seventeenth-century theories of rhetoric in American colleges led away from such public discourse by assigning argument to the realm of logic and retaining only "pleasing expression" in rhetoric, as well as by ignoring vernacular English in favor of Greek and Latin. In the eighteenth century, a more "classical" conception of rhetoric recovered invention, arrangement, and audience, and English became the language of formal academic disputation, which dealt more often with public concerns. In the nineteenth century, emphasis shifted to written products, to the "modes" of discourse, and to correctness, and away from invention and public discourse. These changes were closely related to the dominance of belletristic aesthetics, to the specialization of the curriculum that presented knowledge in small course-units, and to a shift in the function of education from preparation for public service to preparation for personal advancement. Many aspects of classical rhetoric are being revived, but public discourse has not yet reemerged.

83 Horner, Winifred Bryan, ed. *Historical Rhetoric: An Annotated Bibliography of Selected Sources in English.* Boston: G. K. Hall, 1980.

Selected primary and secondary sources, divided into five areas: the classical period, the Middle Ages, the Renaissance, the eighteenth century, and the nineteenth century. Each chapter has an introduction, primary sources listed chronologically, and secondary sources listed alphabetically. Most entries are annotated.

84 Horner, Winifred Bryan, ed. *The Present State of Scholarship in Historical and Contemporary Rhetoric.* Rev. ed. Columbia: Univ. of Missouri Press, 1990.

An indispensable collection of six bibliographic essays by eminent scholars in each period: Richard Leo Enos and Ann M. Blakeslee, "The Classical Period"; James J. Murphy and Martin Camargo, "The Middle Ages"; Don Paul Abbott, "The Renaissance"; Winifred Bryan Horner and Kerri Morris Barton, "The Eighteenth Century"; Donald C. Stewart, "The Nineteenth Century"; and James L. Kinneavy, "Contemporary Rhetoric." The authors also identify areas where further study is needed.

85 Horner, Winifred Bryan. *Nineteenth-Century Scottish Rhetoric: The American Connection.* Carbondale: Southern Illinois Univ. Press, 1993.

Often treated as insignificant by historians of rhetoric, nineteenth-century Scottish rhetoric was in fact "important not only in rhetoric but also in twentieth-century education as a whole and . . . [in] the twentieth-century American composition course" (3). With their mission of serving the business class, Scottish universities were quick to expand their scientific and technical curricula, and they embraced other innovations—such as the new discipline of English literature—as well. Advances in rhetoric in this period have been obscured, however, because nineteenth-century Scottish professors of rhetoric did not publish their lectures, as their more famous eighteenth-century predecessors had done. But meticulous student notes on their lectures are preserved. Horner reviews the history of the period, then identifies and summarizes the archives available at the universities of Edinburgh, Glasgow, St. Andrews, and Aberdeen, and concludes by outlining the connections to American composition theories.

86 Howell, Wilbur Samuel. *Eighteenth-Century British Logic and Rhetoric*. Princeton: Princeton Univ. Press, 1971.

Classical rhetoric and logic remained influential throughout the eighteenth century, though challenged by the new rhetoric and logic of science. Classical logic, which came from Aristotle, aimed to deduce new truths from those already known and to communicate them to a learned audience. Classical rhetoric was of three kinds: Ciceronian rhetoric aimed to communicate truths to a popular audience; stylistic rhetoric analyzed orations and literary works; and elocutionary rhetoric, a new form, prescribed methods of delivery for public speaking, stage acting, and polite conversation. In contrast, the new logic propounded by Francis Bacon and John Locke worked inductively, testing ideas against perceived reality. The new rhetoric claimed to be a general theory of communication, learned as well as popular, advocating inductive reasoning and plain style. Adam Smith and George Campbell were its chief proponents.

87 Howell, Wilbur Samuel. *Logic and Rhetoric in England, 1500–1700*. Princeton: Princeton Univ. Press, 1956.

In Renaissance England, a persistent metaphor likened logic, the discourse of science, to a closed fist (tight and rigorous) and rhetoric, the discourse of popularized knowledge, to an open hand (loose and popular). In the early sixteenth century, rhetorical study had three patterns: the Ciceronian pattern focused on the five rhetorical arts; the stylistic pattern concerned the study of tropes and figures; and the formulary pattern was the study of models for imitation. Later in the sixteenth century, Ramism reformed dialectic and rhetoric (see "A Brief History of Rhetoric and Composition"). At the end of the seventeenth century, the *Port-Royal Logic* popularized Cartesian logic. Bacon's logic and rhetoric paralleled this development and led to the Royal Society's project for language reform. Howell's work is the standard history of this important period in the history of rhetoric.

88 Jarratt, Susan. *Rereading the Sophists: Classical Rhetoric Refigured*. Carbondale: Southern Illinois Univ. Press, 1991.

The Greek Sophists of the fifth century B.C.E. developed a theory and practice of socially constructed discourse, focused on the historical contingency and democratic usefulness of strategies of persuasion, and delighted in the play of language. Recovered from its denigration by Plato and Aristotle, sophism provides a good model for understanding the political effects and goals of feminist discourse and critical-education discourse today.

89 Johnson, Nan. *Nineteenth-Century Rhetoric in North America*. Carbondale: Southern Illinois Univ. Press, 1991.

Nineteenth-century rhetoric was a synthesis of classical elements (the canons of invention, arrangement, and style), belletrism (focusing on criticism and literary taste), and epistemological ideas about the relation of language and persuasion to the mental "faculties" (will, imagination, understanding, and passions). All three of these approaches developed in the eighteenth century and found a solid place in the discipline of rhetoric, in theoretical treatises as well as textbooks. The civic and cultural status of rhetoric was as yet secure in the nineteenth century: It was still seen as a significant factor in maintaining social and political order, as well as in formulating the conventions for scientific and philosophical communication. Both oratory and composition were firmly within its purview. "Nineteenth-century rhetoricians claimed for rhetoric the status of science, practical art, and civil servant. In laying this claim, they addressed and confirmed the dominant intellectual and cultural values of their era" (246).

90   Kennedy, George A. *The Art of Persuasion in Greece.* Princeton: Princeton Univ. Press, 1963.
Volume 1 of Kennedy's history of classical rhetoric (see [91]), the standard work on the period, treats individual rhetoricians and their works and supplies historical background. Kennedy emphasizes that Greek rhetoric was overwhelmingly an art of oral discourse. He discusses the conflict between rhetoric and philosophy, and traces the development of the great central theory of rhetoric to which all classical rhetoricians contributed, foreshadowing Greek influence on the Romans.

91   Kennedy, George A. *The Art of Rhetoric in the Roman World 300 B.C.–A.D. 300.* Princeton: Princeton Univ. Press, 1972.
This is volume 2 of Kennedy's history of classical rhetoric (see [90]), the standard work on the period. It treats individual rhetoricians and their works in detail, supplies much historical background, and traces the fall and rise of persuasion as the main focus of rhetoric under Roman influence. Kennedy has two chapters on Cicero, two on Augustan rhetoric, one on Quintilian, and two on later Greek rhetoric.

92   Kennedy, George A. *Classical Rhetoric and Its Christian and Secular Tradition from Ancient to Modern Times.* Chapel Hill: Univ. of North Carolina Press, 1980.
Originally formulated in ancient Greece as an art, rhetoric later developed into three types. Technical rhetoric prescribed the correct forms for invention, organization of speeches, and style. Sophistic rhetoric, taught by imitation, emphasized the speaker's ethos and the magical powers of stylistic display, and philosophical rhetoric sought to discover truth and convey it to audiences for their good. Kennedy traces these lines of rhetorical study up to the 1700s, chiefly through summaries of the contributions of important rhetoricians.

93   Kimball, Bruce A. *Orators and Philosophers: A History of the Idea of Liberal Education.* New York: Teachers College Press, 1986.
The history of liberal education from the Middle Ages to the present can be seen as a struggle between two kinds of teacher-scholars. *Orators* stressed citizenship education, emphasized commonly held ("liberal") notions of the good, and valued rhetoric as a method of creating consensus on public issues. *Philosophers* stressed education for the pursuit of pure truth, supported education for the elite by defining "liberal" as liberation from worldly cares (hence, freedom to pursue the

truth), and denigrated rhetoric in their search for a language transparent to the truth. Philosophers have come to dominate Western education through the force of science and technology, but the influence of the Orators ought to be restored.

94 Kitzhaber, Albert. *Rhetoric in American Colleges, 1850–1900.* Dallas: Southern Methodist Univ. Press, 1990.

The first publication of Kitzhaber's 1953 dissertation, a comprehensive examination of higher education and the development of rhetoric in a critical period. Kitzhaber sees the end of the nineteenth century as a time of transition and reform as rhetorical theory struggled to adjust to changes in psychology and education theory, the expansion of science and technology, and the influence of the new German model of the university on departments and curriculum. Kitzhaber describes the changes at Harvard; presents British and American rhetorical theories; assesses the work of A. S. Hill, Genung, Wendell, and Scott; examines speech and belletrism in rhetorical theory; and concludes with several chapters on the emergence of composition theory.

95 Lunsford, Andrea A., ed. *Reclaiming Rhetorica: Women in the Rhetorical Tradition.* Pittsburgh: Univ. of Pittsburgh Press, 1995.

Sixteen original essays examine the contribution to rhetorical theory of women such as Aspasia (Susan Jarratt and Rory Ong), Diotima (Jan Swearingen), Christine de Pisan (Jenny Refern), Mary Astell (Christine Mason Sutherland), Margaret Fuller (Annette Kolodny), Ida B. Wells (Jacqueline Jones Royster), Sojourner Truth (Drema R. Lipscomb), Suzanne K. Langer (Arabella Lyon), and Louise Rosenblatt (Annika Hallin).

See: Andrea A. Lunsford and Lisa S. Ede, "Classical Rhetoric, Modern Rhetoric, and Contemporary Discourse Studies" [147].

96 Marrou, H. I. *A History of Education in Antiquity.* Trans. George Lamb. New York: Sheed & Ward, 1956.

The standard introduction to the subject. Marrou describes the origins of classical education from Homer to Isocrates and traces primary, secondary, and postsecondary education from Greek and Roman times to early Christian schooling and Byzantine and monastic education.

97 Murphy, James J. *Rhetoric in the Middle Ages.* Berkeley: Univ. of California Press, 1974.

Saint Augustine turned the prescriptive Aristotelian and Ciceronian rhetorics to Christian use by arguing that rhetoric is neither empty nor merely ornamental if it is filled with religious truth and dedicated to saving souls. Medieval rhetoricians, following Augustine, made the art of preaching one of the three chief rhetorical genres. The others were letter writing, devoted to political ends, and prescriptive grammar, which was studied by writing and analyzing poetry. Prescriptive rhetoric, based on fragmentary knowledge of classical texts, declined after the rediscovery in the 1400s of complete copies of Quintilian's *Institutio* and Cicero's *De Oratore.*

98 Murphy, James J., ed. *The Rhetorical Tradition and Modern Writing.* New York: MLA, 1982.

Twelve essays treat the place of classical, eighteenth-century, and nineteenth-century rhetoric in the modern curriculum and analyze the work of Cicero, John Locke, Alexander Bain, and other premodern rhetoricians. Essays include James J. Murphy, "Rhetorical History as a Guide to the Salvation of American Reading and Writing: A Plea for Curricular Courage"; James L. Kinneavy, "Restoring the Humanities: The Return of Rhetoric from Exile"; Susan Miller, "Classical Practice and Contemporary Basics"; S. Michael Halloran and Merrill D. Whitburn, "Ciceronian Rhetoric and the Rise of Science: The Plain Style Reconsidered"; Winifred Bryan Horner, "Rhetoric in the Liberal Arts: Nineteenth-Century Scottish Universities"; Donald C. Stewart, "Two Model Teachers and the Harvardization of English Departments."

99   Murphy, James J., ed. *A Short History of Writing Instruction from Ancient Greece to Twentieth Century America.* Davis, Calif.: Hermagoras Press, 1990.

Seven essays focus on the contributions of rhetoricians to writing instruction: Kathleen Welch, "Writing Instruction in Ancient Athens After 450 B.C."; James J. Murphy, "Roman Writing Instruction as Described in Quintilian"; Marjorie Woods, "The Teaching of Writing in Medieval Europe"; Don Paul Abbott, "Rhetoric and Writing in Renaissance Europe and England"; Winifred Bryan Horner, "Writing Instruction in Great Britain: Eighteenth and Nineteenth Centuries"; S. Michael Halloran, "From Rhetoric to Composition: The Teaching of Writing in America to 1900"; James A. Berlin, "Writing Instruction in School and College English, 1890–1985." Includes glossary and bibliography.

100   Murphy, James J., ed. *A Synoptic History of Classical Rhetoric.* Davis, Calif.: Hermagoras Press, 1983.

Six essays provide an introductory overview of rhetoric in Greek and Roman culture and include summaries of major works: James J. Murphy, "The Origins and Early Development of Rhetoric"; Forbes I. Hill, "The *Rhetoric* of Aristotle"; James J. Murphy, "The Age of Codification: Hermagoras and the Pseudo-Ciceronian *Rhetorica ad Herennium*"; Donovan J. Ochs, "Cicero's Rhetorical Theory"; Prentice A. Meador, Jr., "Quintilian and the *Institutio Oratoria*"; James J. Murphy, "The End of the Ancient World: The Second Sophistic and Saint Augustine." Also includes a basic bibliography on classical rhetoric compiled by Michael C. Leff.

See: Jasper Neel, *Plato, Derrida, and Writing* [151].

101   North, Stephen M. *The Making of Knowledge in Composition: Portrait of an Emerging Field.* Upper Montclair, N.J.: Boynton/Cook, 1987.

Composition is an interdisciplinary field comprising three methodological communities: first, the practitioners, who generate lore about writing instruction through classroom experience; second, the scholars, whose research produces histories and philosophical works; and third, the researchers, whose empirical methods include protocol analysis and ethnography. At present, scholars and researchers are battling for control of the field and for the allegiance of the practitioners—whose status has been downgraded by the implication that they should adopt one or the other of these ways of making knowledge. North summarizes and critiques examples of work in each of the communities.

102   Ong, Walter J., S.J. *Ramus, Method, and the Decay of Dialogue.* 1958. Rpt. New York: Farrar, Straus and Giroux, 1974.

Although the works of Peter Ramus decisively changed rhetoric, he was heavily influenced by his scholastic predecessors. Like them, he attempted to describe a universal method for systematizing knowledge into academic disciplines that could be easily taught to the young boys who attended the university. Unlike them, Ramus lived in a world in which printed texts were increasingly available. He came to conceive of knowledge as broken up into "fields" (like the visual field of the printed page), composed of discrete bits of information (like printed letters), and hence susceptible to quantification. Ramus "reformed" classical rhetoric by moving invention and arrangement to the realm of dialectic and by treating dialectic as the arranging of bits of information in dichotomies, which presumably convince by virtue of their logical structure alone. Ramus dropped memory and delivery because they are not necessary for print communication. Rhetoric itself has to do only with style, and, because the dichotomies of Ramist dialectic convey rational truth, rhetoric need be used only when a recalcitrant audience required ornamentation of the truth to induce belief. Ramus's view of the quantifiable nature of knowledge contributed to the development of empirical scientific method, and his plain style seemed the appropriately neutral medium for scientific study. Ong argues that Ramus himself cared little about advancing knowledge of the external world or rescuing language from the "distortions" of rhetorical ornamentation.

103   Rudolph, Frederick. *Curriculum: A History of the American Undergraduate Course of Study since 1636.* San Francisco: Jossey-Bass, 1977.

An invaluable history of the establishment and development of colleges in the United States, their curricula, student populations, purposes for education and certification, and the rationale in each period and at key colleges for determining what counts as knowledge.

104   Russell, David R. "Romantics on Writing: Liberal Culture and the Abolition of Composition Courses." *Rhetoric Review,* 6 (Spring 1988), 132–48.

The required composition course has, during its hundred-year history, frequently been attacked by proponents of Arnoldian "liberal culture," who advocate an elitist view of education and oppose the democratic, professional, and scientific character of the modern university. In the view of Thomas Lounsbury, Oscar James Campbell, and others, writing is a creative act that cannot be taught; the required composition course is stultifying to students, instructors, and the English department as a whole; and writing ability should therefore be regarded as an admission criterion, not a college course. The combination of composition with an introduction to literature in many programs reflects the influence of the liberal-culture argument. In recent times, the assumptions underlying calls for abolition of the composition course persist in conflicts over the status of composition in English departments, in expressivist composition theories, and in policy decisions about admissions standards.

105   Russell, David R. *Writing in the Academic Disciplines, 1870–1990: A Curricular History.* Carbondale: Southern Illinois Univ. Press, 1991.

In a long flirtation with writing instruction in the disciplines, universities have begun hundreds of programs to teach writing across the curriculum in the twentieth century, all of which became marginalized. Writing was not integrated in content learning, and professors continued to resist teaching writing and reading papers. These failures reflect the persistent attitude that writing is a skill, a form of recorded speech, that writing instruction is remediation, and that the academy is a single discourse community. They also reflect the myth of transcience, the belief that students' inability to write is a problem that will soon, or eventually, be solved. The structure of the university makes cross-disciplinary conversation unproductive, hence the fantasy that the academy is a single discourse community, for to acknowledge the diversity of discourse conventions would require more attention to one's own conventions and present a clear necessity to teach them. General education reforms reinforced this delusion, as well as the myth of transcience, by calling for a unified society and explicitly remedial writing courses. Writing in the disciplines is much more difficult to learn under these conditions, which contributes to the perceived high status of the disciplines, but also opposes social equity by creating a hurdle that many students cannot vault. Writing across the curriculum has been more influential since 1970, but the same forces of resistance are still at work.

106   Swearingen, C. Jan. *Rhetoric and Irony: Western Literacy and Western Lies.* New York: Oxford Univ. Press, 1991.

Is language a lie, a fiction capable of creating only fictive meanings and identities? Preplatonic philosophers resisted the idea that language was deceptive and began to develop a writing-based technical rhetoric to anatomize arguments and cast them in forms reflecting truth. Plato tried to scuttle this movement, proposing instead that only honest dialogue could attain truth. Plato condemned the self-consciously manipulative rhetor as an "eiron," regarding the manipulator as a liar. Technical rhetoric nevertheless triumphed with Aristotle, progenitor of the "linear-monological-grammatical-logical systems" that have dominated rhetoric in the west. Cicero tried, too, to combat technical rhetoric in favor of dialogue, an effort blocked and obscured by the loss of his mature works. Augustine criticized mendacity in language, also connected, for him, to the deceptive techniques of rhetoric, which were to be corrected by sermonic teaching and inner dialogues between self and soul. The dialogic rhetorics of Plato, Cicero, and Augustine are pertinent to our own age, when textual literacy is being challenged by new technologies and linear-logical argument forms are regarded as too restrictive and abstract.

107   Woodward, William Harrison. *Studies in Education during the Age of the Renaissance, 1400–1600.* Cambridge: Cambridge Univ. Press, 1906.

In what is still an authoritative source for the period, Woodward describes the Quattrocento beginnings of humanist education, traces its influence in Europe by examining the careers of important educators (including Guarino, Agricola, Erasmus, Vives, and Melanchthon), examines Italian and English doctrines of courtesy, and reviews the humanist education of Elizabethan aristocrats.

108   Wozniak, John Michael. *English Composition in Eastern Colleges, 1850–1940.* Washington, D.C.: Univ. Press of America, 1978.

A detailed history of composition courses, textbooks, methods, rationales, and instructors, interwoven with an analysis of theories and purposes and a general history of institutional development.

Rhetoric and Composition Theory

109   Bartholomae, David. "Inventing the University." In *When a Writer Can't Write.* Ed. Mike Rose [177].
Students must learn to sound like experts when they write, and they thus adopt personae that seem to them authoritative and academic. The errors of inexperienced writers should be seen as the result of this effort to approximate and finally to control a complex and alien discourse. Students "extend themselves, by successive approximations, into the commonplaces, set phrases, rituals and gestures, habits of mind, tricks of persuasion, obligatory conclusions and necessary connections" that constitute knowledge in academic communities. Writer, audience, and subject are all located in discourses that exist outside the individual, and it requires an act of courage to penetrate such discourses and earn the right to speak in them.

110   Bartholomae, David. "Writing with Teachers: A Conversation with Peter Elbow." *CCC*, 46 (February 1995), 62–71.
"Academic writing—writing done in the shadow of others—is the real work of the academy and therefore the key term for teaching writing. To pretend otherwise is to withhold from students knowledge of the politics of discursive practice. Student writing is situated in a heavily populated textual space in an institution where power is unequally distributed. The image of a free space for expression, found in Peter Elbow's work, reflects a desire to be outside of history and culture, a desire for a common language, free of jargon and full of presence; a desire for an autonomous author and a democratic classroom. If we wish to help students become aware of the forces at work in producing knowledge, we need, rather, to invoke the reality of the classroom as a substation in the cultural network, not disguise it as a utopian space. Critical knowledge requires working with texts, understanding the possibilities beyond quotation, and not pretending that writing is purely one's own. Composition should not foster the genre of sentimental realism and pretend it is transcendent, but preside over critical writing, academic writing. See Elbow [133].

111   Bazerman, Charles. "What Written Knowledge Does: Three Examples of Academic Discourse." *Philosophy of the Social Sciences,* 11 (September 1981), 361–87. Rpt. in Bazerman, *Shaping Written Knowledge.* Madison, Wis.: Univ. of Wisconsin Press, 1988.
We can study the way written knowledge contributes to a discipline by analyzing how writers in different disciplines use specialized lexicons, citations, tacit knowledge, and personae. Examples from biochemistry, sociology of science, and literary criticism illustrate the ways in which discourse constitutes knowledge in each field.

112   Berlin, James A. "Poststructuralism, Cultural Studies, and the Composition Classroom." *Rhetoric Review,* 11 (Fall 1992), 16–33.

The postmodern critique of traditional liberal-humanist epistemology has been useful to social-epistemic rhetoricians. In place of the traditional view of the individual as a unified consciousness unencumbered by historical circumstances, postmodernism posits a subject shaped by history and conflicting discourses, making individual consciousness contradictory and mutable. In place of the view of language as a neutral device for conveying truth, postmodernism sees language as constructing reality and deriving its meaning from differences among the signs themselves. Postmodernism critiques master narratives of human experience as part of, not external to, experience, and locates their meanings in what they exclude. These views mesh with the social-epistemic treatment of the writer as a construct, the audience as an unstable repertoire of constructed selves, and language as the constructive medium—hence as the site of the struggle to define reality in one's best interests. All texts are thus ideological. In studying texts, rhetoric cannot accept claims of transcendence. The writing course, then, should study many ways of using language, emphasizing the need to negotiate among textual and contextual meanings. This approach fosters democratic values by enabling students to analyze claims made on them by competing discourses.

113   Berlin, James A. "Rhetoric and Ideology in the Writing Class." *CE*, 50 (September 1988), 477–94.
Rhetoric has generally been seen as the arbiter of ideological claims, but rhetorical theories are themselves ideological constructs. Three rhetorics that have had significant influence in composition classrooms—cognitive psychology, expressionism, and the social-epistemic—have distinctive ideological bases. Cognitive psychology claims to be scientific and ideologically neutral. Moreover, it offers no critique of epistemology, the formation of values, or the arrangements of power. In this way, it accepts and therefore advances the current hegemonic political and social order. Its rationalization of the writing process is an extension of rationalized economic activity. Expressionism begins with a critique of oppressive social and political constraints, positing that writing is liberating for the individual. But its critical position is vitiated by the romantic and individualistic approach that fends off collective opposition to oppression. If individualism modulates into entrepreneurship, expressivism becomes a capitalist tool. The social-epistemic approach attempts to keep ideological analysis at its center, to recognize that the self, the community, and the material conditions of existence are in dialectical tension. In this view, rhetoric is the study of how knowledge comes into existence: it asks how the perception of reality is structured, how values are formed, and how change is constrained or enabled.

114   Berlin, James A., and Robert P. Inkster. "Current-Traditional Rhetoric: Paradigm and Practice." *Freshman English News*, 8 (Winter 1980), 1–4, 13–14.
The late-nineteenth-century textbooks that model current-traditional rhetoric synthesized eighteenth-century rhetorical theory and retained its epistemology: belief in a fixed external world that could be apprehended by the senses; "faculty" psychology in which rhetoric appeals to the understanding, imagination, passions, or will; the vitalist position

that the content of each discourse is unique, which excludes invention from rhetoric and focuses on style, arrangement, and the writer's genius; and an emphasis on logical argument in rhetoric. Modern textbooks work within this epistemology, assuming that knowledge exists independently of the mind, that emotion does not contribute to knowledge, and that reality is not probabilistic. Thus, "exposition" is the favored mode of discourse. Invention and the composing process are reduced to exhortations about finding a thesis and good ideas. Writer and audience have little importance because the goal of discourse is simply to report on reality. Only style distinguishes one piece of discourse from another. Those who teach composition as stylistic correctness, as well as those who teach it as an act of genius, share in the current-traditional paradigm, which is entrenched in an outdated, even dangerous, epistemology that ignores the problematic nature of knowledge.

115   Berthoff, Ann E. "Is Teaching Still Possible? Writing, Meaning, and Higher Order Reasoning." *CE,* 46 (December 1984), 743–55. Rpt. in Berthoff, *The Sense of Learning* (Portsmouth, N.H.: Heinemann, Boynton/Cook, 1990).
The human capacity for thinking about thinking is "the ground of hope in the enterprise of teaching reading and writing." A positivist view of language as a medium cannot account for meaning and leads to models of cognitive stages and composing processes that misapply psychology, overestimate empirical research, and rely on shaky analogies. Positivist research leads to teaching by exhortation and away from the consciousness of consciousness that allows us to make meaning. A pedagogy of knowing, on the other hand, works from the premise that language can both name (hypostatize) the world and allow us to reflect on it in discourse: to abstract and then to generalize. Teaching can develop this ability when it does not run aground on spurious developmental concepts. See also Berthoff [116, 180].

116   Berthoff, Ann E. *The Making of Meaning: Metaphors, Models and Maxims for Writing Teachers.* Upper Montclair, N.J.: Boynton/Cook, 1981.
Teachers should see composing as the active formation of understanding by the imagination, an act of sorting and selecting experiences according to our needs and purposes. To study composing is to study how we use language to interpret and know the world. In this collection of essays, Berthoff connects the theories of Richards [160], Vygotsky, and Tolstoy and the pedagogies of Paulo Freire [257], Sylvia Ashton-Warner, Jane Addams, and others. A useful book for teachers at all levels.

117   Bitzer, Lloyd F. "The Rhetorical Situation." *Philosophy and Rhetoric,* 1 (Winter 1968), 1–14. Rpt. in Johannesen [144].
Rhetorical discourse is determined by its situation, which has three constituent elements: exigence, the complex of people, events, and objects that create a need that rhetorical discourse attempts to satisfy; audience, the people who, if persuaded, will act on the exigence; and constraints, the audience's beliefs, traditions, and interests and the rhetor's ethos, style, and logic, all of which bear on the persuasive power of the discourse. Some discourse, such as scientific and poetic discourse, is not rhetorical.

118 Bitzer, Lloyd F., and Edwin Black, eds. *The Prospect of Rhetoric.* Englewood Cliffs, N.J.: Prentice-Hall, 1971.

Proceedings of the Wingspread Conference, at which leading figures from speech communication and English addressed common theoretical concerns about rhetoric. Fourteen essays include Richard McKeon, "The Uses of Rhetoric in a Technological Age: Architectonic Productive Arts"; Henry W. Johnstone, Jr., "Some Trends in Rhetorical Theory"; Wayne C. Booth, "The Scope of Rhetoric Today: A Polemical Excursion"; Chaim Perelman, "The New Rhetoric"; and Wayne E. Brockriede, "Trends in the Study of Rhetoric: Toward a Blending of Criticism and Science."

119 Bizzell, Patricia. *Academic Discourse and Critical Consciousness.* Pittsburgh: Univ. of Pittsburgh Press, 1992.

Bizzell traces the development of her thought about discourse communities, basic writers, and education for critical consciousness in this collection of eleven previously published and two new essays, with a lengthy introduction. Includes "The Ethos of Academic Discourse," "Thomas Kuhn, Scientism, and English Studies" [123], "Cognition, Convention, and Certainty: What We Need to Know About Writing" [120], "Academic Discourse and Critical Consciousness: An Application of Paulo Freire," "What Happens When Basic Writers Come to College?" [332], "Composing Processes: An Overview," "Foundationalism and Anti-Foundationalism in Composition Studies" [122], "What Is a Discourse Community?" and "Beyond Anti-Foundationalism to Rhetorical Authority: Problems Defining 'Cultural Literacy.'"

120 Bizzell, Patricia. "Cognition, Convention, and Certainty: What We Need to Know about Writing." *PRE/TEXT,* 3 (Fall 1982), 213–43. Rpt. in Bizzell [119] and in Vitanza [163].

Composition research has proceeded along two theoretical lines: inner-directed research that looks at the writer's cognitive processes, and outer-directed research that looks at the social context of language use. Inner-directed researchers look for innate processes and mental structures, but they regard these processes as teachable. Linda Flower and John Hayes, for example, claim to have described a set of thought processes that produce writing. They assert that the process followed by good writers should be taught to students. Their model separates thought ("planning") from writing ("translating") and fails to account for the writer's knowledge or sense of context. Outer-directed research examines the dialectical relationship between thought and language by describing the intentions, genres, communal expectations, and knowledge that shape language use. In the Flower and Hayes model, basic writers are cognitively deficient, whereas in the sociolinguistic model, they are simply alien to the community in which they are being judged. Inner-directed models seek scientific certainty, while outer-directed models examine political, ethical, and social dynamics. What we need to know about writing will emerge from the debate between these two camps.

121 Bizzell, Patricia. "Contact Zones and English Studies." *CE,* 56 (February 1994), 163–69.

Multiculturalism is stalled by the outdated national and chronological structure of English studies. Adding new materials to the old categories will not suffice. New categories like feminism continue to essentialize and separate. But the contact-zone notion conceptualized by Mary Louise Pratt provides a way of seeing how diverse literatures may come into productive dialogue with each other. A contact zone is an historical time and space in which a cultural struggle occurs. Instead of seeing literature as a monolingual exchange, the contact zone casts it as a negotiation among people with different languages attempting to represent themselves each to the others. America has always been a congeries of overlapping contact zones, and the growing diversity of our classrooms brings this out. Contact-zone categories release us from evaluating the literary goodness of a text: Instead, we look at the rhetorical effectiveness of a writer in dealing with the matter at hand. This approach reconnects literature with composition and rhetoric, not only through rhetorical criticism but also by casting student writing as contending in contact zones and engaging in the arts of cultural mediation.

122   Bizzell, Patricia. "Foundationalism and Anti-Foundationalism in Composition Studies." *PRE/TEXT,* 7 (Spring–Summer 1986), 37–56. Rpt. in Bizzell [119].
"Foundationalism" is the philosophical position that there are absolute and knowable standards for judging truth. "Antifoundationalism" holds that such standards are nonexistent or unknowable and that, therefore, human judgments of truth must be relative to personal emotions, social circumstances, and historical conditions. Stanley Fish has argued that antifoundationalists slide back into foundationalism by treating the antifoundational method itself as a detached and privileged means of judging the truth. This error is committed by those who first claim that language and knowledge are socially constructed and then argue that academic-discourse literacy (or, similarly, metadiscursive awareness) confers critical powers. These are avoidable errors: antifoundationalism is a significant position, linked to the social turn in the theories of many disciplines and pointing to the significance of teaching rhetoric as the study of the personal, social, political, and historical elements in human discourse.

123   Bizzell, Patricia. "Thomas Kuhn, Scientism, and English Studies." *CE,* 40 (March 1979), 764–71. Rpt. in Bizzell [119].
Kuhn's description of paradigms and paradigm shifts in the sciences has led to speculation about an impending paradigm shift in the field of composition. Presumably, this shift, based on empirical research, will put composition studies on a scientific basis. But such speculations betray a desire to escape into scientific "certainty" and fundamentally misread Kuhn's thesis that knowledge in all disciplines develops by a rhetorical process of debate. Thus, Kuhn teaches us to study the ways in which rhetoric constitutes knowledge. Cf. Bazerman [111].

124   Bloom, Lynn Z., Donald A. Daiker, and Edward M. White. *Composition in the 21st Century: Crisis and Change.* Carbondale: Southern Illinois Univ. Press, 1995.
Sixteen paired essays and a response to each pair, on issues that face the profession in the near future. Originally papers presented at the Confer-

ence on Composition in the 21st Century, most offer challenges and warnings. Selections include: David Bartholomae, "What Is Composition and (if you know what that is) Why Do We Teach It?"; Sylvia Holladay, "Order Out of Chaos: Voices from the Community College"; Robert Connors, "The New Abolition Debate in Composition: A Short History"; Peter Elbow, "Writing Assessment in the 21st Century: A Utopian View"; Anne Ruggles Gere, "The Long Revolution in Composition"; John Trimbur, "Writing Instruction and the Politics of Professionalization"; Stephen North, "The Death of Paradigm Hope, the End of Paradigm Guilt, and the Future of (Research in) Composition"; James Berlin, "English Studies, Work, and Politics in the New Economy"; Shirley Brice Heath, "Work, Class, and Categories: Dilemmas in Identity"; Linda Flower, "Literate Action"; and Andrea Lunsford, "Intellectual Property in an Age of Information."

125   Booth, Wayne C. "The Rhetorical Stance." *CCC,* 14 (October 1963), 139–45. Rpt. in Winterowd [165] and in Young and Liu [189].
Good writing takes a "rhetorical stance," a conscious balance between subject, audience, and the writer's persona. Writing, as traditionally taught, overvalues the subject, fostering the "pedant's stance," which produces dry, obscure work. In reaction, some newer writing pedagogies have overvalued the audience-persona relationship, fostering the "entertainer's stance," which produces charming vacuities.

See: Doug Brent, *Reading as Rhetorical Invention* [181].

126   Bruffee, Kenneth A. "Collaborative Learning and the 'Conversation of Mankind.'" *CE,* 46 (November 1984), 635–52.
Psychologists contend that the ability to think is not innate but is developed socially. As children converse with those around them, they learn how to think in ways the community sanctions. Children internalize this conversation, which becomes reflective thought, and finally, when learning to write, externalize their thought in a social medium. Thus both thought and writing are transformations of oral conversation. William Perry, Stanley Fish, and Richard Rorty argue that knowledge, like thought, is socially generated and authorized. They describe a process of "conversation," spoken and written, which constitutes knowledge for participants in a discourse community. If students are to think and write according to academic standards, they must have opportunities for academic talk, as they have in collaborative learning—in a writing workshop, for example, with peer tutors. If students lack academic knowledge, teachers can structure collaborative tasks to generate this knowledge. Teachers should emphasize that academic discourse is not intended to stifle creativity: It is only one of many available discourses the student can choose. Mastery of any community's discourse, however, should be understood as acculturation, which may change the student profoundly. See also Olson [432].

127   Bullock, Richard, and John Trimbur. *The Politics of Writing Instruction, Postsecondary.* Portsmouth, N.H.: Heinemann, Boynton/Cook, 1991.
Eighteen original essays (and a Foreword by Richard Ohmann) that develop a political critique of writing instruction and demonstrate the

inseparability of teaching writing from social, cultural, and economic forces. Essays include: James S. Slevin, "Depoliticizing and Politicizing Composition Studies"; James A. Berlin, "Rhetoric, Poetic, and Culture: Contested Boundaries in English Studies"; Susan Miller, "The Feminization of Composition"; Robert Connors, "Rhetoric in the Modern University: The Creation of an Underclass"; Bruce Herzberg, "Composition and the Politics of the Curriculum"; Elizabeth Flynn, "Composition Studies from a Feminist Perspective"; Richard Bullock, "Autonomy and Community in the Evaluation of Writing"; Robert Schwegler, "The Politics of Reading Student Papers"; Victor Villanueva, Jr., "Considerations of American Freireistas"; and John Trimbur, "Literacy and the Discourse of Crisis." Winner of the CCCC Outstanding Book Award for 1993.

128   Burke, Kenneth. *A Grammar of Motives.* Englewood Cliffs, N.J.: Prentice-Hall, 1945. Excerpted in Johannesen [144].
The "basic forms of thought . . . are exemplified in the attributing of motives." Thought and language are modes of action, and all action can be regarded as dramatic. The dramatistic method analyzes motives by dividing motivated action into a dramatic pentad: act, scene, agent, agency, and purpose. Composition specialists have extracted Burke's pentad from this rich book of philosophy and literary criticism and have used it as a heuristic (see Comprone [183]). For Burke's comments on this use of the pentad, see "Questions and Answers About the Pentad." *CCC*, 29 (December 1978), 330–35, and Winterowd [165].

129   Burke, Kenneth. *A Rhetoric of Motives.* Englewood Cliffs, N.J.: Prentice-Hall, 1950. Excerpted in Johannesen [144].
The persuasive power of rhetoric lies in "identification": The persuader convinces the audience that they share traditions, experiences, and values, all embodied in their shared language. The use of identification for persuasion need not be deliberate, nor acquiescence to identification conscious, except for the desire to identify. Thus, rhetoric is an instrument of socialization, and all social interactions are rhetorical.

130   Clark, Gregory. *Dialogue, Dialectic, and Conversation: A Social Perspective on the Function of Writing.* Carbondale: Southern Illinois Univ. Press, 1990.
Through collaborative textual exchange, readers and writers construct their collectivity, negotiating beliefs, values, and actions. Dialogue, as defined by Bakhtin and others, is the conscious cooperative exchange of discourse in this process of social construction. Dialectic, in both classical and modern definitions, is the process of constructing knowledge collaboratively. Conversation, as social science research confirms, is the actual experience of persuading and compromising through which dialogue and dialectic are enacted. Many disciplines today share and develop this perspective on the creation of knowledge in communities, suggesting that social life is essentially a rhetorical process. The social theory of discourse entails an ethics of reading that places the responsibility for a text's social force and function on its readers, whose criticism should be public. We should teach composition students to read and write as a democratic practice, as an exercise in public discourse that collaboratively constructs and sustains the community.

131   Clifford, John, and John Schilb, eds. *Writing Theory and Critical Theory.* New York: MLA, 1994.

Historiography, cultural studies, rhetoric, social construction, politics, discourse communities, social construction, narrative, postmodernism, and the move to theory itself—the dominant concerns of composition theory today—are analyzed and criticized in these essays. Fourteen essays comprise the three main sections of the book. Essays include: Susan Miller, "Composition as a Cultural Artifact: Rethinking History as Theory"; James Slevin, "Reading and Writing in the Classroom and the Profession"; Kurt Spellmeyer, "On Conventions and Collaboration: The Open Road and the Iron Cage"; Suzanne Clark, "Rhetoric, Social Construction, and Gender: Is It Bad to Be Sentimental?"; Susan Wells, "The Doubleness of Writing and Permission to Lie"; Beth Daniell, "Theory, Theory Talk, and Composition"; Joseph Harris, "The Rhetoric of Theory"; Judith Summerfield, "Is There a Life in This Text? Reimagining Narrative"; Lester Faigley, "Street Fights over the Impossibility of Theory: A Report of a Seminar"; and Linda Brodkey, "Making a Federal Case out of Difference: The Politics of Pedagogy, Publicity, and Postponement." These are followed by three responses to Brodkey and a symposium, "Looking Backward and Forward," with Louise Rosenblatt, Robert Scholes, W. Ross Winterowd, Elizabeth Flynn, Sharon Crowley, and Victor Villanueva.

See: William A. Covino and David Jolliffe, *Rhetoric: Concepts, Definitions, Boundaries* [75].

132   Dillon, George L. *Constructing Texts.* Bloomington: Indiana Univ. Press, 1981.

Psycholinguists, deconstructionists, and reader-response critics agree that to read is to create meaning, not merely to decode what the text encodes. The reader is enabled to create meaning by prior knowledge of the conventions governing text formation in a given discourse community and of patterns of concepts, or schemata, familiar within the discourse community. Conventions and schemata are cognitive in function, but they are not cognitively determined according to fixed, innate rules: they change gradually as the community itself changes. Writing instruction should reflect this flexible definition of conventions and schemata rather than persist in treating writing as encoding information. Dillon criticizes Hirsch's *Philosophy of Composition* for such cognitive determinism.

133   Elbow, Peter. "Being a Writer vs. Being an Academic: A Conflict in Goals." *CCC*, 46 (February 1995), 72–83.

While it would be best if students could be comfortable in both the role of the writer and of the academic, freshman composition cannot aim at both. The role of the writer is preferable. Writing should be the predominant course activity, with reading secondary. Academics are chiefly readers and their courses privilege reading—input—over writing. Academic readers exercise control over the text by nullifying the author, while writers seek a reader who believes in them. Similarly, academics get to be readers of student texts and decide what they mean. Writers must be free to insist that readers cannot ignore intentions and searches for meaning; they must be free to ignore readers. Writing teachers who wish to foster the writer's role should primarily *understand* what writers are saying and only secondarily point out where that understanding is difficult to attain. The writing course need not situate writers in the ongoing intellectual conversation, but can pretend that no authorities have written on students' topics before. Students should see themselves at the center, not the periphery, of discourse. See Bartholomae [110].

134 Elbow, Peter. *Embracing Contraries: Explorations in Learning and Teaching.* New York: Oxford Univ. Press, 1986.
Twelve essays trace Elbow's thinking since the late 1960s about the complexity—even messiness—of the learning process, the conflicts raised by assumptions about teaching and its goals, the authority of teachers, the mystifications of evaluating students, and the philosophical basis for embracing contraries through dialectical thinking. Includes "Cooking" (from *Writing without Teachers* [307]), "The Pedagogy of the Bamboozled" (on American attempts to use Freire [257]), "Trying to Teach While Thinking about the End" (on competency-based teaching), "Evaluating Students More Accurately," "The Value of Dialectic," and "Methodological Doubting and Believing." Also includes a bibliography of Elbow's works on writing and teaching.

135 Emig, Janet. *The Web of Meaning: Essays on Writing, Teaching, Learning, and Thinking.* Ed. Dixie Goswami and Maureen Butler. Upper Montclair, N.J.: Boynton/Cook, 1983.
Eleven selections trace the development of Emig's thought from 1963 to 1982, including Chapters 4, 6, and 7 from *The Composing Processes of Twelfth Graders* [168]; "Hand, Eye, Brain: Some 'Basics' in the Writing Process"; "Writing as a Mode of Learning" [184]; and "Non-Magical Thinking: Presenting Writing Developmentally in Schools." Mina P. Shaughnessy Prize winner.

136 Faigley, Lester. *Fragments of Rationality.* Pittsburgh: Univ. of Pittsburgh Press, 1992.
The postmodern era is characterized by randomness of experience, unopposed by any transcendent terms, a randomness that terrifies with the prospect of total dissolution while exhilarating with the possibility of free play of identities and social locations—that is, of subject positions. Composition pedagogy is often unresponsive to postmodernity, continuing to assume that unitary selves compose purposeful, linearly structured, generically recognizable texts. While this focus is often promoted by academic institutions as serving the practical ends of efficient communication, composition scholars increasingly resist it as oppressive to diverse students. A more postmodern composition study entails looking at how discourses, and the unequal power relations among them, are historically produced. Yet the field is still reluctant to abandon a unitary notion of students' subjectivities. The field needs the kind of destabilized, decentered view that characterizes the networked classroom, where on-line discussion allows free play with different personae and even "forbidden" discourses (e.g., homophobic, racist, sexist). The problem that remains is how to establish an ethics of engagement for social action against the oppressive economic and discursive structures that postmodern analysis purports to reveal. Winner of CCCC Outstanding Book Award for 1994.

137   Fogarty, Daniel, S.J. *Roots for a New Rhetoric.* New York: Bureau of Publication; Teachers College, Columbia Univ., 1959. Rpt. New York: Russell and Russell, 1968.

Aristotelian rhetoric is based on four elements: thought-word-thing relationships, abstraction, definition, and argumentation. The "current-traditional" writing course using this rhetoric is inadequate for modern communication situations. A consideration of how the four elements are treated in the work of I. A. Richards, Kenneth Burke, and the general semanticists provides the roots for a new rhetoric that encompasses the study of all kinds of symbolic behavior using insights from the human sciences.

138   Fulkerson, Richard. "Composition Theory in the Eighties: Axiological Consensus and Paradigmatic Diversity." *CCC,* 41 (December 1990), 409–29.

Composition studies has reached a significant consensus on what constitutes good writing. Of the four possible positions, three are in decline. Expressivism is no longer widely defended. Formalism appears to be strong in some classrooms, but is not defended in print. And mimeticism (concern for logic or informational accuracy) has never been strong. Rhetorical axiology, the fourth position, has taken over textbooks and is reflected in scholarly concerns such as audience, writing across the curriculum, and the social conception of writing. Despite this consensus, there is still a great diversity of theoretical positions because the goal (defined by axiological commitment) does not determine theories of text creation, pedagogical approach, or epistemology. Collaborative writing, for example, although a social form of text creation, is not necessarily the best way to produce texts understood as socially mediated. James Berlin's epistemological categories [62, 113] conflate axiology, process, pedagogy, and epistemology, but it is clear that the four elements of theory are not uniquely dependent. On the other hand, there are undoubtedly conflicts between some combinations, such as a rhetorical axiology taught by outlining.

139   Gere, Ann Ruggles. *Into the Field.* New York: MLA, 1993.

Twelve essays explore the connections between composition and other disciplines as forms of *restructuring*—the idea that interaction between fields is not simply borrowing but reconceptualizing, repositioning on disappearing, contested, or negotiated boundaries. Essays include: Kurt Spellmeyer, "Being Philosophical about Composition: Hermeneutics and the Teaching of Writing"; Brenda Deen Schildgen, "Reconnecting Rhetoric and Philosophy in the Composition Class"; George Disson, "Argumentation and Critique: College Composition and Enlightenment Ideals"; James Berlin, "Composition Studies and Cultural Studies: Collapsing Boundaries"; John Trimbur, "Composition Studies: Postmodern or Popular"; Irene Papoulis, "Subjectivity and Its Role in 'Constructed' Knowledge: Composition, Feminist Theory, and Psychoanalysis"; and David Bleich, "Ethnography and the Study of Literacy: Prospects for Socially Generous Research."

140   Giroux, Henry A. *Schooling and the Struggle for Public Life: Critical Pedagogy in the Modern Age.* Minneapolis: Univ. of Minnesota Press, 1988.

The discourse of democracy and citizenship must be reclaimed by progressive educators to counteract the historical amnesia promoted by the New Right. A critical theory of citizenship reveals the ideological conflicts in American history, opposes chauvinism (especially in media images), and envisions a public philosophy that truly honors equality, liberty, and human life. Questions about the student's voice, literacy, and teacher authority are central to this project.

141 Hairston, Maxine. "Diversity, Ideology, and Teaching Writing." *CCC*, 43 (May 1992), 179–93. Rpt. in Tate, Corbett, and Myers [162].

Making ideology and social goals the center of a writing course or program, as many theorists have advocated, threatens the low-risk, student-centered classroom in which writing is not about anything other than itself. The leftward political move is the result of critical theories in English departments trickling down to the freshman English floors below. Composition theorists who are part of English departments naturally seek approval from the power structure, which favors political theories. But writing classes should focus on student writing, and writing teachers are not qualified to teach complex issues such as racial discrimination and class or gender inequities. Moreover, no classroom should be the forum for the professor's political agenda. Students learn to write by writing about what they care about, not by conforming to a political position and stifling their creative impulses. A diverse student body writing about and sharing their own experiences will produce real cultural diversity. [Responses appear in *CCC,* 42 (May 1993).]

142 Harkin, Patricia, and John Schilb, eds. *Contending with Words: Composition and Rhetoric in a Postmodern Age.* New York: MLA, 1991.

"A collection of essays for college and university teachers of English who believe that the study of composition and rhetoric is not merely the service component of the English department, but also an inquiry into cultural values" (3). Twelve essays on the general theme of the discursive formation of knowledge contend with the many current attempts to formulate the aims of composition programs and courses: Don Bialostosky, "Liberal Education, Writing, and the Dialogic Self"; William A. Covino, "Magic, Literacy, and the *National Enquirer*"; John Clifford, "The Subject in Discourse"; Patricia Bizzell, "Marxist Ideas in Composition Studies"; Bruce Herzberg, "Michel Foucault's Rhetorical Theory"; Lynn Worsham, "Writing against Writing: The Predicament of *Ecriture Feminine* in Composition Studies"; Susan Jarratt, "Feminism and Composition: The Case for Conflict"; Patricia Harkin, "The Postdisciplinary Politics of Lore"; Victor Vitanza, "Three Countertheses: Or, A Critical In(ter)vention into Composition Theories and Pedagogies"; John Schilb, "Cultural Studies, Postmodernism, and Composition"; and two reflections on the collection itself by Sharon Crowley and James Sosnoski.

143 Harris, Joseph. "The Idea of Community in the Study of Writing." *CCC*, 40 (February 1989), 11–22.

The concept of discourse community has helped reveal the ways that writers' intentions emerge not from within but through interaction with communal projects. The image of "community," notably, is entirely positive and unified. Thus, David Bartholomae [109, 280, 330] and Patricia Bizzell [120, 122, 123, 332] suggest that students must completely abandon other discourse communities in order to fully enter the academic community. The idea of community should instead acknowledge the normal presence of internal conflict and competing voices. Braddock Award winner.

144   Johannesen, Richard L., ed. *Contemporary Theories of Rhetoric: Selected Readings.* New York: Harper & Row, 1971.
Rhetoricians from English and speech communication explain and evaluate the work of Kenneth Burke, I. A. Richards, Chaim Perelman, Richard Weaver, Steven Toulmin, and Marshall McLuhan. Excerpts from these theorists and twenty-two essays, including Wayne E. Brockriede, "Toward a Contemporary Aristotelian Theory of Rhetoric"; Kenneth Burke, from *A Grammar of Motives* and *A Rhetoric of Motives* [128, 129]; I. A. Richards, from *The Philosophy of Rhetoric* [160]; Richard Weaver, "Language Is Sermonic" [164]; Chaim Perelman and L. Olbrechts-Tyteca, from *The New Rhetoric* [158]; Wayne E. Brockriede and Douglas Ehninger, "Toulmin on Argument: An Interpretation and Application"; Marshall McLuhan, from *Understanding Media*; Douglas Ehninger, "On Systems of Rhetoric"; Maurice Natanson, "The Limits of Rhetoric"; and Lloyd F. Bitzer, "The Rhetorical Situation" [117].

145   Kent, Thomas. *Paralogic Rhetoric: A Theory of Communicative Interaction.* Lewisburg, Pa.: Bucknell Univ. Press, 1993.
Expressivism, cognitivism, and social constructionism all construe the mind and external reality as completely separate, with contact mediated by transcendent mental forms, cognitive processes, or discourse conventions respectively. The mind is thus unable to get in touch with other minds—the mediating structure is always in the way. The mind is also unable to verify the structure it must use. Relativism is the inescapable conclusion of such views. Philosopher Donald Davidson suggests a better model of communication as a triangulated process in which two people compare their impressions of a shared sensory stimulus, each guessing what the other has in mind. To the extent that they are able to communicate, they may ascertain whether these guesses are correct. This process is paralogical, not logical, because it it not reducible to rules. It follows that the communication process cannot be taught as there are no rules to teach. Communication can only be practiced, collaboratively. Winner of CCCC Outstanding Book Award for 1995.

146   Kinneavy, James L. *A Theory of Discourse.* Englewood Cliffs, N.J.: Prentice-Hall, 1971. Rpt. New York: Norton, 1980.
Discourse can be divided into four main types: reference, persuasive, literary, and expressive, each emphasizing a particular element in the exchange between writer and audience about the subject of the discourse. Reference discourse emphasizes the subject, which it presents with as little interference as possible from writer, reader, or language itself. In persuasive discourse, the aim is to move the reader, and the other elements—writer, subject, and language—are subordinated to that end. Literary discourse focuses on language itself: writer, reader, and

subject are incidental. Expressive discourse emphasizes the writer, suiting subject and language to the writer's need for self-expression. A complex and influential work in the study of discourse. See also James L. Kinneavy, "The Basic Aims of Discourse," *CCC*, 20 (December 1969), 297–304; rpt. in Tate, Corbett, and Myers [162].

147   Lunsford, Andrea A., and Lisa S. Ede. "Classical Rhetoric, Modern Rhetoric, and Contemporary Discourse Studies." *Written Communication*, 1 (January 1984), 78–100.
Some proponents of the "new rhetoric" claim that in classical rhetoric humans are regarded as rational beings moved chiefly by logic but subject to the coercion of rhetors. Grimaldi shows, however, that for Aristotle, both inductive argument (by example) and deductive argument (by enthymeme) rely on all three appeals (logos, pathos, and ethos) in order to discover contingent truths. Thus, classical rhetoric is similar to modern rhetoric as a cross-disciplinary enterprise. But unlike modern rhetoric, classical rhetoric relied on oral language and searched for stable truths in the world.

148   McClelland, Ben W., and Timothy R. Donovan, eds. *Perspectives on Research and Scholarship in Composition.* New York: MLA, 1985.
Thirteen essays review the history and theory of the main branches of composition scholarship, including C. H. Knoblauch, "Modern Rhetorical Theory and Its Future Directions"; John Clifford and John Schilb, "Composition Theory and Literary Theory"; John Trimbur, "Collaborative Learning and Teaching Writing"; and Andrea A. Lunsford, "Cognitive Studies and Teaching Writing."

149   Miller, Susan. *Rescuing the Subject: A Critical Introduction to Rhetoric and the Writer.* Carbondale: Southern Illinois Univ. Press, 1989.
The story of instruction in language use must be liberated from the traditional major-texts approach. Premodern rhetoric cannot provide an adequate theoretical base for modern composition studies, first, because it focuses on oratory and neglects intertextuality, and second, because it focuses on officially sanctioned forms of language use and neglects adventitious and popular uses. We need a textual rhetoric that highlights intertextuality while avoiding the social and historical decontextualization of writing that besets contemporary literary studies. This approach includes a complex view of the writing subject that avoids both the naive classical definition of the rhetor as a "good man speaking well" and the postmodern reduction of the person to a discursive position.

150   Miller, Susan. *Textual Carnivals: The Politics of Composition.* Carbondale: Southern Illinois Univ. Press, 1991.
Composition teachers submit to the continuing subordination of composition to literature and even unwittingly reinforce the perception of composition as a merely practical art without disciplinary status or intellectual rigor. Like other groups marginalized by race, gender, or class, composition teachers have created self-images of sacrifice and rebellion that actually maintain their inequality, reproduce the received history of composition's inferiority, and hide the institutional agendas that stig-

matize it. To change the story told about composition requires a close examination of the connections between it and literature, a critique of received history, and an effort to "endow agency and dignity" on the protagonists of the story: students, teachers (like the "sad women in the basement"), and program administrators. Includes an Appendix, "The Status of Composition: A Survey of How Its Professionals See It." Winner of CCCC Outstanding Book Award for 1992.

151   Neel, Jasper. *Plato, Derrida, and Writing.* Carbondale: Southern Illinois Univ. Press, 1988.
Plato and Derrida launch much the same attack on writing, denying that the process of writing can generate transcendent truth. Plato argued that the rhetor must find truth by philosophical means before attempting to convey it and should convey it by speech rather than writing, because interlocutors cannot interrogate a text about its method. Derrida denies Plato's contentions that philosophy can attain transcendent truth and that dialogue gives access to the philosophical method. Instead, says Derrida, we have only the fictions constructed by writing, a web of texts accumulating over time, allusively linked. Derrida argues correctly that transcendent truth does not exist (or at least that such truth is unknowable), but he is mistaken when he concludes that no *usable* truth exists. There is sufficient truth to serve as a basis for decisions about social action in the "strong discourse" of Sophists—be they Isocrates and Gorgias or the leaders of modern democracies. The strong discourse of probabilistic rhetoric is not mere propaganda, as Plato argued, if only because such discourse tends to generate competing discourses that test its claims. Composition studies can work to free rhetoric from the strictures of philosophy so that it can fulfill its political mission.

152   Ohmann, Richard. *English in America.* New York: Oxford Univ. Press, 1976.
The professional, institutional, and economic structures within which we teach severely constrain the efficacy of liberalizing curricular reforms. Universities continue to serve the needs of government and industry for efficient, docile communicators, while teachers resist acknowledging the political implications of their control of knowledge. This book includes a chapter by Wallace Douglas on English education in America in the 1800s, focusing on the influence of Channing of Harvard.

153   Olson, Gary A., ed. *Philosophy, Rhetoric, Literary Criticism: (Inter)views.* Carbondale: Southern Illinois Univ. Press, 1994.
Six interviews with scholars outside of composition—philosopher Donald Davidson, literary theorists Stanley Fish, bell hooks, J. Hillis Miller, and Jane Tompkins, and philosopher Stephen Toulmin—are each followed by two response essays by composition scholars. The responses explore the applications of "outside" theories to composition and sometimes react contentiously to them. Response essays are by Susan Wells, Reed Way Dasenbrock, Patricia Bizzell, John Trimbur, Joyce Irene Middleton, Tom Fox, Patricia Harkin, Jasper Neel, Susan Jarratt, Elizabeth Flynn, Arabella Lyon, and C. Jan Swearingen. Includes a Foreword by Clifford Geertz, Introduction by Patricia Bizzell, and Commentary by David Bleich.

154   Olson, Gary A., and Sidney I. Dobrin, eds. *Composition Theory for the Postmodern Classroom.* Albany: SUNY, 1995.

Twenty-two essays originally published in the *Journal of Advanced Composition* [10], including: James Kinneavy, "The Process of Writing: A Philosophical Base in Hermeneutics"; Jasper Neel, "Dichotomy, Consubstantiality, Technical Writing, Literary Theory: The Double Orthodox Curse"; Patricia Sullivan, "Writing in the Graduate Curriculum: Literary Criticism as Composition"; David Smit, "Some Difficulties with Collaborative Writing"; Thomas Fox, "Repositioning the Profession: Teaching Writing to African American Students"; W. Ross Winterowd, "Rediscovering the Essay"; Robert Wood, "The Dialectic Suppression of Feminist Thought in Radical Pedagogy"; Henry Giroux, "Paulo Freire and the Politics of Postcolonialism"; Joseph Harris, "The Other Reader"; John Trimbur, "Articulation Theory and the Problem of Determination: A Reading of *Lives on the Boundary*"; J. Hillis Miller, "Nietzsche in Basel: Writing Reading"; and Richard Coe, "Defining Rhetoric—and Us: A Meditation on Burke's Definitions."

155   Olson, Gary A., and Irene Gale, eds. *(Inter)views: Cross-Disciplinary Perspectives on Rhetoric and Literacy.* Carbondale: Southern Illinois Univ. Press, 1991.

Seven interviews with scholars outside of composition—Mary Field Belenky, Noam Chomsky, Jacques Derrida, Paulo Freire, Clifford Geertz, Richard Rorty, and Gayatri Spivak—each followed by two response essays by composition scholars. The responses explore and criticize the applications of their theories to composition. Response essays are by Elizabeth Flynn, Marilyn Cooper, James Sledd, Sharon Crowley, Jasper Neel, James Berlin, C. H. Knoblauch, Linda Brodkey, Kenneth Bruffee, and Thomas Kent. Includes a Foreword by David Bleich and an Afterword by Andrea Lunsford.

156   Owens, Derek. *Resisting Writings (and the Boundaries of Composition).* Dallas: Southern Methodist Univ. Press, 1994.

Composition courses that teach only academic discourse or the personal essay are ethnocentric. Rather, the introductory course should survey kinds of writing produced in different cultures, in feminist work, and in experimental writing inspired by electronic media in which fiction and nonfiction are often blurred. Upper-division courses could be devoted to each of these kinds. Additionally, academics should push for a wider variety of writing to be acceptable in all undergraduate and graduate courses and in scholarly publications. Only this way will American education's "process of rigid mechanization and self-effacement" be resisted creatively by students and teachers alike, with healthy results for social justice.

157   Perelman, Chaim. *The Realm of Rhetoric.* Trans. William Kluback. Notre Dame, Ind.: Univ. of Notre Dame Press, 1982. Trans. of *L'Empire Rhetorique.* 1977.

A summary of *The New Rhetoric* [158].

158   Perelman, Chaim, and L. Olbrechts-Tyteca. *The New Rhetoric: A Treatise on Argumentation.* Trans. John Wilkinson and Purcell Weaver. 1958. Rpt. Notre Dame, Ind.: Univ. of Notre Dame Press,

1969. Excerpted in Bizzell and Herzberg [39] and in Johannesen [144].

Rhetoric is the art of gaining adherents to propositions that cannot be verified through calculations. All rhetorical discourse, then, is argumentation. Some arguments aim to convince only a particular audience, whereas others try to persuade all rational people—the imagined "universal audience." Arguments can be evaluated rationally and good reasons given for or against adherence to them, both for particular and for "universal" audiences. Such evaluations, though rational, are conditioned by the culture of the evaluator's discourse community—its traditions, language-using conventions, and beliefs. This book exhaustively catalogs the kinds of arguments that can be used in most Western discourse communities, with numerous examples from canonical works in philosophy, literature, history, and other fields. A seminal work in discourse theory.

159   Pratt, Mary Louise. "Arts of the Contact Zone." *Profession 91* (1991), 33–40.

Contact zones are social spaces where cultures meet and clash, often in contexts of highly asymmetrical power relations, such as colonialism or its aftermath. In such situations we find examples of texts that subordinate groups produce to describe themselves to the dominant group and engage with representations others have made of them. Such texts selectively use the forms and idioms of the other group (a part of the process of transculturation) and may, as in the case of Guaman Poma's Andean text addressed to the king of Spain, be a marginalized group's entry into literacy. Such texts seem chaotic unless read as expressions of those who live in a contact zone. The utopian image of a unified speech community with shared norms is challenged by such texts. What are we to do when the classroom community, another imagined utopia, is challenged by unsolicited oppositional discourse, as is happening more frequently? Multicultural curricula can and should create contact zones in which all interests are represented, where mulitple cultural histories intersect, where there are ground rules for communication across lines of difference and hierarchy, and where there is a systematic approach to cultural mediation.

160   Richards, I. A. *The Philosophy of Rhetoric.* New York: Oxford Univ. Press, 1936. Excerpted in Bizzell and Herzberg [39] and in Johannesen [144].

All discourse allows multiple meanings, but most interpretations of discourse are based on cultural conventions and the widespread idea that words have single determinate meanings. Rhetoric is the study of the misunderstandings that arise from such interpretations. Rhetoric looks at the "context" of disputed passages—the surrounding text, which constrains the meaning of the passage. Because meaning is determined by context, usage must be based on appropriateness to context rather than on fixed standards. Rhetoric must rely on Coleridge's idea that all language is metaphor and that we understand the world through the resemblances offered by language. See also Berthoff [116].

161   Selzer, Jack, ed. *Understanding Scientific Prose.* Madison: Univ. of Wisconsin Press, 1993.

Thirteen essays analyze a single scientific essay, "The Spandrels of San Marco," by Stephen Jay Gould and R. C. Lewontin. Each analysis uses a different critical method in order to "domesticate new methods of practical criticism," to show their usefulness when applied to scientific discourse, and to reveal the complexities of scientific prose. Essays include: Charles Bazerman, "Intertextual Self-Fashioning: Gould and Lewontin's Representations of the Literature"; Susan Wells, "'Spandrels,' Narration, and Modernity"; Carl G. Herndl, "Cultural Studies and Critical Science"; Mary Rosner and Georgia Rhoades, "Science, Gender, and 'The Spandrels of San Marco'"; Carolyn Miller and S. Michael Halloran, "Reading Darwin, Reading Nature; or, On the Ethos of Historical Science"; John Lyne, "Angels in the Architecture: A Burkean Inventional Perspective on 'Spandrels'"; Gay Gragson and Jack Selzer, "The Reader in the Text of 'The Spandrels of San Marco'"; Debra Journet, "Deconstructing 'The Spandrels of San Marco'"; Greg Myers, "Making Enemies: How Gould and Lewontin Criticize"; and Stephen Jay Gould, "Fulfilling the Spandrels of World and Mind." Includes the original article by Gould and Lewontin.

162   Tate, Gary, Edward P. J. Corbett, and Nancy Myers. *The Writing Teacher's Sourcebook*, 3rd ed. New York: Oxford Univ. Press, 1994.

Thirty-four previously published essays (fifteen of which appeared in the second edition) on immediate pedagogical concerns of writing teachers, divided into nine sections: Perspectives, Teachers, Classrooms, Composing and Revising, Assigning and Responding, Audiences, Styles, Basic Writing, and Computers. Essays include: Richard Fulkerson, "Four Philosophies of Composition"; James Berlin, "Contemporary Composition: The Major Pedagogical Theories"; Maxine Hairston, "Diversity, Ideology, and Teaching Writing" [141]; Donald Lazere, "Teaching the Political Conflicts: A Rhetorical Schema"; Peter Elbow, "Embracing Contraries in the Teaching Process"; Susan Jarratt, "Teaching across and within Differences"; Terry Dean, "Multicultural Classrooms, Monocultural Teachers" [336]; Harvey Wiener, "Collaborative Learning in the Classroom: A Guide to Evaluation" [312]; Hephzibah Roskelly, "The Risky Business of Group Work"; Sondra Perl, "Understanding Composing"; Nancy Sommers, "Between the Drafts"; Jeanne Fahnestock and Marie Secor, "Teaching Argument: A Theory of Types" [194]; Brooke Horvath, "The Components of Written Response: A Practical Synthesis of Current Views" [244]; Douglas Park, "The Meanings of 'Audience'" [207]; Lisa Ede and Andrea Lunsford, "Audience Addressed/Audience Invoked: The Role of Audience in Composition Theory and Pedagogy" [202]; Peter Elbow, "Closing My Eyes as I Speak: An Argument for Ignoring Audience" [203]; Richard Ohmann, "Use Definite, Specific, Concrete Language" [228]; Winston Weathers, "Teaching Style: A Possible Anatomy" [229]; David Bartholomae, "The Study of Error" [330]; and Mike Rose, "Remedial Courses: A Critique and a Proposal."

163   Vitanza, Victor, ed. *PRE/TEXT: The First Decade*. Pittsburgh: Univ. of Pittsburgh Press, 1993.

Ten essays from the journal: Paul Kameen, "Rewording the Rhetoric of Composition"; Louise Wetherbee Phelps, "The Dance of Discourse"; Patricia Bizzell, "Cognition, Convention, and Certainty" [120]; S. Michael Halloran, "Rhetoric in the American College Curriculum" [82]; C.

Jan Swearingen, "The Rhetor as Eiron"; William Covino, "Thomas De Quincey in a Revisionist Rhetoric"; Charles Bazerman, "The Writing of Scientific Non-Fiction"; Sharon Crowley, "Neo-Romanticism and the History of Rhetoric"; John Schilb, "The History of Rhetoric and the Rhetoric of History"; and Susan Jarratt, "Toward a Holistic Historiography." Includes a history of the journal by Vitanza, a comment by James Berlin, and afterwords by David Bartholomae and Steven Mailloux.

164   Weaver, Richard M. "Language Is Sermonic." In *Dimensions of Rhetorical Scholarship*. Ed. Robert E. Nebergall. Norman: Univ. of Oklahoma Dept. of Speech, 1963, pp. 49–64. Rpt. in Bizzell and Herzberg [39] and in Johannesen [144].

Rhetoric should be restored to its once prominent place in the curriculum, for it is "the most humanistic of the humanities," concerned with the intimate details of human feelings, needs, and historical pressures in its attempt to find ways to persuade people to right action. Rhetoric is therefore incompatible with science—the search for universals. To study rhetoric is to evaluate the force of appeals to action—an "existential, not hypothetical" concern. Finally, all speech is rhetorical—intended to persuade, never neutral—and all language is value laden, a system for making predications and propositions: "we are all of us preachers."

165   Winterowd, W. Ross, ed. *Contemporary Rhetoric: A Conceptual Background with Readings*. New York: Harcourt Brace Jovanovich, 1975.

This important collection of twenty-four theoretical essays includes the complete exchange between Janice Lauer and Ann E. Berthoff on the imagination. It also includes Wayne C. Booth, "The Rhetorical Stance" [125]; Janice Lauer, "Heuristics and Composition"; Ann E. Berthoff, "The Problem of Problem-Solving"; Richard L. Larson, "Discovery Through Questioning: A Plan for Teaching Rhetorical Invention"; Kenneth Burke, "The Five Key Terms of Dramatism"; W. Ross Winterowd, "The Grammar of Coherence" [200]; Francis Christensen, "A Generative Rhetoric of the Paragraph" [191]; and Francis Christensen, "A Generative Rhetoric of the Sentence" [214].

Composing Processes

Composing Processes

166   Britton, James, et al. *The Development of Writing Abilities (11–18)*. London: Macmillan Education, 1975.

A study of about two thousand papers written by British schoolchildren between the ages of eleven and eighteen suggests that their writing falls into three categories: transactional (communicating information); poetic (creating beautiful verbal objects); and expressive (exploring ideas and relating them to feelings, intentions, and other knowledge). Most school writing is transactional, but this emphasis is wrong because children use expressive writing as a mode of learning. Transactional writing, with its complex sense of audience, can develop only from expressive facility. Transactional writing puts the writer in a passive, spectator role, whereas expressive writing encourages an active, participant role.

167   Cooper, Marilyn M. "The Ecology of Writing." *CE,* 48 (April 1986), 364–75. Rpt. in Cooper and Holzman [335].

Cognitive-process models of composing rely too heavily on the image of a solitary author. A better, ecological model would situate the writer and the writer's immediate context in larger social systems, of which there are several. The system of ideas integrates private experience with public knowledge. The system of purposes links the actions of many different writers. The system of interpersonal relations connects writers in terms of social and linguistic conventions. The system of cultural norms reflects the attitudes of social groups to which writers belong. The system of textual forms marks generic conventions and innovations. These systems make up the material circumstances that constrain writers and are in turn subject to the writer's power to shape and change them through interpretation.

168   Emig, Janet. *The Composing Processes of Twelfth Graders.* Urbana, Ill.: NCTE, 1971.

Eight twelfth graders were asked to "compose aloud" while writing three essays. Extensive interviews with one of the students form a case study showing that twelfth graders compose in two modes: reflexive and extensive. Reflexive writing concerns the writer's feelings and personal experience. The style is informal, and several kinds of exploratory writing accompany drafts. The student usually initiates reflexive writing and is its primary audience. Extensive writing focuses on information to be conveyed to a reader. The style is more formal, and much less time is spent on planning and drafting than in the reflexive mode. The directive to write usually comes from the teacher, who is the primary audience. Twelfth graders write much more often, though less well, in the extensive than in the reflexive mode. They should have more opportunities to write reflexively in school. This study has been influential because of its conception of composing as a process, its suggestion that the composing process should be taught and studied, and its method of composing aloud.

169   Faigley, Lester. "Competing Theories of Process: A Critique and a Proposal." *CE,* 48 (October 1986), 527–42. Rpt. in Graves [285] and in Perl [176].

Three theories of the composing process—expressive, cognitive, and social—characterize the discipline of composition. The expressive theory embodies a neoromantic view of process that invokes the ideas of integrity, spontaneity, and originality. Integrity—or sincerity—becomes an evaluative category; spontaneity suggests the organic unfolding of writing; and originality changes from genius to self-actualization. The cognitive theory uses notions of cognitive development to explain how writing is learned, while using a cybernetic model (feedback, memory, processing) of the individual composing process. Cognitive theory created a science consciousness in composition researchers. Several lines of research—poststructuralism, sociology of science, ethnography, and Marxism—combine to form the social theory, which explains writing as a function of the activities of the writer in a discourse community. These process methods are superior to previous methods; they validate student writing, examine writing behavior, and investigate the social systems that stand in relation to the act of writing.

170   Flower, Linda. *The Construction of Negotiated Meaning: A Social Cognitive Theory of Writing.* Carbondale: Southern Illinois Univ. Press, 1994.

Literacy is a constructive process, an attempt to create meaning as part of social action. Literacy is shaped by literate, social, and cultural practices of a community, but, at the same time, it is a personal attempt to communicate. The issues of positioning within a community, communicative intent, and mediating social practices overshadow the mechanical concerns usually associated with literacy. A social-cognitive view of literacy, which situates the individual within a social context, explains more of the diversity and complexity of literate action. Such action occurs between the poles of thought (interpreting, problem solving, reflecting) and culture (the texts, voices, and knowledge out of which interpretetions are built). To examine an individual's thinking within the context of literate action can reveal the underlying logic of literate performance. Other metaphors for meaning-making, such as reproduction and conversation, are too limited to account for the individual's engagement in the process. Negotiation better describes the individual's agency within social constraints. Writers can articulate their strategic knowledge (goals, strategies, and awareness) to reveal their processes of meaning-construction in social settings.

171   Flower, Linda S. "The Construction of Purpose in Writing and Reading." *CE,* 50 (September 1988), 528–50.

Purpose emerges from the interactions of individual language users with social and cultural contexts. A cognitive view of a writer's purpose would see it not as a unitary, conscious intention but rather as a web of intertwined goals and plans, not all of which are fully conscious or rationally attributable to immediate context and text content. The writer deals with this web through a constructive planning process in which goals are prioritized to help guide the composing process even as the goal hierarchy may be revised during composing. Good planners are opportunistic. A reader constructs a similar web or scenario made up of goals and plans (again not necessarily fully conscious) for using or responding to the reading. The reader's web also includes estimates of the author's purposes, forecasts of what may be coming next in a difficult or lengthy text, and so on. Framing such scenarios helps a reader group information and responses drawn from a text and isolate trouble spots that need more interpretation. Expert writers and readers generate more complex webs than do novices.

172   Flower, Linda S., and John R. Hayes. "A Cognitive Process Theory of Writing." *CCC,* 32 (December 1981), 365–87.

The structure of the composing process is revealed by "protocol analysis"—asking writers to think aloud while writing and then analyzing the writers' narratives. The three elements of the composing process are the task environment, which includes such external constraints as the rhetorical problem and text produced so far; the writer's long-term memory, which includes knowledge of the subject and knowledge of how to write; and the writing processes that go on inside the writer's head. This last category comprises a planning process, subdivided into generating, organizing, and goal setting; a translating process, in which thoughts are put into words; and a reviewing process, subdivided into evaluating and revising. The whole process is regulated by a monitor that switches from one stage to another. The process is hierarchical and recursive. All writers exhibit this process, but poor writers carry it out ineffectively.

173   Flower, Linda, David L. Wallace, Linda Norris, and Rebecca E. Burnett, eds. *Making Thinking Visible: Writing, Collaborative Planning, and Classroom Inquiry.* Urbana, Ill.: NCTE, 1994.
A report on Carnegie Mellon's Making Thinking Visible project, a four-year collaboration among thirty-three high-school and college teachers, in which students and teachers attempted to document the processes of thinking about writing and teaching writing. Some of the twenty-seven chapters are brief accounts of classroom and teaching discoveries. Others are full essays, including: Linda Flower, "Teachers as Theory Builders"; Linda Flower, "Writers Planning: Snapshots from Research"; David Wallace, "Teaching Collaborative Planning: Creating a Social Context for Writing"; Leslie Byrd Evans, "Transcripts as a Compass to Discovery"; James Brozick, "Using the Writing Attitude Survey"; David Wallace, "Supporting Students' Intentions for Writing"; and Wayne Peck, "The Community Literacy Center: Bridging Community- and School-Based Literate Practices."

174   Fox, Tom. *The Social Uses of Writing: Politics and Pedagogy.* Norwood, N.J.: Ablex, 1990.
Case studies show how freshmen use writing to negotiate conflicts between academic values and values they hold as a consequence of race, gender, and class. Teachers' responses to the students' writing are affected, in turn, by their own culturally constructed values. These tensions between culture-based values can be the topic of study in an interactive pedagogy that helps students see how such socially constructed values as beauty, objectivity, and upward mobility affect their writing. Interactive pedagogy, moreover, seeks to replace evaluation with interpretation and to bring student and academic discourse together instead of seeking to move students to a univocal academic discourse.

See: George Hillocks, Jr., *Research on Written Composition* [34].

175   Penrose, Ann M., and Barbara M. Sitko, eds. *Hearing Ourselves Think: Cognitive Research in the College Writing Classroom.* New York: Oxford Univ. Press, 1993.
Cognitive research, investigating the relationship between how writers think about the writing process and the way they engage in the process, reveals much about the factors that determine how easy and successful

writing will be. Process research in the classroom—methods for critical reflection on ways of learning and writing—can lead to an understanding by students and teachers of the ways that writers choose and can improve their writing strategies. Ten essays explain cognitive classroom research and its application to teaching: Ann Penrose and Barbara Sitko, "Introduction: Studying Cognitive Processes in the Classroom"; Christina Haas, "Beyond 'Just the Facts': Reading as Rhetorical Action"; Stuart Greene, "Exploring the Relationship between Authorship and Reading"; Ann Penrose, "Writing and Learning: Exploring the Consequences of Task Interpretation"; Lorraine Higgins, "Reading to Argue: Helping Students Transform Source Texts"; Jennie Nelson, "The Library Revisited: Exploring Students' Research Processes"; Rebecca Burnet, "Decision-Making During the Collaborative Planning of Coauthors"; Karen Schriver, "Revising for Readers: Audience Awareness in the Writing Classroom"; Barbara Sitko, "Exploring Feedback: Writers Meet Readers"; and Betsy Bowen, "Using Conferences to Support the Writing Process."

176 Perl, Sondra, ed. *Landmark Essays on Writing Process.* Davis, Calif.: Hermagoras Press, 1994.

Eighteen essays, arranged chronologically, beginning with Janet Emig's "The Composing Process: Review of the Literature" (1971). Essays include: Sondra Perl, "The Composing Processes of Unskilled College Writers"; Linda Flower and John Hayes, "The Cognition of Discovery: Defining a Rhetorical Problem"; Nancy Sommers, "Revision Strategies of Student Writers and Experienced Adult Writers" [211]; Mike Rose, "Rigid Rules, Inflexible Plans, and the Stifling of Language: A Cognitivist Analysis of Writer's Block"; Sondra Perl, "Understanding Composing"; Ann Berthoff, "The Intelligent Eye and the Thinking Hand"; James Reither, "Writing and Knowing: Toward Redefining the Writing Process"; Lester Faigley, "Competing Theories of Process: A Critique and a Proposal" [169]; Min-zhan Lu, "From Silence to Words: Writing as Struggle" [345]; Elizabeth Flynn, "Composing as a Woman" [361]; and Nancy Sommers, "Between the Drafts."

177 Rose, Mike, ed. *When a Writer Can't Write: Studies in Writer's Block and Other Composing Process Problems.* New York and London: Guilford Press, 1985.

Eleven essays address the social and psychological constraints that contribute to serious hesitations and false starts in writing. They include Donald H. Graves, "Blocking and the Young Writer"; Stan Jones, "Problems with Monitor Use in Second Language Composing"; David Bartholomae, "Inventing the University" [109]; and Mike Rose, "Complexity, Rigor, Evolving Method, and the Puzzle of Writer's Block: Thoughts on Composing Process Research."

178 Rose, Mike. *Writer's Block: The Cognitive Dimension.* Carbondale and Edwardsville: Southern Illinois Univ. Press, 1984.

A number of case studies of students who frequently experienced writer's block and some who seldom blocked show that writers who block frequently may rely on context-independent rules for good writing, edit individual sentences as they are being written, plan only after beginning to write, or interpret writing assignments too narrowly in light of their limited knowledge of discourse modes. Writers who seldom block are "opportunists" who treat what they know about writing as strategies, not rules, which can be varied in different writing situations. The capacities to write well and to enjoy writing are not related to blocking. This study suggests that no composing method should be taught as if applicable to all writing situations.

179   Tobin, Lad, and Thomas Newkirk, eds. *Taking Stock: The Writing Process Movement in the 90s.* Portsmouth, N.H.: Heinemann Boynton/Cook, 1994.

Sixteen essays examine the history, theory, successes, problems, and prospects of writing-process pedagogy. Essays include: James Moffett, "Coming Out Right"; Lisa Ede, "Reading the Writing Process"; Donald Murray, "Knowing Not Knowing"; Ken Macrorie, "Process, Product, and Quality"; Mary Minock, "The Bad Marriage: A Revisionist View of James Britton's Expressive Writing Hypothesis in American Practice"; Peter Elbow, "The Uses of Binary Thinking: Exploring Seven Productive Oppositions"; Thomas Recchio, "On the Critical Necessity of 'Essaying'"; and James Britton, "There is One Story Worth Telling."

Invention: Heuristics and Pre-Writing

180   Berthoff, Ann E. *Forming/Thinking/Writing: The Composing Imagination.* Rochelle Park, N.J.: Hayden, 1978.

Writing is a process of making meaning, of discovering how we think and feel about the world as we try to shape our thoughts in language. This textbook offers a series of "assisted invitations" to explore the composing process, from simple observation to forming concepts and writing critically about one's own knowledge.

181   Brent, Doug. *Reading as Rhetorical Invention: Knowledge, Persuasion, and the Teaching of Research-Based Writing.* Urbana, Ill.: NCTE, 1992.

A rhetoric of discourse consumption explains how people come to be persuaded by the texts they read and how they decide among texts' competing claims. Assuming that texts can convey shareable good reasons for belief, readers adjudicate among them, granting or withholding assent on the basis of the text's match with what the reader already knows and believes. The richer the reader's repertoire of knowledge and examined belief, the more readily she can learn from reading. This ability to learn from texts is the fundamental academic research skill. It can be taught, even to beginners, by emphasizing that the purpose of research is not to retrieve data but to converse about it, that all texts are biased, that gut feelings of commitment to one text over another can be trusted, and that research is recursive.

182   Coe, Richard M. "If Not to Narrow, Then How to Focus: Two Techniques for Focusing." *CCC*, 32 (October 1981), 272-77.

The typical advice of textbooks to narrow a topic to one of its parts or to focus on one aspect of a topic may limit students to trivial topics or choke off development of ideas. Instead, students should shape a topic by looking for a contradiction in it and resolving the contradiction as the thesis of the essay.

183 Comprone, Joseph. "Kenneth Burke and the Teaching of Writing." *CCC,* 29 (December 1978), 336–40.
Burke's theory of language as symbolic action is applicable to writing as an active process. The pentad can be used as a heuristic in the invention stage by focusing on agent and scene as a way to interpret experience and, later, in the drafting stage by focusing on agency and purpose as a way to move the audience. Burke's concept of "terministic screens" can help writers understand the need to translate their world-views for an audience, and the concept of "identification" can point to persuasive techniques. Comprone restates the pentad as a set of questions for the writer. Cf. Burke [128, 129].

See: Sharon Crowley, *The Methodical Memory* [76].

184 Emig, Janet. "Writing as a Mode of Learning." *CCC,* 28 (May 1977), 122–28. Rpt. in Young and Liu [189].
Writing is a uniquely valuable mode of learning. It simultaneously engages the hand, the eye, and both hemispheres of the brain. Writing requires an emotional commitment and is self-paced. The written product provides immediate feedback on learning and a record that can be reconsidered and revised at leisure. The stages of the writing process, embodied in notes, outlines, and drafts, also provide a record of the growth of learning.

185 Harrington, David V., et al. "A Critical Survey of Resources for Teaching Rhetorical Invention: A Review Essay." *CE,* 40 (February 1979), 641–61.
A discussion of research works and textbooks on neoclassical invention, pre-writing, tagmemic invention and linguistic theory, dramatistic methods, and speech communication.

186 LeFevre, Karen Burke. *Invention as a Social Act.* Carbondale: Southern Illinois Univ. Press, 1987.
American composition pedagogy has long been based on the Platonic view that invention is the act of the individual writer who searches for truth by self-examination. This view is supported by ubiquitous myths of individualism in America. Although there is real value in this perspective, a more complete account must recognize that invention is social and collaborative: the individual author has been influenced by society; all human acts are dialectical responses to context; writing refers to an audience, internal or external; and the classical context of rhetoric is explicitly social. Thus, there are four perspectives on invention. In the Platonic view, invention is private. The internal-dialogic view projects a Freudian self made up of contesting inner voices, strongly influenced by internalized social values. The collaborative view follows George Herbert Mead in locating meaning in the symbolic interactions of a group of people. And the collective view follows Emile Durkheim's theory that social institutions and cultural traditions affect individual choices. The social view of invention suggests ways that

composition research and pedagogies can go beyond personal assumptions about authorship.

187. Murray, Donald M. "Write before Writing." *CCC,* 29 (December 1978), 375–82.

Professionals go through an elaborate pre-writing process, for which teachers would do well to allow time. The first stage is delay, when the writer collects information, develops a concern for the subject and a sense of the audience, and feels the deadline approaching. Next comes rehearsal, talking about what will be written and making notes, outlines, and finally a tentative draft. Eight signals—such as genre, the sense that one's writing is fitting into a known form, or point of view, the development of a strong position on the subject—help the writer to the final draft.

188 Young, Richard E., Alton L. Becker, and Kenneth L. Pike. *Rhetoric: Discovery and Change.* New York: Harcourt, Brace and World, 1970.

Rhetoric is the study of methods for discovering ideas and changing the attitudes of one's audience about those ideas. Humans render the chaos of external reality intelligible through three cognitive activities: sorting perceptions by simple comparison and contrast with other perceptions, looking at the range of variation among the set of similar perceptions, and looking at the distribution of these perceptions across a range of experience. The subject can be considered in three ways in each activity: as an isolated "particle," in itself; as a dynamic "wave" and as a "field," in relation to other subjects. Out of this nine-part heuristic comes an understanding of the subject as a problem to be solved in writing. To persuade the audience, it is better to avoid an adversary posture and to adopt a three-step method devised by psychotherapist Carl Rogers: (1) convince your reader that you truly understand his position; (2) compare the worldviews that support your position and your reader's, to exploit the similarities between those views; and (3) move your reader toward your position. This textbook, seldom used in undergraduate courses, was a very influential work on invention and persuasion methods derived from psychology and linguistics.

189 Young, Richard, and Yameng Liu, eds. *Landmark Essays on Rhetorical Invention in Writing.* Davis, Calif.: Hermagoras Press, 1994.

Nineteen essays arranged chronologically, beginning with Kenneth Burke, "The Five Master Terms" (1943). Essays include: Wayne Booth, "The Rhetorical Stance" [125]; Kenneth Pike, "Beyond the Sentence"; D. Gordon Rohman, "Pre-Writing: The Stage of Discovery in the Writing Process"; Chaïm Perelman, "Rhetoric and Philosophy"; S. Michael Halloran, "On the End of Rhetoric, Classical and Modern"; Janet Emig, "Writing as a Mode of Learning" [184]; Walter Ong, "Literacy and Orality in Our Times" [271]; James Britton, "Shaping at the Point of Utterance"; Douglas Park, "The Meanings of 'Audience'" [207]; and James Kinneavy, "Kairos: A Neglected Concept in Classical Rhetoric."

Arrangement and Argument

190 Braddock, Richard. "The Frequency and Placement of Topic Sentences in Expository Prose." *Research in the Teaching of English,* 8 (Winter 1974), 287–302.

Do good expository paragraphs begin with explicit topic sentences? In twenty-five essays by professional writers, fewer than half of the paragraphs have topic sentences at all, and fewer than half of those topic sentences are simple and direct. Other kinds of topic sentences are delayed completion, assembled (in which the topic-sentence ideas are scattered through the paragraph), and inferred. First Braddock Award winner.

191 Christensen, Francis. "A Generative Rhetoric of the Paragraph." *CCC,* 16 (October 1965), 144–56. Rpt. in *The Sentence and the Paragraph* [198], in Francis Christensen, *Notes Toward a New Rhetoric: Six Essays for Teachers* (New York: Harper & Row, 1967); and in Francis Christensen and Bonniejean Christensen, eds., *Notes Toward a New Rhetoric: Nine Essays for Teachers* (New York: Harper & Row, 1978).

Paragraph structure resembles sentence structure (cf. [214]). The topic sentence, usually the first sentence, is analogous to the main clause, and supporting sentences, working at lower levels of generality, are analogous to modifying phrases. Relations between sentences in a paragraph are coordinate or subordinate. Most paragraphs exhibit both kinds of relation, even when there is no topic sentence or when the paragraph includes unrelated sentences. Students should practice diagramming paragraphs by level of generality to see where coordinate and subordinate additions are needed. Cf. Braddock [190].

192 D'Angelo, Frank J. "Topoi and Form in Composition." In *Linguistics, Stylistics, and the Teaching of Composition.* Ed. Donald McQuade. Carbondale: Southern Illinois Univ. Press, 1986.

Paradigms—such as classification, exemplification, and cause-to-effect—are, like the classical topoi, patterns for essays. Unlike the more static topoi, however, paradigms stimulate and guide invention and arrangement during the composing process. Paradigms have a unifying effect because they are based on typical human thought patterns. Consciously using paradigms will improve students' ability to organize abstract thinking.

193 Eden, Rich, and Ruth Mitchell. "Paragraphing for the Reader." *CCC,* 37 (December 1986), 416–30, 441.

While research shows that paragraphs in admired professional writing don't necessarily contain topic sentences or follow prescribed patterns, textbooks continue to offer these "rules." Writers should be taught, instead, reader-oriented paragraphing. Readers expect to see paragraphs and project several qualities upon them. Most importantly, readers will always treat the first sentence of a paragraph as the orienting statement, so writers should ask only if their first sentence orients the reader as they wish. Moreover, this consideration should only arise during the editing procress and not—as generative theories of paragraphing suggest—during composing itself. Paragraphing shapes the reader's interpretation of the text. Ineffective paragraphing usually comes from thinking of paragraphs as formal structures related only to the material.

194   Fahnestock, Jeanne, and Marie Secor. "Teaching Argument: A Theory of Types." *CCC,* 34 (February 1983), 20–30. Rpt. in Tate, Corbett, and Myers [162].

Argument can be taught by the logical/analytic, content/problem-solving, or rhetorical/generative approaches. The first does not work because formal logic is not the logic of discourse, as shown by Toulmin [199] and Perelman [157]. The second approach works better because students infer argumentative techniques by taking stands on controversial issues, but the issues tend to take over the course. The rhetorical/generative approach is best because it teaches forms of argument that are transferable to a wide variety of situations. Most arguments take one of four forms: categorical propositions, causal statements, evaluations, and proposals. Students should learn to write an argument of each kind, in this sequence, on their own topics.

195   Gage, John T. "Teaching the Enthymeme: Invention and Arrangement." *Rhetoric Review,* 2 (September 1983), 38–50.

Structural formulae for constructing essays do not acknowledge the extent to which audience affects invention and arrangement. The enthymeme, however, properly understood as a large-scale heuristic and not a sentence-level device, can help the writer consider the questions that concern a particular audience, the probable answers to those questions, potential strategies for presenting those answers, and the shared premises that make reasons persuasive. It can thus provide the basic structure of a whole argument. Teaching the enthymeme helps writers see their rhetorical situation and understand logic as a function of audience assumptions.

196   Kneupper, Charles W. "Teaching Argument: An Introduction to the Toulmin Model." *CCC,* 29 (October 1978), 237–41.

Stephen Toulmin's model of argumentation has three parts: the claim or issue, which concludes the argument; the data, or evidence for the claim; and the warrant, which is the general principle that links data and claim. In simple arguments, the warrant may be assumed. If the warrant is specified, then three more elements enter the model: the qualifier, an acknowledgment that the claim is probably but not certainly true; the reservation, which spells out constraints on the warrant; and the backing, which supports the warrant. Teaching students to analyze essays according to this model will improve their ability to write coherently and argue reasonably. Cf. Toulmin [199].

197   Rodgers, Paul C., Jr. "A Discourse-Centered Rhetoric of the Paragraph." *CCC,* 17 (February 1966), 2–11. Rpt. in *The Sentence and the Paragraph* [198].

The principal organization unit of the essay is the "stadium," which may or may not be a paragraph. A stadium is a completed movement in the flow of an author's thought. Coherence in students' papers will improve if they see essays as a sequence of stadia, and paragraphs as a form of punctuation that guides the reader through the stadia. Paragraphs may be needed to signal a logical break, to break up a long passage for the reader's convenience, or to improve rhythm. See also Paul Rodgers, Jr., "The Stadium of Discourse," *CCC*, 18 (October 1967), 178–85.

198 *The Sentence and the Paragraph.* Urbana, Ill.: NCTE, 1963.
This important collection comprises essays by Francis Christensen on the generative rhetoric of the sentence and the paragraph [214, 191] as well as his "Notes Toward a New Rhetoric: Sentence Openers; A Lesson from Hemingway." It also includes Alton L. Becker, "A Tagmemic Approach to Paragraph Analysis"; and a symposium on the paragraph by Francis Christensen, Alton L. Becker, Paul C. Rodgers, Jr., Josephine Miles, and David H. Karrfalt.

199 Toulmin, Stephen. *The Uses of Argument.* New York: Cambridge Univ. Press, 1964. Excerpted in Bizzell and Herzberg [39].
The persuasiveness of our arguments ("claims") depends upon both the general principles ("warrants") that underlie our interpretations of data and the reasons we provide for them. See Kneupper [196].

200 Winterowd, W. Ross. "The Grammar of Coherence." *CE,* 31 (May 1970), 328–35. Rpt. in Winterowd [165] and in Tate, Corbett, and Myers [162].
Transformational grammar shows how case and syntax hold sentences together, but these features do not fully explain the coherence either of sentences or of larger units of discourse. Seven transitional relations account for coherence: coordinate (expressed, for example, by *and)*; obversative *(but)*; causative *(for)*; conclusive *(so)*; alternative *(or)*; inclusive (the colon); and sequential *(first . . . second)*.

201 Witte, Stephen P., and Lester Faigley. "Coherence, Cohesion, and Writing Quality." *CCC,* 32 (May 1981), 189–204.
According to M. A. K. Halliday and Ruqaiya Hasan, cohesive ties, the semantic relations that hold a text together, fall into five classes: substitution and ellipsis, more common in speech than in writing; reference (the use of pronouns and definite articles); conjunction; lexical reiteration (repeating words or synonyms); and collocation (common word groups). Better writers use more ties. Coherence, however, depends on more than cohesive ties. It also requires setting discourse in the appropriate context for the audience. Collocation may be the best indicator of coherence.

Audience

202 Ede, Lisa, and Andrea Lunsford. "Audience Addressed/Audience Invoked: The Role of Audience in Composition Theory and Pedagogy." *CCC*, 35 (May 1984), 155–71. Rpt. in Tate, Corbett, and Myers [162].
Two divergent views of audience face the writing teacher, one claiming that it is crucial to writing instruction to identify a real audience (the

audience addressed), the other claiming that the audience is fictional and a function of signals given in texts (the audience invoked). Both views miss the dynamic quality of rhetorical situations and the interdependence of reading and writing. To emphasize the audience as addressed tends to undervalue both invention and ethics of language use in the effort to adapt to the "real" audience. On the other side, Ong's view of the audience as a fiction (see [206]) which contrasts the speaker's real, present audience with the writer's distant one, tends to overstate the reality of the speaker's audience as compared with the writer's. Rather, both senses of audience must be understood within the larger rhetorical situation and the many possible roles that may be taken by real readers and imagined by the writer. Braddock Award winner.

203   Elbow, Peter. "Closing My Eyes as I Speak: An Argument for Ignoring Audience." *CE*, 49 (January 1987), 50–69. Rpt. in Graves [285] and in Tate, Corbett, and Myers [162].
Writers should think about their audience, but not always. Some audiences help writers think better, others inhibit or intimidate. Faced with the latter, it is better to ignore the audience or pretend the audience is friendly during the early stages of writing. Not only can this overcome a block, it may lead to new thinking and knowledge. Indeed, this writer-based prose can be better than reader-based prose, in the same way that journal writing can be stronger than formal audience-directed writing. Writing to an audience has been characterized as the higher level cognitively, yet the ability to turn off the audience, to experiment with a more poetic form of language, should be seen as a higher level still.

204   Kirsch, Gesa, and Duane H. Roen. *A Sense of Audience in Written Communication.* Newbury Park, Calif.: Sage Publications, 1990.
Ten essays on the history and theory of audience as a rhetorical concern and six essays reporting on empirical studies of writers' conceptions and use of audience include R. J. Willey, "Pre-Classical Roots of the Addressed/Invoked Dichotomy of Audience"; Stuart Brown and Thomas Willard, "George Campbell's Audience"; Barbara Tomlinson, "Ong May Be Wrong: Negotiating with Nonfictional Readers"; Bennett Rafoth, "The Concept of Discourse Community: Descriptive and Explanatory Adequacy"; Louise Wetherbee Phelps, "Audience and Authorship: The Disappearing Boundary"; Gesa Kirsch, "Experienced Writers' Sense of Audience and Authority: Three Case Studies."

205   Kroll, Barry M. "Writing for Readers: Three Perspectives on Audience." *CCC*, 35 (May 1984), 172–85.
Three conceptions of audience are influential in composition teaching: rhetorical, informational, and social. The rhetorical perspective draws from classical theory and recommends adapting speech or writing to the characteristics of the audience. This advice is generally good, but the perspective is flawed: It casts audiences as adversarial, it ignores the impossibility of characterizing most audiences, and it takes an unsophisticated view of reader psychology. The second approach is that writing must convey information to the reader effectively, by attending to the difficulties readers have extracting meaning from texts. But this model, criticized thoroughly by Dillon [132], tends to give a mechanis-

tic and reductive account of text-processing. The third approach is that writing is a social activity like all communication, requiring a decentering from the self that allows the speaker or writer to take another's perspective. Collaborative writing and reader feedback support this approach pedagogically. The "sense of audience" promoted here, though, is vague and it can be objected that writing is not social but rhetorical, more connected to genre and convention than to social knowledge.

206   Ong, Walter J., S.J. "The Writer's Audience Is Always a Fiction." *PMLA,* 90 (January 1975), 9–21.
Writers project audiences for their work by imagining the presumptive audiences of other pieces of writing. Readers seem willing to be fictionalized in this way—to be the audience projected by the writer—as long as the reader's role is familiar or the writer creates a new role persuasively. Thus, the writer's style or voice is a way of addressing an imagined audience that will respond in the desired way.

207   Park, Douglas. "The Meanings of 'Audience.'" *CE*, 44 (March 1982), 246–57. Rpt. in Tate, Corbett, and Myers [162] and in Young and Liu [189].
Audience, a crucial part of teaching writing, is difficult to define and to apply. The meanings tend to diverge, on the one hand, toward real people with a set of beliefs and expectations to which the discourse must be adjusted, and, on the other, toward a fictional audience implied by the text itself. In both cases, audience refers to aspects of knowledge and motivation that form the contexts for discourse. Even when identified, its characteristics remain complex; the general audience is that much more elusive. Instead of asking about audience, we might more usefully ask about the conventions that make a piece of writing meaningful to a range of readers, beginning with generally accepted conventions of form and moving toward more particular conventions associated with the subject or genre. Using the class as audience does not solve the problem of defining the appropriate rhetorical contexts. We ask our students to act in sophisticated ways when we call for sensitivity to audience, but we lack a clear understanding of the kinds of writing we ought to teach and fall instead into teaching vaguely defined general writing skills.

Revision

208   Beach, Richard. "Self-Evaluation Strategies of Extensive Revisers and Non-Revisers." *CCC,* 27 (May 1976), 160–64.
In a limited study of revising, the students who typically revised drafts very little tended to evaluate their drafts in terms of form: "choppy," "awkward," "wordy," and the like. They did not consider content important when revising. The more extensive revisers tended to locate the "centers of gravity" in early drafts and to evaluate drafts in terms of the development of ideas. The extensive revisers found that their evaluations of each draft were helpful guides to further revision and occasions for predicting solutions to problems in a draft.

209   Faigley, Lester, and Stephen P. Witte. "Analyzing Revision." *CCC,* 32 (December 1981), 400–414.

Revisions can be classified as either surface changes or text-based changes. Surface changes do not affect the information content of the text. They can be subdivided into formal changes, such as spelling, and meaning-preserving changes, such as substitutions. Text-based changes do affect the content. They can be subdivided into microstructure changes, which affect local content only, and macrostructure changes, which affect the gist of the whole text. This taxonomy complements studies of revision such as Sommers's [211] by providing a way of indicating the significance of revision changes. "The major implication of this study . . . is that revision cannot be separated from other aspects of composing." Revision studies have not determined what causes writers to revise.

210   Flower, Linda S., John R. Hayes, Linda Carey, Karen Schriver, and James Stratman. "Detection, Diagnosis, and the Strategies of Revision." *CCC,* 37 (February 1986), 16–55.

Successful writers revise in order to adapt the text to their goals. Revision requires knowledge about texts, knowledge about strategies for revising, and a clear intention to use this knowledge to achieve a goal. Beginning writers must clear three hurdles in learning revision: detecting problems in the text, diagnosing the problems, and selecting a strategy. Detecting problems calls for a review of the text, testing it against an imagined ideal text that fulfills the writer's intentions. Many beginning writers see not the actual text but the intended text when they read their own drafts and many do not form a clear sense of the gist of their own writing. These problems are often compounded by too narrow an intention or the lack of a clear sense of intention. Intention reflects knowledge, so beginning writers may focus on proofreading, which they know to be a feature of finished writing. A stronger sense of purpose and audience brings other features into focus. Diagnosis places problems, once detected, into conceptual categories related, for example, to style or audience. Writers may detect problems and simply do local rewriting. But diagnosis suggests more elaborate revising strategies in response to well-defined problems of knowledge and intention. Braddock Award winner.

211   Sommers, Nancy. "Revision Strategies of Student Writers and Experienced Adult Writers." *CCC,* 31 (December 1980), 378–88. Rpt. in Enos [338], and in Perl [176].

Revision is a recursive process essential to developing ideas, not merely the last stop in a train of writing tasks. Students usually describe revision as choosing better words and eliminating repetition. They revise to develop ideas only when redrafting the opening paragraph. Adults, on the other hand, usually describe revision as the process of finding the form of an argument and accommodating the audience. Adult writers are more likely to add or delete material and to rearrange sentences and paragraphs as they revise.

Style, Grammar, and Usage

(212) Baron, Dennis. *Guide to Home Language Repair.* Urbana, Ill.: NCTE, 1994.

Based on Baron's radio call-in show on grammar and the vagaries of English. Baron answers questions (as "Dr. Grammar") and offers advice on dealing with the Language Police (William Safire and his ilk), the demands of politically correct language, the peculiarities of English spelling, jargon, plagiarism, and sundry other topics.

(213) Baron, Dennis E. *Grammar and Good Taste: Reforming the American Language.* New Haven: Yale Univ. Press, 1982.

After the Revolution, English supplanted Latin and Greek as the dominant language of instruction in American schools. Patriots sought to differentiate American from British English by establishing native standards of spelling, grammar, and pronunciation. Some advocated the formation of an American Academy, like the French Academy, to set these standards. The authors of popular grammar textbooks also attempted to set standards. Although no uniform "Federal grammar" emerged, the link between correct grammar and patriotism led to the association of correctness with good morals in general, and hence with social prestige. The link between grammar and morality also fostered intense anxiety about correctness that continues to this day.

See: Francis Christensen, "A Generative Rhetoric of the Paragraph" [191].

214 Christensen, Francis. "A Generative Rhetoric of the Sentence." *CCC,* 14 (October 1963), 155–61. Rpt. in *The Sentence and the Paragraph* [198]; in Francis Christensen, *Notes Toward a New Rhetoric: Six Essays for Teachers* (New York: Harper & Row, 1967); in Francis Christensen and Bonniejean Christensen, eds., *Notes Toward a New Rhetoric: Nine Essays for Teachers* (New York: Harper & Row, 1978); and in Winterowd [165].

Professional writers write "cumulative" sentences, in which modifying words and phrases are added before, within, or after the base clause. The modifiers work at different levels of abstraction and add to the sentence's texture. Students should practice writing cumulative descriptions of objects and events in single sentences, which will make style and content more complex simultaneously. See also Christensen [191].

215 Corbett, Edward P. J. "Approaches to the Study of Style." In *Teaching Composition: Twelve Bibliographic Essays.* Ed. Gary Tate [38].

This bibliographic essay discusses works on literary style and stylistics, the history of English prose style, theories of style, teaching the analysis of prose style, and teaching students how to improve their writing style.

216 Crew, Louie. "Rhetorical Beginnings: Professional and Amateur." *CCC,* 38 (October 1987), 346–50.

Most amateurs begin an essay by stating their purpose, giving background, or telling results. Professionals hold those moves in reserve. Sixty percent of professionals, compared with 10 percent of student amateurs (in the given sample), begin with narratives. Such openings dramatize the subject and are brief. Professionals use indirection, drop hints or cite experts in order to contradict them, and use oblique quotations, whereas amateurs attempt to be direct. Amateurs use rhetorical questions and truisms, while professionals rarely do. But when these professional strategies are pointed out, student amateurs learn them quickly.

217   D'Eloia, Sarah. "The Uses—and Limits—of Grammar." *Journal of Basic Writing,* 1 (Spring–Summer 1977), 1–20. Rpt. in Tate, Corbett, and Myers [162] and in Enos [338].

Students should learn grammar as part of the writing process. Mina Shaughnessy's work [354] helps us distinguish between true grammar errors and merely accidental errors in student writing. Teachers can address the grammar-based errors through such techniques as dictation, narrowly focused editing, paraphrasing, and imitation. D'Eloia gives much useful advice for teaching grammar.

See: Erasmus, *Copia* [45].

218   Faigley, Lester. "Names in Search of a Concept: Maturity, Fluency, Complexity, and Growth in Written Syntax." *CCC,* 31 (October 1980), 291–300.

Recent research on syntactic maturity in student writing has relied too uncritically on the measures of complexity devised by Kellogg Hunt. Such research, aimed at testing the efficacy of sentence combining, finds increased T-unit and clause lengths in student writing, but no connection has been established between such complexity and the overall quality of the writing. Moreover, designating writing as more or less mature on the basis of such measures is problematic because T-unit and clause length in adult writing vary with discourse aims. Similarly, fluency depends on intersentence, not intrasentence, relations. We have no adequate description of syntactic complexity because we have no reliable generative grammar. Nonetheless, writing pedagogy emphasizes syntax to the detriment of coherence in the essay as a whole.

219   Finegan, Edward. *Attitudes toward English Usage.* New York: Teachers College Press, 1980.

The war between prescriptive grammar and descriptive linguistics has a long history—from Swift and Johnson to the battle of *Webster's Third.* In the attempt to halt the "degradation" of English, prescriptivists developed the doctrine of correctness, the idea that there are right and wrong grammatical forms. This doctrine dominated language study through the 1800s and continues to dominate teaching and public attitudes toward language. Descriptive linguistics holds that usage determines the language, that different forms have different functions, that spoken language is the language, and that change is inevitable. Although this position has led to modern forms of linguistics, it has not, apparently, changed the general attitude that links "correct" grammar to propriety and even morality. Finegan wittily summarizes the work of teachers and writers on both sides of the war, popular and scholarly, including excellent discussions of the NCTE, Noam Chomsky, Labov [343], and others.

220   Flannery, Kathryn T. *The Emperor's New Clothes: Literature, Literacy, and the Ideology of Style.* Pittsburgh: Univ. of Pittsburgh Press, 1995.

There is no inherently good style. Rather, the style preferred by socially powerful groups becomes established as good. This style is part of the group's cultural capital, helping them maintain their power. Since the late Renaissance, the clear, simple, objective style praised by the Royal Society has been promoted by Western educational institutions. Behind "style talk" that treats style as politically neutral is a conservative agenda of maintaining the cultural status quo, as can be seen in T. S. Eliot's elevation of Francis Bacon's work as model prose. E. D. Hirsch follows the same agenda with his doctrine of "communicative efficiency" in *The Philosophy of Composition.* Literacy education has the institutional role of teaching the plain style to the masses, while literature, with its premium on artifice, remains privileged discourse. Resisting this agenda requires a rhetorical conception of style that valorizes artifice and a range of styles for everyone.

221   Harris, Muriel, and Katherine E. Rowan. "Explaining Grammatical Concepts." *Journal of Basic Writing,* 6 (Fall 1989), 21–41.

Editing is a process of detection, diagnosis, and rewriting, not a single final step in the composing process. But prescriptive grammar often does not help unpracticed writers. As Patrick Hartwell [222] argues, most grammar rules are COIK—clear only if known. Learning grammatical terminology, however, is not the same as learning the grammatical concepts necessary for editing. To help students learn the concepts, four techniques are useful: provide background information (i.e., prerequisite concepts) when needed; define critical attributes of the concept; use a variety of examples; and in practice sessions, lead students to formulate questions they can ask themselves.

222   Hartwell, Patrick. "Grammar, Grammars, and the Teaching of Grammar." *CE,* 47 (February 1985), 105–27. Rpt. in Enos [338].

The debate about whether grammar instruction improves writing will not be resolved by empirical studies. These studies suggest that grammar instruction has no effect on writing, and they have been attacked by proponents of such instruction. Grammar may be defined in five ways: (1) The internalized rules shared by speakers of a language. These rules are difficult to articulate and are learned by exposure to the language. (2) The scientific study of the internalized rules. Different theories of language generate different systems of rules. These rules do not dictate the actual use of grammar in the first sense. Researchers find no correlation between learning rules and using them, or between using rules and articulating them. (3) The rules promulgated in schools. These are simplifications of scientific grammars and are therefore even farther from grammar as used by speakers of the language. They reflect the questionable belief that poor grammar is a cognitive deficiency. Metalinguistic awareness, including some knowledge of grammar, seems to be central to print literacy, but the awareness appears to follow, not generate, print literacy. (4) Grammar as usage: a set of exceptions to grammar rules. (5) Grammar as style: the use of grammatical terms in manipulating style. Much research suggests that active use of language improves writing more than instruction in any grammar.

See: Richard Haswell, "Minimal Marking" [243].

223   Haussamen, Brock. *Revising the Rules: Traditional Grammar and Modern Linguistics.* Dubuque: Kendall Hunt, 1993.
The prescriptive rules of grammar were divorced from descriptive linguistics in the nineteenth century and trying to remarry them is difficult. The tradition of grammar handbooks is long and deeply ingrained, while linguistics has focused on oral language and theory. Descriptive grammar does, however, have much to offer about grammar conventions that can enliven and improve the grammar we teach to students. Haussamen, a community college teacher, offers new descriptions of old conventions including verb tense, agreement, passive voice, pronoun agreement, and punctuation, all in aid of a more rhetorical approach to grammar.

224   Hunter, Susan, and Ray Wallace, eds. *The Place of Grammar in Writing Instruction: Past, Present, Future.* Portsmouth, N.H.: Heinemann, Boynton/Cook, 1995.
Grammar was long regarded as an essential element in the teaching of writing, an attitude criticized and discarded in more recent times. However, the usefulness and methods of grammar instruction are still debated, with some good arguments appearing for at least limited grammar instruction keyed to students' writing. Sixteen essays explore grammar instruction past, present, and future, including: Cheryl Glenn, "When Grammar Was a Language Art"; Gina Claywell, "Reasserting Grammar's Position in the Trivium in American Composition"; John Edlund, "The Rainbow and the Stream: Grammar as System Versus Language in Use"; R. Baird Shuman, "Grammar for Writers: How Much Is Enough?"; Stuart Brown, Robert Boswell, and Kevin McIlvoy, "Grammar and Voice in the Teaching of Creative Writing"; and David Blakesly, "Reconceptualizing Grammar as an Aspect of Rhetorical Invention."

225   Kline, Charles, R., Jr., and W. Dean Memering. "Formal Fragments: The English Minor Sentence." *Research in the Teaching of English,* 11 (Fall 1977), 97–110.
Grammar handbooks, if they do not simply forbid using sentence fragments, give few guidelines for using them effectively. A survey of samples of formal prose shows that accomplished writers use fragments often and in predictable ways. Kline and Memering list and explain the conditions in which fragments are effectively used and argue that such effective fragments should be called "minor sentences" (following Richard Weaver's suggestion) and taught as a stylistic option.

226   Lanham, Richard A. *Analyzing Prose.* New York: Scribner's, 1983.
The dominant theory of prose style prizes clarity, brevity, and sincerity. This theory tries to make prose transparent; it reduces rhetoric to mere ornament; it runs counter to common sense, to what we value in literature, and to the fact that context defines its three main terms. Classical rhetorical terms provide an alternative way to describe prose style. Noun style relies on "be" verbs, prepositional phrases, and nominalized verbs. Verb style uses active verbs. Parataxis is the absence of connect-

ing words between phrases and clauses, and paratactic style uses simple sentences and prepositional phrase strings. Hypotaxis is the use of connecting words, hence a highly subordinated style. Either style may use asyndeton (few connectors) or polysyndeton (many connectors). The "running" style uses parataxis: it is characterized by a serial record of ideas with many parenthetical additions. "Periodic" style is hypotactic: highly organized, reasoned, and ranked. Other stylistic devices (isocolon, chiasmus) affect these styles differently. Descriptive analysis should also account for visual and vocal form, the use of several common and effective tropes and schemes, and high and low diction. The reader's self-consciousness about style tends to direct judgments of style as clear or opaque, but determining the appropriateness of style to a range of purposes through descriptive analysis is a better way to judge prose.

227   O'Hare, Frank. *Sentence-Combining: Improving Student Writing without Formal Grammar Instruction.* Urbana, Ill.: NCTE, 1973.
Although teaching transformational grammar is no more helpful in improving student writing than instructing in traditional grammar, practice in sentence combining (originally used as a way of teaching grammar) leads to increased syntactic maturity, even in the absence of formal grammar training of any kind. See: Donald Daiker, Andrew Kerek, and Max Morenberg, "Sentence-Combining and Syntactic Maturity in Freshman English," *CCC*, 29 (February 1978), 36–41. Cf. Faigley [218].

228   Ohmann, Richard. "Use Definite, Specific, Concrete Language." *CE*, 41 (December 1979), 390–97. Rpt. in Tate, Corbett, and Myers [162].
One of the most common revision maxims given in rhetoric textbooks is to substitute concrete for abstract language. This advice springs from an ideology of style that values ahistoricism (focus on the present moment), empiricism (focus on sensory data), fragmentation (objects seen outside the context of social relations), solipsism (focus on individual's perceptions), and denial of conflict (reported facts have the same meaning for everyone). Following this advice may trap students in personal experience and inhibit their ability to think critically about the world. Students need to practice the relational thinking made possible by abstractions and generalizations.

See: *The Sentence and the Paragraph* [198].

229   Weathers, Winston. "Teaching Style: A Possible Anatomy." *CCC*, 21 (May 1970), 144–49. Rpt. in Tate, Corbett, and Myers [162].
To teach style, we must convince students that they must master style to express themselves with individuality and to communicate vividly. We must give students a way to recognize and imitate different styles, to incorporate them into extended discourse, and to suit style to the rhetorical situation. Finally, we must demonstrate our own ability to vary style in writing done in front of the class.

See: Yancey, *Voices on Voice* [321].

Response and Evaluation

230 Anson, Chris M. *Writing and Response: Theory, Practice, and Research*. Urbana, Ill.: NCTE, 1989.

Seventeen essays include Anson, "Response to Writing and the Paradox of Uncertainty"; David Bleich, "Reconceiving Literacy: Language Use and Social Relations"; Louise Phelps, "Images of Student Writing: The Deep Structure of Teacher Response"; Martin Nystrand and Deborah Brandt, "Response to Writing as a Context for Learning to Write"; Susan Wall and Glynda Hull, "The Semantics of Error: What Do Teachers Know?"; Thomas Newkirk, "The First Five Minutes: Setting the Agenda in a Writing Conference"; Richard Beach, "Demonstrating Techniques for Assessing Writing in the Writing Conference" [302].

See: Richard Beach, "Demonstrating Techniques for Assessing Writing in the Writing Conference" [302].

231 Belanoff, Pat. "The Myth of Assessment." *Journal of Basic Writing*, 10 (Spring 1991), 54–66.

There are four myths of assessment. The first is that we know what we're testing for. Tests assume, falsely, that we can judge when writing is good enough for some purpose, to satisfy a requirement or to graduate, and they assume that we know what constitutes improvement. The second myth is that we know what we are testing. We cannot test ability, though: we simply judge the quality of a hastily written product, the result of a meaningless task, without reference to the writer at all. The third is that we agree both on criteria and on whether individual papers meet the criteria. But because texts do not contain meaning, readers inevitably differ about whether abstract criteria have been met. The final myth is that there is a standard of good writing that can be applied uniformly, an obvious misapprehension. Even communal portfolio assessment does not eliminate differences in judgment, but, by promoting discussion of teaching and criteria, it improves teaching, and, moreover, appears to be the best way to approach consensus.

232 Belanoff, Pat, and Marcia Dickson. *Portfolios: Process and Product*. Portsmouth, N.H.: Heinemann, Boynton/Cook, 1991.

Twenty-three essays on both practical and theoretical dimensions of portfolio assessment. Units cover proficiency testing, program assessment, using portfolios in courses, and political issues. Essays include: Peter Elbow and Pat Belanoff, "State University of New York at Stony Brook Portfolio-based Evaluation Program"; David Smit, Patricia Kolonosky, and Kathryn Seltzer, "Implementing a Portfolio System"; Roberta Rosenberg, "Using the Portfolio to Meet State-Mandated Assessment"; Anne Sheehan and Francine Dempsey, "Bridges to Academic Goals: A Look at Returning Adult Portfolios"; Richard Larson, "Using Portfolios in the Assessment of Writing in the Academic Disciplines"; Jeffery Sommers, "Bringing Practice in Line with Theory: Using Portfolio Grading in the Composition Classroom"; Pamela Gay, "A Portfolio Approach to Teaching a Biology-Linked Basic Writing Course"; and Marcia Dickson, "The WPA, The Portfolio System, and Academic Freedom." Includes a cumulative bibliography of works cited.

233   Belanoff, Pat, and Peter Elbow. "Using Portfolios to Increase Collaboration and Community in a Writing Program." *WPA,* 9 (Spring 1986), 27–40.

Students prepare portfolios of three composition-course papers—one narrative or expressive, one formal essay conceptually organized, and one text analysis—plus cover sheets describing their writing processes and an unrevised piece of in-class writing. Students submit one or two pieces at midsemester to be evaluated without prejudice. Grades are pass-fail only, assigned by a group of teachers. The student's own teacher can ask for a second reading. This testing process, unlike the proficiency exam, rewards the student for collaboration and revision. It also builds community among the teachers, who have two chances each semester to discuss writing and grading standards and slowly work toward consensus on some issues. The portfolio system encourages collaboration between teachers and students and gives the teacher's coaching role more credibility. Finally, the system increases collaboration between teachers and program directors by bringing the course content into the open.

234   Black, Laurel, Donald A. Daiker, Jeffrey Sommers, and Gail Stygall, eds. *New Directions in Portfolio Assessment: Reflective Practice, Critical Theory, and Large-Scale Scoring.* Portsmouth, N.H.: Heinemann, Boynton/Cook, 1994.

Twenty-six essays representing a variety of research approaches to the questions of the validity and perceived benefits of portfolio assessment. Essays include: Pat Belanoff, "Portfolios and Literacy: Why?"; Edward White, "Portfolios as an Assessment Concept"; Peter Elbow, "Will the Virtues of Portfolios Blind Us to Their Potential Dangers?"; James Berlin, "The Subversions of the Portfolio"; Glenda Conway, "Portfolio Cover Letters, Students' Self-Presentation, and Teachers' Ethics"; John Beall, "Portfolios, Research, and Writing about Science"; James Reither and Russell Hunt, "Beyond Portfolios: Scenes for Dialogic Reading and Writing"; Nedra Reynolds, "Graduate Writers and Portfolios: Issues of Professionalism, Authority, and Resistance"; Irwin Weiser, "Portfolios and the New Teacher of Writing"; Gail Stygall, et al., "Gendered Textuality: Assigning Gender to Portfolios"; Robert Broad, "'Portfolio Scoring': A Contradiction in Terms"; David Smit, "A WPA's Nightmare: Reflections on Using Portfolios as a Course Exit Exam"; and Carl Lovitt and Art Young, "Portfolios in the Disciplines: Sharing Knowledge in the Contact Zone."

235   Charney, Davida. "The Validity of Using Holistic Scoring to Evaluate Writing: A Critical Overview." *Research in the Teaching of English,* 18 (February 1984), 65–81.

A good test of writing ability must be both reliable (it must provide reproducible results) and valid (it must actually test what it claims to test). Many writing teachers have rejected quantitative tests as invalid, feeling that they do not actually measure writing ability. But qualitative tests are often unreliable, as raters disagree over what constitutes good writing. The use of holistically scored writing samples is now widely regarded as a reliable and valid testing method. But holistic scorers are often influenced by legibility, length, and unusual diction, casting doubt on the validity of this method.

236   Cooper, Charles R., and Lee Odell, eds. *Evaluating Writing: Describing, Measuring, Judging.* Urbana, Ill.: NCTE, 1977.

Six essays explain current techniques for assessing students' writing, including measures of syntactic complexity, intellectual maturity, and self-evaluating ability. Two important testing methods are described in Cooper and Odell, "Holistic Evaluation of Writing," and Richard Lloyd-Jones, "Primary Trait Scoring."

237   Diederich, Paul. *Measuring Growth in English.* Urbana, Ill.: NCTE, 1974.

Diederich discusses factor analysis of readers' responses to essay tests; avoidance of reader bias; reliability of statistical results; standard deviation; comparative reliability of objective and essay tests; and design of tests. Appendices describe criteria for evaluating essay tests, sample essay topics, and sample objective questions. See Cooper and Odell [236] for newer testing methods, but Diederich's work is essential for explaining statistical problems.

238   Faigley, Lester, Roger D. Cherry, David A. Jolliffe, and Anna M. Skinner. *Assessing Writers' Knowledge and Processes of Composing.* Norwood, N.J.: Ablex, 1985.

Current methods of evaluating writing do not adequately reflect the research on composing that has prompted many writing programs to teach the composing process. Better evaluation would consider the literary, cognitive, and social dimensions of composing, and measure what writers know as well as what they do. Two methods developed for this study attempt to assess knowledge and process. In the first method, writers describe the knowledge they will apply to a given writing task (about situation, form, content, and so on). The second method is a "process log" of the actual writing experience. This book presents an extensive overview of research; the results of a study of writers' planning, writing, and revising and their task-related knowledge; and a thorough discussion of the relationship between theories of composing and theories of assessment.

239   Garrison, Roger. "One-to-One: Tutorial Instruction in Freshman Composition." *New Directions for Community Colleges,* 2 (Spring 1974), 55–84.

Professional writers learn their craft by writing with the help of an editor. Freshman writers can learn the same way if the classroom is set up as a workshop in which students work independently, at their own pace, and consult the instructor for editorial guidance in brief conferences. The instructor should suggest writing projects tailored to each student's personal or career interests. Garrison provides detailed advice on commenting effectively in a short conference.

240   Greenberg, Karen. "Validity and Reliability Issues in the Direct Assessment of Writing." *WPA: Writing Program Administration,* 16 (Fall–Winter 1992), 7–22.

Writing teachers prefer direct assessment—that is, holistically scored essay tests—to indirect, multiple-choice tests. Yet direct assessment is still criticized by the College Board on grounds of inter-rater unreliability, based on studies through the years that show greater reliability for indirect measures. But multiple-choice tests, scored mechanically, will always produce high reliability. Such tests, moreover, focus on the less important components of writing and reflect cultural bias. Differences in judgment on essays reflect the complexity of reading and writing, and good scoring procedures increase reliability. The validity of indirect assessment has long been challenged, yet the College Board—despite the evidence of their own study showing that a writing sample calling for two or more rhetorical tasks has greatest construct validity—champions a cost-effective test that includes multiple choice. Portfolio assessment is clearly more relevant to theory and classroom practice, but it does not yet include a model of good writing that will boost construct validity. Though research is needed in this area, there is sufficient reason to be comfortable with a commitment to direct assessment.

241   Greenberg, Karen, Harvey S. Wiener, and Richard A. Donovan, eds. *Writing Assessment: Issues and Strategies.* New York and London: Longman, 1986.

Twelve essays and an annotated bibliography (fifty-three entries) collected by the National Testing Network in Writing, which is based at the City University of New York. Included are Stephen P. Witte, Mary Trachsel, and Keith Walters, "Literacy and the Direct Assessment of Writing: A Diachronic Perspective"; Edward M. White, "Pitfalls in the Testing of Writing"; Gertrude Conlon, "'Objective' Measures of Writing Ability"; Roscoe C. Brown, Jr., "Testing Black Student Writers"; Gordon Brossell, "Current Research and Unanswered Questions in Writing Assessment."

242   Harris, Muriel. *Teaching One-to-One: The Writing Conference.* Urbana, Ill.: NCTE, 1986.

Conferences should be an integral part of teaching writing. Many teachers find conferences their most helpful pedagogical strategy, useful at every stage of the writing process, and capable of improving the writer's sense of audience and purpose. To have successful conferences, teachers should consider their goals, their role in the conference, meeting formats, and scheduling. Conversation should be purposefully directive or nondirective in keeping with the immediate goals. To diagnose student difficulties and provide help in solving problems, teachers should begin by diagnosing their own criteria, their teaching methods, and the composing styles of the students. Diagnosis leads to strategies for overcoming writer's block, for recognizing cultural differences, and for dealing with learning disabilities. Finally, the conference is a good setting for teaching grammar.

243   Haswell, Richard H. "Minimal Marking." *CE*, 45 (October 1983), 600–4.

Marking compositions is unpleasant and largely unproductive as well: Correcting surface errors has virtually no effect on students' writing. A way to address this level of writing, though, is not to correct errors but to indicate their presence in a line of writing by a check in the margin. This method challenges the student to find and correct the errors, most of which turn out to be careless. Conceptual errors are now easier to address; the teacher's commenting time can be spent on substance; and students move more effectively to mastery.

244   Horvath, Brooke K. "The Components of Written Response: A Practical Synthesis of Current Views." *Rhetoric Review,* 2 (January 1985), 136–56. Rpt. in Tate, Corbett, and Myers [162].

The consensus of advice on formative evaluation (feedback on drafts as opposed to summative evaluation of final products) suggests that teachers should avoid correcting and rewriting students' papers and should instead ask questions, suggest changes, and assign new tasks. The goal of formative evaluation is to promote learning and help students approximate skilled writers' behavior. Teachers should remember to put responses in appropriate order (large-scale concerns before mechanics), leave the authorship with the student, and avoid unhelpful comments. Bibliography contains eighty-one annotated items.

245   Rubin, Donnalee. *Gender Influences: Reading Student Texts.* Carbondale: Southern Illinois Univ. Press, 1993.

Reader-response theories argue that men and women respond differently to literary texts. Nevertheless, research in which a group of male and female teachers were asked to evaluate unidentified essays reveals little gender bias. Longitudinal study of two teachers, one male and one female, also reveals little bias. The better a teacher knows his or her students—through, for example, a pedagogy that uses frequent conferencing—the less gender bias the teacher exhibits. Blind evaluation increases the chance of distortion by essay topics or styles uncongenial to the evaluator's gender identity. A maternal model of teaching, which gives a responsive reading to all students, attends to the contexts of writing, and encourages independence, most tends to obviate gender bias.

246   Sommers, Nancy. "Responding to Student Writing." *CCC,* 32 (May 1982), 148–56. Rpt. in *Teaching Writing: Theories and Practices.* Ed. J. Travers. Glenview, Ill.: Scott, Foresman, 1988.

"Teachers' comments can take students' attention away from their own purposes in writing a particular text and focus that attention on the teachers' purpose in commenting." In this study, comments by teachers directed students to edit sentences and to rethink and expand the topic at the same time. This is contradictory advice, urging students to treat the text as finished while treating the subject as unfinished. Instead of using comments to justify grades, teachers should respond to the meaning and purpose of early drafts and leave editing corrections for later, thus encouraging students to revise more extensively rather than to patch up the text. Braddock Award winner.

247   Walvoord, Barbara E. Fassler. *Helping Students Write Well: A Guide for Teachers in All Disciplines.* 2nd ed. New York: MLA, 1990.

To help students write well, teachers should communicate expectations clearly, respond to writing without rewriting students' papers for them, and use grades to coach as well as evaluate writing. Walvoord provides a wealth of practical advice, primarily for the novice writing teacher, with sample assignments, student papers, and comments.

248 White, Edward M. *Teaching and Assessing Writing.* 2nd ed. San Francisco and London: Jossey-Bass, 1994.

Assessment can have a damaging influence on writing instruction, but, used properly, may improve teaching and demonstrate the value of what we do. Formative assessment should be used to help students progress and to understand that product assessment is the inevitable end of writing in college. Writing teachers should, for example, help students learn how to take essay tests, which they will encounter frequently. External or summative assessment is similarly inevitable, and writing program administrators are well advised to understand the language of testing from a variety of perspectives, in an effort to produce fair and satisfactory tests. White offers much commonsense advice on testing, organizing holistic tests, program evaluation, and using testing and evaluation in teaching.

Literacy

249 Bernstein, Basil. *Class, Codes, and Control.* New York: Schocken, 1975.

School writing and speaking tasks call for the use of the elaborated code—a formal way of using language that explicitly identifies context and carefully fills in transitions and details for an anonymous reader. Most everyday speech, however, calls only for the restricted code, which is highly context dependent. Socioeconomic class tends to determine whether children learn how to use the elaborated code at home, hence whether they can readily perform the kind of linguistic tasks assigned and expected at school. Working-class children experience social relations in which elaborated code use is rare, unlike middle-class children, who can distinguish the codes and when to use them. Thus, working-class children are often judged to be stupid when they only lack access to school-like linguistic forms.

250 Bleich, David. *The Double Perspective: Language, Literacy and Social Relations.* New York: Oxford Univ. Press, 1988.

We learn how to communicate by internalizing the double perspective of speaker and interlocutor first experienced as small children in dialogue with our parents. Effective adult communication is never an assertion of will but part of an oscillation between socially constructed pairs of opposing concepts. In teaching, a productive oscillation is needed between the classroom, in which subjective expression and collaboration are encouraged, and the academy, which valorizes "objective" scholarship produced by "independent" thought. In this as in other pairs of perspectives, one term must not be privileged: A double perspective is to be maintained. Bleich gives many examples of assignments and student work to illustrate his pedagogy.

251   Bloome, David, ed. *Classrooms and Literacy*. Norwood, N.J.: Ablex, 1989.

Eleven essays explore the idea that literacy education is a function of the curriculum as a whole and the school as a social institution. Includes: David Bloome, "Beyond Access: An Ethnographic Study of Reading and Writing in a Seventh Grade Classroom"; Catherine Snow, et al., "Giving Formal Definitions: An Oral Language Correlate of School Literacy"; Thomas Eisemon and Theresa Rogers, "The Acquisition of Literacy in Religious and Secular Schools"; Jay Lemke, "Social Semiotics: A New Model for Literacy Education"; and Patricia Stock and Jay Robinson, "Literacy as Conversation: Classroom Talk as Text Building."

252   Brandt, Deborah. *Literacy as Involvement: The Acts of Writers, Readers, and Texts*. Carbondale: Southern Illinois Univ. Press, 1990.

The oral-literate dichotomy and the accompanying assumption that text literacy requires the ability to manage decontextualized language are in error. Rather, all forms of literacy are deeply context-bound, and reading and writing are forms of social interaction and intersubjectivity.

253   Chiseri-Strater, Elizabeth. *Academic Literacies: The Public and Private Discourse of University Students*. Portsmouth, N.H.: Heinemann, Boynton/Cook, 1991.

Detailed case studies of two college writers reveal linguistic resources that are not always recognized by the university. The academy favors lecture-recitation and combative debate formats that suited one of the students, while the other found less agonistic ways of communicating and learning. Both students used nonverbal expression, like visual images and dance, as aids to learning, even though these media were rarely valued in coursework. The development of multiple literacies can be fostered by adopting collaborative learning strategies and writing assignments that breach the traditional separation between public knowledge and private life.

254   Cook-Gumperz, Jenny. *The Social Construction of Literacy*. Cambridge: Cambridge Univ. Press, 1986.

Ten essays investigate the settings in which and means by which literacy is acquired. Includes: Jenny Cook-Gumperz, "Literacy and Schooling: An Unchanging Equation?"; John Gumperz, "Interactional Sociolinguistics in the Study of Schooling"; Gordon Wells, "The Language Experience of Five-Year-Old Children at Home and at School"; James Collins, "Differential Instruction in Reading Groups"; Herbert Simons and Sandra Murphy, "Spoken Language Strategies and Reading Acquisition."

255   Daniell, Beth. "Against the Great Leap Theory of Literacy." *PRE/TEXT*, 7 (Fall–Winter 1986), 181–93.

Literacy scholarship is divided into two camps, those who embrace and those who oppose the Great Leap theory. This theory holds that literacy shifts a culture's perception from holistic to analytic. It is advanced by Eric Havelock [261], Walter Ong, S.J. [271, 272], and Thomas Farrell

[256]. But the conflation of thought itself with the qualities of formal discourse prejudices the characterization of oral communities, equating Western forms of academic thinking with human intelligence. The theory also permits broad generalization about language competence and cognitive ability from small language samples. Many researchers oppose this theory, having found that a continuum from oral to literate or a complex intermixing of these forms of discourse more accurately describes the language use of particular societies.

See: Janet Carey Eldred and Peter Mortensen, "Reading Literacy Narratives" [322].

256   Farrell, Thomas J. "I.Q. and Standard English." *CCC,* 34 (December 1983), 470–84.
There is no genetic cause for Black children's persistently lower scores on I.Q. tests. Black English communities, however, exhibit many patterns of oral, rather than literate, language use. If I.Q. tests measure cognitive abilities valued by society, and if the acquisition of literacy confers these abilities, the low I.Q. scores of Black children can be attributed to their orality—their ignorance of Standard English, which is shaped by literacy. Thus, their cognitive abilities may be enhanced by teaching them to speak and write Standard English. See also "Responses to Thomas J. Farrell, 'I.Q. and Standard English,'" *CCC,* 35 (December 1984), 455–77.

257   Freire, Paulo. *Pedagogy of the Oppressed.* Trans. Myra Bergman Ramos. New York: Seabury, 1968.
Pedagogy can be liberating if it truly enables the oppressed to name the world for themselves rather than merely imposing the knowledge of the dominant group. The banking approach to education, in which the teacher knows, thinks, speaks, and disciplines, treats people as adaptable and manipulable, rather than as agents in the world with the power to create and transform. Liberating education consists of acts of cognition, not transfers of information. Teaching from generative themes drawn from the lives of the students can lead to critical consciousness as the students come to understand the situation in which they live, gain the power to name it, and see the possibility of changing it themselves.

258   Freire, Paulo, and Donaldo Macedo. *Literacy: Reading the Word and the World.* South Hadley, Mass.: Bergin & Garvey, 1987.
Literacy is a form of cultural politics, in the United States as elsewhere. It may reproduce the existing social formation or promote emancipatory change. Critical literacy encourages cultural production rather than reproduction, enabling people to tell their own stories about their individual and collective experience.

259   Graff, Harvey. *The Labyrinths of Literacy: Reflections on Literacy Past and Present.* Pittsburgh: Univ. of Pittsburgh Press, 1995.
Sixteen previously published essays by Graff exploring the history of literacy and the implications of that history. Present-day conceptions of literacy are historically grounded, reflecting the oversimple view of literacy as the key to civilization (dominant until quite recently) yet serving as the basis of a more complex understanding of literacy at pre-

sent. The connection between literacy and social development was based on untested assumptions and ideological predispositions: Literacy was mistaken for a neutral technology; alphabetic literacy was extolled, to the exclusion of other significant literacies; a false dichotomy was discerned between literacy and orality; and a hierarchy that irrevocably harmed individuals and societies perceived as illiterate was erected. Critical theory and social history have worked to test and correct these conceptions, revealing a far more complex understanding of the nature and types of literacy, the ways that literacies are learned and used, the functions of literacy in communities, and the policies that have been employed to foster—or impede—literacy.

260   Graff, Harvey J. *The Legacies of Literacy: Continuities and Contradictions in Western Culture and Society.* Bloomington: Indiana Univ. Press, 1987.
Graff reviews classical and medieval education but concentrates on the advent of print literacy in the Renaissance, exploring its consequences for popular schooling in eighteenth- and nineteenth-century Europe and America. He examines literacy in the social context to determine who achieves literacy, what kind of literacy is achieved, and what purposes literacy serves.

261   Havelock, Eric. *Preface to Plato.* Cambridge: Belknap Press of Harvard Univ. Press, 1963.
Plato's attack on poetry was in fact an attack on the use of oral poetry as the archive of Greek culture and the means of cultural instruction. Poetry distorts truth, Plato charges, making it entirely inappropriate for this task. Behind this attack is a rejection of oral forms of cultural preservation and transmission. In nonliterate societies, oral literature is the only means of preserving and handing on collective knowledge. Oral literature is didactic, teaching accepted beliefs and practices. Poetic form is an aid to memorization. Writing, which developed between the time of Homer and Plato, changes all of this by allowing cultural information to be stored more permanently and transmitted more reliably. Poetic form is no longer necessary, as a result of which, propositional forms, including logic, developed. The effect was a cognitive revolution based on alphabetic literacy, changing fundamentally the way that people thought.

262   Heath, Shirley Brice. *Ways with Words: Language, Life, and Work in Communities and Classrooms.* New York: Cambridge Univ. Press, 1983.
Research in three Carolina communities reveals socially conditioned patterns of oral and written language use, but no clear distinctions between literate and oral or preliterate groups.

263   Hirsch, E. D. *Cultural Literacy: What Every American Needs to Know.* Expanded ed. New York: Vintage, 1988.
Effective communication requires not only encoding and decoding skills—technical literacy—but also background knowledge shared among interlocutors—cultural literacy. Effective communication in a democracy requires a shared national culture. The contents of this culture, in the United States, have been largely determined by history:

knowledge that has traditionally been important continues to be so for that very reason. Thus the cultural knowledge of dominant groups tends to predominate. Nevertheless, this cultural knowledge need not be elitist if it is taught to everyone in school and becomes the property of all. Curriculum planning should attend to conveying this cultural literacy. Includes an appendix listing several hundred names, dates, and ideas put forward as the basis of American cultural literacy.

264 Horsman, Jennifer. *Something in My Mind besides the Everyday: Women and Literacy.* Toronto: Women's Press, 1990.

Literacy programs often assume that their clients are completely illiterate and even unintelligent, that traditional school literacy is what they need, and that any failure to complete the program is owing to the individual's lack of motivation. Interviews with twenty-three women enrolled in literacy programs and ten workers in the programs suggest, to the contrary, that learners have varied abilities and a variety of personal and career goals related to literacy. They want to end their dependence on social-service agencies. They are often hampered in their efforts by the complex demands of life in disadvantaged socioeconomic settings and by the debilitating links between many literacy programs and the very social agencies they wish to escape. Literacy programs need to listen more to learners' self-definitions of their needs and to encourage the use of literacy for social criticism.

265 Kintgen, Eugene R., Barry M. Kroll, and Mike Rose, eds. *Perspectives on Literacy.* Carbondale: Southern Illinois Univ. Press, 1988.

Twenty-eight major essays on the theory, history, and pedagogical and social implications of literacy. Essays include Jack Goody and Ian Watt, "The Consequences of Literacy"; Walter J. Ong, S.J., "Some Psychodynamics of Orality"; Sylvia Scribner and Michael Cole, "Unpackaging Literacy"; Harvey J. Graff, "The Legacies of Literacy"; Eric A. Havelock, "The Coming of Literate Communication to Western Culture"; David R. Olson, "From Utterance to Text"; John U. Ogbu, "Literacy and Schooling in Subordinate Cultures"; Yetta Goodman, "The Development of Initial Literacy"; Shirley Brice Heath, "Protean Shapes in Literacy Events"; Paulo Freire, "The Adult Literacy Process as Cultural Action for Freedom"; Carl Kaestle, "The History of Literacy and the History of Readers"; Jay Robinson, "The Social Context of Literacy"; David Bartholomae, "Inventing the University" [109]; Kyle Fiore and Nan Elsasser, "'Strangers No More': A Liberatory Literacy Curriculum" [339]; and William Diehl and Larry Mikulecky, "The Nature of Reading at Work."

266 Knoblauch, C. H., and Lil Brannon. *Critical Teaching and the Idea of Literacy.* Portsmouth, N.H.: Heinemann, Boynton/Cook, 1993.

Critical teaching aims to prepare students to live comfortably with cultural diversity and to work actively for social and economic justice. These goals have been hampered by the scare tactics of those who, like Dinesh D'Souza, deride political correctness but have much more power than those they warn against. Critical teaching is also thwarted by limiting models of literacy: the functionalist model, emphasizing supposedly practical skills; the cultural-literacy model, inculcating

Western culture; and the expressivist model, celebrating personal growth while disguising political realities. A preferable model is critical literacy, which, as Paulo Freire argues, empowers students to name the inequities in their world and work to change them.

267   Lunsford, Andrea A., Helene Moglen, and James Slevin, eds. *The Right to Literacy.* New York: MLA, 1990.

Twenty-nine compact essays address the public and professional issue of literacy, the literacy problems of particular social groups, and political and pedagogical concerns. Essays include Theodore Sizer, "Public Literacy: Puzzlements of a High School Watcher"; Jacqueline Jones Royster, "Perspectives on the Intellectual Tradition of Black Women Writers"; James Moffett, "Censorship and Spiritual Education"; Deborah Brandt, "Literacy and Knowledge"; Glynda Hull and Mike Rose, "Toward a Social-Cognitive Understanding of Problematic Reading and Writing"; and Shirley Brice Heath, "The Fourth Vision: Literate Language at Work."

268   Macedo, Donaldo. *Literacies of Power: What Americans Are not Allowed to Know.* Boulder: Westview Press, 1994.

Drills in discrete skills give people sufficient literacy to decode but not to demystify government propaganda. Adding a cultural-literacy component to education perpetuates cultural genocide on those who do not belong to the majority culture, if the model favors Western culture, as does E. D. Hirsch's. Following Paulo Freire, we should encourage multilingual, multicultural literacy education in order to effect change toward social justice. Macedo testifies to the value of such education from personal experience.

269   Moss, Beverly J. *Literacy across Communities.* Cresskill, N.J.: Hampton, 1994.

Five of the six essays in this collection study nonacademic literacy practices in mainstream communities: Marcia Farr, "En Los Dos Idiomas: Literacy Practices Among Chicano Mexicanos"; Gail Weinstein-Shr, "From Mountaintops to City Streets: Literacy in Philadelphia's Hmong Community"; Daniel McLaughlin, "Toward a Dialogical Understanding of Literacy: The Case of Navajo Print"; Jabari Mahiri, "Reading Rites and Sports: Motivation for Adaptive Literacy of Young African-American Males"; and Beverly Moss, "Creating a Community: Literacy Events in African-American Churches." In the final essay, "World Travelling: Enlarging Our Understanding of Nonmainstream Literacies," Elizabeth Chiseri-Strater comments on the preceding studies and recommends, following them, that teachers should function as coaches, not authority figures; that classrooms should be collaborative learning communities; and that school-home communication should become bidirectional.

270   Murray, Denise E., ed. *Diversity as Resource: Redefining Cultural Literacy.* Alexandria, Va.: TESOL, 1992.

Twelve essays illustrate and develop an approach to multicultural literacy that explicitly answers E. D. Hirsch's program for a primarily Western common culture in the United States. Essays include: Keithe Walters, "Whose Culture? Whose Literacy?"; Anna Soter, "Whose Shared Assumptions? Making the Implicit Explicit"; Denise Murray, Patricia Nichlos, and Allison Hecht, "Identifying the Languages and Cultures of Our Students"; Evelyn Baker Dandy, "Sensitizing Teachers to Cultural Differences: An African American Perspective"; Olga Vasquez, "A Mexicano Perspective: Reading the World in a Multicultural Setting"; Ann Johns, "Toward Developing a Cultural Repertoire: A Case Study of a Lao College Freshman"; Daniel McLaughlin, "Power and the Politics of Knowledge: Transformative Schooling for Minority Language Learners"; and Patricia Nichols, "Language in the Attic: Claiming Our Linguistic Heritage."

271 Ong, Walter, J., S.J. "Literacy and Orality in Our Times." *ADE Bulletin,* 58 (September 1978), 1–7. Rpt. in Horner [84], in Enos [338], and in Young and Liu [189].
Writing is essential for analytic, linear, and sequential thought, in contrast to speech, which is "rhapsodic"—loosely constructed of clichés, proverbs, and other "loci" (topoi). Students, particularly those from highly oral cultural communities, must move from the oral to the written form of thought; their writing often has the loose structure of conversation. It can be helpful to teach students about the contrast between oral and written thought, but it is essential for writing teachers to know about the differences. See also Ong [272].

272 Ong, Walter J., S.J. *Orality and Literacy: The Technologizing of the Word.* New York: Methuen, 1982.
Ong applies Eric Havelock's theory of cognitive differences between oral and literate cultures to modern society. See Ong [271]; Daniell [255].

273 Pattison, Robert. *On Literacy: The Politics of the Word from Homer to the Age of Rock.* New York: Oxford Univ. Press, 1982.
Historical and cross-cultural study focusing on ideological implications of different definitions and forms of literacy. Literacy, finally, cannot be defined as a mechanical skill, a touchstone of civility, or a prerequisite for economic advancement but as consciousness of the problems raised by language.

274 Scribner, Sylvia, and Michael Cole. *The Psychology of Literacy.* Cambridge: Harvard Univ. Press, 1981.
Research among the African Vai, a people with widely varying degrees of literacy, reveals no pattern of cognitive gains associated with literacy.

275 Street, Brian, ed. *Cross-Cultural Approaches to Literacy.* Cambridge Univ. Press, 1993.
Opposing a psycholinguistic focus on discrete reading and writing skills, this collection illustrates approaches to literacy informed by anthropology and focused on social contexts and practices. Twelve essays study literacies around the world, many in nonacademic settings. Includes: Kathleen Rockhill, "Gender, Language, and the Politics of Literacy"; Miriam Camitta, "Vernacular Writing: Varieties of Literacy among Philadelphia High School Students"; Amy Shuman, "Collaborative Writing: Appropriating Power or Reproducing Authority?"; Gail Weinstein-Shr, "Literacy and Social Process: A Community in Transition"; and an introduction by Street.

276   Stubbs, Michael. *Language and Literacy: The Sociolinguistics of Reading and Writing.* London: Routledge and Kegan Paul, 1980.
A functional or sociolinguistic theory of literacy accounts for the relationship between spoken and written language and delineates the "communicative functions served by different types of language in different social settings." Although spoken language is usually learned before written language, speech is much more variable than writing, the orthography of which often does not reflect pronunciation. Written language is thus semiautonomous from and often higher in prestige than spoken language. These differences make writing difficult to learn for children whose spoken language varies widely from the written form dominant in school. Psychological theories of verbal deprivation that purport to explain these difficulties are reductive. All languages are equally effective media of communication. Language-learning difficulties must be understood in terms both of children's varied social experiences with language and of their teachers' attitudes toward their preferred language forms.

277   Taylor, Denny, and Catherine Dorsey-Gaines. *Growing Up Literate: Learning from Inner-City Families.* Portsmouth, N.H.: Heinemann, 1988.
Detailed ethnographic study of poor urban Black families, depicting them as creating productive environments for literacy learning.

278   Tuman, Myron C. *A Preface to Literacy: An Inquiry into Pedagogy, Practice, and Progress.* Tuscaloosa: Univ. of Alabama Press, 1987.
Discussions of literacy present conflicting definitions of the term, from transcription of speech and minimal reading ability (the unproblematic model) to sophisticated interpretive skills that require inferring a context to find meaning in a message (the problematic model). These definitions have supported particular ideological agendas that affect our understanding of literacy education.

279   Villaneuva, Victor, Jr. *Bootstraps: From an American Academic of Color.* Urbana, Ill.: NCTE, 1993.
Linguistic deficit theories are grossly inadequate to explain the school difficulties of students from minority social groups, who are stigmatized by color and social class, unlike immigrant students, even if their native language is English. Particularly disadvantaged are students of castelike minorities that have been economically and culturally colonized by dominant U.S. culture. The dominant culture requires racelessness and abandonment of the home culture as conditions of acceptance, making biculturalism a difficult option. These students need to develop a critical consciousness of the historically generated social conditions that block their freedom and to become conscious intellectuals who can lead progressive social change. Educators should hold minority students to high standards while teaching forms of literacy that foster cultural and linguistic diversity, and political analyses that address the economic decline and individualistic fragmentation of postmodern life.

Curriculum Development

Course Development

280   Bartholomae, David, and Anthony R. Petrosky. *Facts, Artifacts and Counterfacts.* Upper Montclair, N.J.: Boynton/Cook, 1986.
Basic writers can learn to use academic discourse in a course that asks them to read difficult nonfiction books and write about their reading processes. The students find that all reading requires interpretation and that interpretive methods are inevitably culture-bound. They thus come to see that their "problem" as basic writers consists in their use of non-academic or imperfectly assimilated academic interpretive methods. As they become more familiar with the language and methods of the university, they can create authoritative, academically successful personae in their writing. This book explains the theory behind the authors' University of Pittsburgh course and reproduces course materials, including twenty-four sequenced writing assignments. It also includes chapters by their colleagues on revising, correcting errors, and using personal writing to develop a dialogue between student and text.

281   Dickson, Marcia. *It's Not Like That Here: Teaching Academic Writing and Reading to Novice Writers.* Portsmouth, N.H.: Heinemann, Boynton/Cook, 1995.
A major problem for novices entering the academic discourse community is that they do not understand how they can use their nonacademic literacies and personal knowledge there. The Distanced/Personal writing course project attacks this problem by having students research and write about a topic like high-school education, about which they have some personal experience, a topic that can be explored both in the library and by ethnographic research in their home communities. Final papers synthesize these disparate sources. Several chapters give advice on how to help students read difficult academic material and interview others effectively.

282   Dixon, John. *Growth through English.* 3rd ed. 1967. Rpt. London: Oxford Univ. Press for the National Association for the Teaching of English, NCTE, and MLA, 1975.
"Language is learnt in operation, not by dummy runs." Children need to do more writing in school for their own purposes of self-exploration or communicating personal experience. The development of writing ability thus becomes a social and cognitive process. English education should be based on a "growth model" rather than a "skills" or "cultural heritage" model. Reporting on his conclusions following the 1966 Dartmouth Conference, Dixon gives examples of student writing and suggestions for classroom practice at the elementary and middle-school levels, but his curriculum theory has also influenced college teachers. In this edition, Dixon recommends paying more attention to the students' social world and encouraging students to write in a wider variety of modes.

283   Elbow, Peter. *Writing with Power.* New York: Oxford Univ. Press, 1981.

Learning to master our writing makes us feel that we can express our ideas powerfully and move our audience. Writing well thus becomes an important way of relating to the world. This book works from the same premises as *Writing without Teachers* [307] with many more teaching suggestions, particularly on making writing responsive to audience.

284   Foster, David. *A Primer for Writing Teachers: Theories, Theorists, Issues, Problems.* 2nd ed. Portsmouth, N.H.: Boynton/Cook, 1993.

The teaching of writing has been influenced by a number of theories and traditions. The handbook tradition of error correcting still wields power in the field, although most writing teachers are now convinced that handbook exercises do not improve writing. The rhetorical tradition, revived in the last two decades, emphasizes the communication situation and connects with poststructuralist focus on context. The work of Piaget, Vygotsky, and Bruner in cognitive psychology has led to the development of a variety of cognitive-process models of writing that have been vastly influential in teaching and research. Constructivist views, drawing on the work of Rorty, Bakhtin, and Freire [257, 258], oppose the cognitivist view of language as expression of thought. Cognitive construction implies that mental constructs shape knowledge and understanding; social construction proposes that meaning is a function of social discourse. This perspective emphasizes the negotiation of communal discourse conventions in learning to write. Several discourse systems offer additional theoretical bases for teachers of writing. Relational systems (Burke [128, 129], Moffett [291], Britton [166]) emphasize the interaction between writer and audience; categorical systems (Kinneavy [146], D'Angelo [192]) classify topics, strategies, forms, and styles; "micro-rhetorics" (Christensen [191, 214], Alton Becker, Rodgers [197]) focus on the shaping of sentences and paragraphs. Writing teachers must also be aware of the relationship between literacy and dialect, the problems of measuring writing skills, and research in basic writing. Foster concludes with a chapter each on course planning and teaching methods.

See: Paulo Freire and Donaldo Macedo, *Literacy: Reading the Word and the World* [258].

285   Graves, Richard L., ed. *Rhetoric and Composition: A Sourcebook for Teachers and Writers.* 3rd ed. Portsmouth, N.H.: Heinemann, Boynton/Cook, 1990.

Thirty-one previously published essays collected as a resource for practicing writing teachers. Few of the essays from the previous edition appear in this one. There are sections on theory, motivating student writing, and style, as well as stories from the writing classroom. Essays include: Maxine Hairston, "The Winds of Change"; Lester Faigley, "Competing Theories of Process" [169]; Robert Brooke, "Underlife and Writing Instruction"; Gabriele Lusser Rico, "Tapping Creative Potential for Writing"; Donald Murray, "Writing and Teaching for Surprise"; Valerie Krishna, "The Syntax of Error"; Francis Christensen, "A Generative Rhetoric of the Sentence" [214]; Winston Weathers, "Grammars of Style: New Options in Composition"; Stephen North, "The Idea of a Writing Center" [431]; Peter Elbow, "Closing My Eyes as I Speak: An Argument for Ignoring Audience" [203]; Linda Brodkey, "On the Subjects of Class and Gender in 'The Literacy Letters'" [333]; and Ann Berthoff, "Paulo Freire's Liberation Pedagogy."

286   Herzberg, Bruce. "Community Service and Critical Teaching." *CCC*, 45 (October 1994), 307–19.
Students in service-learning courses who go into the community as volunteers are performing needed work. Moreover, they report a heightened sense of the reality of homelessness and need. But their perceptions of these problems tend to be personal rather than social and systemic. They see illiteracy, for example, as the consequence of not studying hard enough. Band-aid volunteer work thus masks the causes of social problems. Service learning must promote critical analysis and social change: Students must therefore do more than write about their experiences. Studying and writing about social forces and how they operate through institutions like schools challenges their long-held beliefs in meritocracy and individualism, but finally leads to deeper reflection on the nature of the problems they see in their community-service work.

287   Kail, Harvey. "Narratives of Knowledge: Story and Pedagogy in Four Composition Texts." *Rhetoric Review,* 6 (Spring 1988), 179–89.
A course or a textbook is like a story about acquiring knowledge, a heroic quest; in the texts considered here, it is a myth of separation, initiation, and return. In Young, Becker, and Pike's *Rhetoric: Discovery and Change* [188], the hero's quest is to reunite the post-Babel world of epistemic alienation by overcoming barriers to communication through the exercise of tortuous heuristics and the disarming of opponents by Rogerian rhetoric, at once winning the trust of the audience and a glimpse of unclouded reality. In Berthoff's *Forming/Thinking/Writing* [180], the hero assails the Castle of Positivism to reclaim the imagination, sailing off on assisted invitations to examine magical objects that lead first to chaos and then to self-recognition. In Coles's *Teaching Composing,* the hero awakens from enchantment by the school, abandons its familiar language, enters the gap of silence between languages, and, with the help of classmate-comrades, gains the freedom of true individual identity. These and other such narratives are founded on social traditions—the Christian search for salvation or the romantic quest for a natural form of individual identity.

288   Kiniry, Malcolm, and Ellen Strenski. "Sequencing Expository Writing: A Recursive Approach." *CCC,* 36 (May 1985), 191–202.
The basic-writing program at the University of California at Los Angeles uses a sequence of expository assignments, in order of increasing cognitive complexity, to introduce students to academic writing: listing, definition, seriation (e.g., chronology), classification, summary, comparison/contrast, analysis, and academic argument. These schema, abstracted from a survey of writing assignments in all departments, allow for development, recursivity (repetition of earlier tasks in later assignments), the use of model academic writing, and an introduction to the methods of reasoning in different academic disciplines.

289   Klaus, Carl H., and Nancy Jones, eds. *Courses for Change in Writing: A Selection from the NEH/Iowa Institute.* Upper Montclair, N.J.: Boynton/Cook, 1984.

Twenty essays describe courses designed by Iowa Institute participants. Groups of essays focus on personal writing, research writing, writing as problem solving, writing in literature courses, writing in courses that focus on social issues, and faculty development for writing across the curriculum. Includes a bibliography on curriculum development and an introduction by Klaus describing the institute's educational philosophy. Mina P. Shaughnessy Prize co-winner.

290   Lindemann, Erika. *A Rhetoric for Writing Teachers.* 3rd ed. New York: Oxford Univ. Press, 1995.

Writing is a means of communication (sending a message to a reader in a particular context) as well as a process involving pre-writing, writing, and rewriting. Psychology and linguistics inform modern methods of teaching students to find ideas; choose words; shape effective sentences, paragraphs, and forms of discourse; and revise what they have written. Lindemann provides chapters on each step in the writing process, on premodern rhetoric, on modern grammar, on the evaluation of writing, and on the design of courses. The third edition provides an expanded bibliography and an outline of the history of composition and rhetoric.

291   Moffett, James. *Teaching the Universe of Discourse.* Boston: Houghton Mifflin, 1968.

English classes in grades K through 12 should focus on language as a symbol system that enables increasingly abstract thought. This view of language is realized in a curriculum that moves students through a "spectrum" of kinds of discourse—interior dialogue, conversation, correspondence, public narrative, and public generalization and inference—that are classified according to the distance between speaker/writer, hearer/reader, and subject. Moving through the spectrum requires increasing efforts to imagine one's audience and what they need to be told about the subject. Lessons can begin with drama performed in class, followed by narrative, moving from diaries and letters to memoirs and biographies. As narration becomes more anonymous, older students move to abstract reasoning. This curriculum is student-centered because it reflects children's cognitive development and because student writing is the principal content. An influential curriculum model, based on the principles developed at the 1966 Dartmouth Conference.

292   Muller, Herbert J. *The Uses of English.* New York: Holt, Rinehart and Winston, 1967.

Summarizing the conclusions agreed upon at the 1966 Dartmouth Conference, Muller makes several recommendations. Children in a democratic school system should not be grouped according to ability; the classroom should also be ethnically and socially diverse. The English curriculum should center on the child's cognitive development, and "good English" should not be taught prescriptively. Literature, not literary criticism, should be taught, with respect for personal responses.

English teachers should connect writing with speaking to break down students' tendency to use academic jargon; bring drama into the classroom to foster social maturity and creativity; and use audiovisual media in the classroom and make the study of film, television, and other mass media part of English study. Alternatives to formal examinations should also be sought.

293   Murray, Donald M. *A Writer Teaches Writing.* 2nd ed. Boston: Houghton Mifflin, 1985.

Murray advocates teaching writing through a workshop approach, in which students and teachers seek the surprise of hearing the written voices that engage readers. Drawing on his experience as a Pulitzer Prize-winning journalist, Murray gives detailed advice on teaching the whole writing process, from syllabus design ("inviting writing") to evaluation (helping students learn to evaluate their own drafts).

294   Peck, Wayne Campbell, Linda Flower, and Lorraine Higgins. "Community Literacy." *CCC,* 46 (May 1995), 199–222.

The Community Literacy Center, a collaboration between a Pittsburgh settlement house and Carnegie Mellon, seeks to foster literacy as action and reflection. It promotes collaborative, intercultural efforts to write public texts as a form of community action. Unlike cultural literacy, which seeks to build community by minimizing difference, and unlike social critique, which seeks community through ideological struggle, community literacy seeks alternative discourses that promote social change, intercultural conversation, inquiry, and strategic rhetoric. Community literacy approaches difference with the goal of negotiating meanings as a way of responding to conflicts. In the CLC collaboration, CMU student mentors do not work to "improve" community residents' writing or help them "find their own voice." Their approach instead is rhetorical: finding ways to use writing as a tool in a literate transaction. This process, to be successful, requires intercultural conversation, problem solving, and negotiation. Several examples illustrate the successes of the community literacy approach.

295   Petrosky, Anthony R., and David Bartholomae, eds. *The Teaching of Writing: Eighty-Fifth Yearbook of the National Society for the Study of Education, Part II.* Chicago: Univ. of Chicago Press, 1986.

Eleven comprehensive essays directed to an audience of educators who are not composition specialists. Included are David Bartholomae, "Words from Afar"; John Gage, "Why Write?"; Patricia Bizzell, "Composing Processes: An Overview"; Arthur N. Applebee, "Problems in Process Approaches: Toward a Reconceptualization of Process Instruction"; Rexford Brown, "Evaluation and Learning"; and Paul Kameen, "Coming of Age in College Composition."

296   Reynolds, Mark, ed. *Two-Year College English: Essays for a New Century.* Urbana, Ill.: NCTE, 1994.

Nineteen essays on a variety of issues facing teachers of English in two-year colleges, including Janice Albert, "I Am Not the Look in Your Eyes"; Mary L. Needham, "This New Breed of College Students"; Mary Kay Morrison, "'The Old Lady in the Student Lounge': Integrating the Adult Female Student into the College Classroom"; Smokey Wilson, "What Happened to Darlene? Reconstructing the Life and Schooling of an Underprepared Learner"; Kate Mangelsdorf, "Latina/o College Writing Students: Linguistic, Cultural, and Gender Issues"; Raelyn Agustin Joyce, "Aliteracy among Community College Students"; Claudia Barrett and Judith Wootten, "Today for Tomorrow: Program and Pedagogy for 21st-Century College Students"; Myrna Goldenberg and Barbara Stout, "Writing Everybody In"; Judith Rae Davis and Sandra Silverberg, "The Integration Project: A Model for Curriculum Transformation"; Ellen Andrews Knodt, "If at First You Don't Succeed: Effective Strategies for Teaching Composition in the Two-Year College"; Nell Ann Pickett, "A Quarter Century and Beyond: My Story of Teaching Technical Writing"; Jean Bolen Bridges, "Honors English in the Two-Year Colleges"; Mark Harris and Jeff Hooks, "Writing in Cyberspace: Communication, Community, and the Electronic Network"; Al Starr, "Community College Teaching: Endless Possibilities"; Bertie E. Fearing, "Renewed Vitality in the 21st Century: The Partnership between Two-Year College and University English Departments"; and Keith Kroll, "(Re)Viewing Faculty Preservice Training and Development."

297   Shor, Ira. *Critical Teaching and Everyday Life.* Boston: South End Press, 1980.

Open-admissions policies have brought increasing numbers of working-class students into American colleges. They need to learn how to distance themselves from their everyday experience in order to analyze it critically, a first step toward understanding and acting on their political situation. Shor shows how to design a writing course that encourages such analysis while reducing the teacher's authority. The most complete application of the ideas of Paulo Freire [257] to American education. Cf. Berthoff [116] and Fiore and Elsasser [339].

298   Small, Robert C., Jr., and Joseph E. Strzepek. *A Casebook for English Teachers: Dilemmas and Decisions.* Belmont, Calif.: Wadsworth, 1988.

Thirty-three cases dramatically present problems that call for ethical and pedagogical solutions, for example, dialect prejudice, sexual stereotyping, hostile reactions to group work, students unprepared for class, plagiarism, grade complaints, failed lessons, boring papers, unwillingness to participate in class discussion, and mechanical errors in papers. Each case is followed by analytic questions, suggestions for approaching the problem from different angles, possible pedagogical solutions or follow-up activities, and reading suggestions. Though designed for secondary-school teachers, most cases apply as well to college classes.

299   Stock, Patricia L., ed. *Fforum: Essays on Theory and Practice in the Teaching of Writing.* Upper Montclair, N.J.: Boynton/Cook, 1983.

These fifty essays on literacy, speaking and writing, reading and writing, writing as a way of learning, and writing and rhetoric are by teachers of science, medicine, and law as well as English and linguistics. They include William E. Coles, Jr., "The Literacy Crisis: A

Challenge How?"; Ken Macrorie, "Language-Using Animals"; Frank J. D'Angelo, "Imitation and the Teaching of Style"; David Bartholomae, "Writing Assignments: Where Writing Begins"; and essays by Peter Elbow, Edward P. J. Corbett, Lee Odell, James Moffett, and others.

300   Summerfield, Judith, and Geoffrey Summerfield. *Texts and Contexts: A Contribution to the Theory and Practice of Teaching Composition.* New York: Random House, 1986.

Human discourse is produced in reaction to social contexts. People adopt a variety of roles constructed in discourse, roles that can be understood as occupying a position on a spectrum from participant in the social context to spectator of it. Participant texts tend to offer many sensory impressions of the context but little explanation of it. They also tend to be structured paratactically. Spectator texts tend to evaluate the social context from a critical distance, to seek connections among contexts, and to be structured hypotactically. Students can be stimulated to write in a variety of participant and spectator roles as they react to texts by others. They can thus test the purposes and effects of taking different roles, develop commitment in writing, and become more critical as readers.

See: Barbara E. Fassler Walvoord, *Helping Students Write Well: A Guide for Teachers in All Disciplines* [247].

301   Williams, James D. *Preparing to Teach Writing.* Belmont, Calif.: Wadsworth, 1989.

Williams offers a straightforward presentation of theory and pedagogical suggestions for teaching writing at the secondary and postsecondary levels. His topics include a review of modern theories and traditional rhetoric, reading and writing connections, grammar, style, nonstandard English and ESL, use of groups, design of assignments, and assessment of writing. Includes bibliography and index.

Collaborative Learning

302   Beach, Richard. "Demonstrating Techniques for Assessing Writing in the Writing Conference." *CCC,* 37 (February 1986), 56–65.

Some students need instruction in assessing writing beyond either reader-based feedback or the teacher's identification of problems in the text. Such instruction can be offered in a conference in which the teacher first demonstrates describing, judging, and selecting appropriate revisions, then describes the rhetorical context of purpose and audience used as criteria for assessment, and finally asks the student to practice this technique. When writers describe their goals in rhetorical terms, they articulate the bases for making judgments, which leads to revision strategies. Students can be given an assessment form before the conference, asking them to describe goals and audience, identify problems, and suggest changes. In conference, the teacher can then focus on the students' difficulties with these categories, helping them see the nature of rhetorical goals, sensing dissonance between goals and the text, and so on.

303   Brooke, Robert. *Writing and Sense of Self: Identity Negotiation in Writing Workshops.* Urbana, Ill.: NCTE, 1991.

Learning to write requires seeing oneself as a person who uses writing to solve problems and accomplish purposes in many areas of one's life, not only in school. To foster this vision, the writing class should encourage students to try on various social roles in their writing and to negotiate a writer's identity for themselves. The teacher should coach apprentices and offer instruction about writing (writing processes, formal rules, etc.) only as needed to help students write what they want. This approach also encourages students to use writing to address public problems beyond the classroom.

304   Brooke, Robert, Ruth Mirtz, and Rick Evans. *Small Groups in Writing Workshops.* Urbana, Ill.: NCTE, 1994.

Writing groups facilitate four elements that are essential to a writer's life: time for writing, ownership of the uses of writing, a community of responders, and exposure to other people's writing. Groups are complex communities, with social and emotional challenges for students. Such challenges are opportunities for learning to deal with differences of many kinds. Teachers are challenged, too, to see themselves as writers in communities and to formulate successful pedagogies. Teachers must, for example, facilitate student role experimentation in groups, design writing activities, provide rules for response, adjust rules as needed, monitor group dynamics, and evaluate group work. The authors give specific, detailed advice about teaching courses with small group workshops.

305   Bruffee, Kenneth A. "The Brooklyn Plan: Attaining Intellectual Growth Through Peer-Group Tutoring." *Liberal Education,* 64 (December 1978), 447–69.

Student tutors are sometimes more effective than teachers in helping other students gain confidence and ability in writing because the students are engaged socially and intellectually at once. In the Brooklyn Plan, tutors who have been trained in an advanced composition course help other students in expository composition. The tutors gain, too, by becoming more committed to quality in their own writing. Bruffee describes the tutor-training program.

See: Kenneth Bruffee, "Collaborative Learning and the 'Conversation of Mankind'" [126].

306   Bruffee, Kenneth A. *Collaborative Learning: Higher Education, Interdependence, and the Authority of Knowledge.* Baltimore: Johns Hopkins Univ. Press, 1993.

Collaborative learning embodies a nonfoundational conception of knowledge as communal consensus achieved by conversation. A foundational or cognitive conception that knowledge is a transferable entity now dominates university teaching. This view maintains the authority of knowledge and the authority of the teacher, challenged by collaboration and its assumption that knowledge is socially constructed. In college, students must enter new communities and cultures. Collaborative learning is the most effective way to gain such acculturation because it works as cultures really do, through social interaction. Conversation allows people to cross boundaries, to become more like others and learn a new discourse. Not only is collaboration more effective than top-down learning, it creates more critical acuity as well. Collaborative teachers use different teaching procedures: setting group tasks, managing the groups, and keeping time. The process teaches interdependence, vital in our interdependent world, while helping students understand the nature of knowledge and its creation.

See: Gregory Clark, *Dialogue, Dialectic, and Conversation* [130].

307   Elbow, Peter. *Writing without Teachers.* New York: Oxford Univ. Press, 1973.

Many writers have been trained to think that good writing proceeds from an organized outline through a near-perfect rough draft to an error-free final draft. This view is wrong for many writers, for it assumes that writers know exactly what they want to say before they begin writing. For those who don't (most of us), a better way to begin is "freewriting," deliberately unfocused but sustained written brainstorming from which a "center of gravity" for an organized essay can emerge. Working on drafts is then a process of "growing," or allowing the organization to remain flexible at first while you generate as many ideas as possible on your subject, and "cooking," or submitting your draft to constructive critical interaction with the demands of fellow writers, literary genres, or your own expectations. A group of people committed to working on their writing in this way can form a teacherless class. They can work on academic writing, too, if they understand that academic work is carried on by the interplay of the "doubting game"—radical skepticism about another's work—and the "believing game"—fully entering another's worldview.

308   Forman, Janis, ed. *New Visions of Collaborative Writing.* Portsmouth, N.H.: Boynton/Cook, 1992.

Nine essays extend the theory and practice of collaborative writing, including: Anne Ruggles Gere and Laura Jane Roop, "For Profit and Pleasure: Collaboration in Nineteenth Century Women's Literary Clubs"; John Trimbur and Lundy Braun, "Laboratory Life and the Determination of Authorship"; Mary Lay, "The Androgynous Collaborator: The Impact of Gender Studies on Collaboration"; John Schilb, "The Sociological Imagination and the Ethics of Collaboration"; and Cynthia Selfe, "Computer-Based Conversations and the Changing Nature of Collaboration."

309   Gere, Anne Ruggles. *Writing Groups: History, Theory, and Implications.* Carbondale: Southern Illinois Univ. Press, 1987.

Since the eighteenth century, American college students have formed literary clubs—essentially writing groups—to coach one another on writing and speaking. Literary clubs that featured formal presentation and critique of papers were also popular among adults, at least until the twentieth century, and offered intellectual opportunities that were especially important to women. Writing groups work against alienation and the solo-performer view of the author. Vygotsky's theory that language development is socially conditioned, along with recent revisionist work on literacy as a communal phenomenon, partly explains why group work helps students write better. Groups work best when all members have agreed on clearly defined tasks and on ways to evaluate their performance on these tasks. Includes an extensive annotated bibliography.

See: Karen Burke Lefevre, *Invention as a Social Act* [186].

See: Joan Mullin and Ray Wallace, *Intersections* [429].

310   Spear, Karen. *Sharing Writing: Peer Response Groups in English Classes.* Portsmouth, N.H.: Heinemann, Boynton/Cook, 1988.
Peer-response groups must first learn how groups work. Peer interaction needs to be seen as part of the composing process, and students need instruction in how to read each other's drafts to overcome confusion about sharing writing. Students' tendency to stand in for the teacher should be replaced by real collaborative behavior. The teacher's role is to recognize successful group work and foster it. Spear offers detailed advice on running a class with groups, focusing on interpersonal relationships.

311   Trimbur, John. "Consensus and Difference in Collaborative Learning." *CE,* 51 (October 1989), 602–16.
The purpose of collaborative learning as described by Bruffee [305] and Wiener [312] is to help students experience the process of negotiating and reaching consensus. This goal has been attacked on the ground that it subjects individual students to leveling peer pressure. But since individuals must face peer pressure as part of living in society, collaborative learning can help them learn how to deal with it. Moreover, the collaborative approach can teach students how to deflect control by authorities to which they might be subject as isolated individuals. Some critics of collaborative learning caution that consensus may actually be acquiescence to prevailing social attitudes; consensus would thus reproduce the oppressions of a nonegalitarian social structure. Richard Rorty, whose views are called upon to support collaborative learning, seems to exacerbate that danger by presenting consensus as a seamless conversational web that can be ruptured only occasionally by individuals. But, contrary to Rorty's thinking, most people participate in a variety of overlapping discourses that often come into conflict. Thus, a collaborative classroom would treat "dissensus," however muted, as the normal state of affairs in most discourse communities and would teach students to think of genuine consensus, following Habermas, not as something achievable but as a commitment to engage in polyvocal conversations as free from relations of domination as possible.

312   Wiener, Harvey S. "Collaborative Learning in the Classroom: A Guide to Evaluation." *CE,* 48 (January 1986), 52–61. Rpt. in Tate, Corbett, and Myers [162].
In a collaborative classroom, students work in small groups on a task designed by the teacher. Each group reports its results to the whole class while the teacher mediates differences and highlights important features of the task. The teacher can be evaluated in several roles: as a task-setter who must design problems that involve students in complex negotiations and provide guidelines for reaching consensus; as a classroom manager who must organize groups efficiently; as a facilitator

who must help all students to participate while intervening minimally; and as a synthesizer who must help the class compare the groups' results and lead them to appreciate the intellectual purposes of the task rather than simply to seek the right answers.

Essay and Personal Writing

313   Anderson, Chris, ed. *Literary Nonfiction: Theory, Criticisms, Pedagogy.* Carbondale: Southern Illinois Univ. Press, 1989.
New Journalism and personal essays by contemporary men and women of letters are often studied in composition classes. This intersection of literature and rhetoric is explored in the seventeen essays in this volume, presenting readings of individual authors, theoretical commentary on the essay form, and pedagogical strategies. Essays include Charles Schuster, "The Nonfictional Prose of Richard Selzer"; Suzanne Clark, "Annie Dillard"; Carl H. Klaus, "Essayists on the Essay"; George L. Dillon, "Fiction in Persuasion: Personal Experience as Evidence and Art"; Peter Elbow, "Gretel Ehrlich and Richard Selzer"; John Clifford, "Responding to Loren Eiseley's 'The Running Man'"; and Pat Hoy II, "Students and Teachers under the Influence: Image and Idea in the Essay."

See: Akua Duku Anokye, "Oral Connections to Literacy" [329].

314   Coles, William E., Jr. *The Plural I: The Teaching of Writing.* New York: Holt, Rinehart and Winston, 1978. Rpt. Upper Montclair, N.J.: Boynton/Cook, 1988.
Students produce "themewriting"—correct but meaningless prose—when teachers correct only for mechanics and style and never comment on content. Coles sets forth a thirty-lesson writing course that focuses on content by identifying an intellectual problem that the class will work on together throughout the semester. Assignments pose increasingly difficult questions about the common problem. Class discussion of students' essays creates a productive self-consciousness about using language.

315   Connors, Robert J. "Personal Writing Assignments." *CCC,* 38 (May 1987), 166–83.
Through most of its history, instruction in rhetoric aimed to equip students to write or speak on any *objective* topic. The rhetor was to be knowledgeable and impersonal in treating subjects. In the seventeenth and, especially, the eighteenth centuries, personal tastes and feelings became more acceptable, particularly in essays and narratives. Nineteenth-century romanticism brought a dramatic shift in the direction of personal writing, and rhetoric instruction, following suit, came to emphasize everyday language (as opposed to Ciceronian high style), assignments that called upon personal experience (rather than abstract ideas), and invention methods for probing personal experience (rather than for searching academic knowledge). By the early twentieth century, novelty—one's own new experience—became a criterion for good writing. Several objective modes remained—impersonal or public topics were still assigned for exposition

and argument exercises—but personal assignments have remained an important, if contested, element of the composition curriculum.

316   Elbow, Peter, ed. *Landmark Essays on Voice and Writing*. Davis, Calif.: Hermagoras Press, 1994.

Seventeen essays, beginning with an analytical introduction by Elbow and including: Mikhail Bakhtin, "Discourse in Life and Discourse in Art"; Walker Gibson, "The 'Speaking Voice' and the Teaching of Composition"; Barbara Johnson, "Translator's Introduction to Dissemination"; bell hooks, "When I Was a Young Soldier for the Revolution: Coming to Voice"; June Jordan, "Nobody Mean to Me Than You: And the Future Life of Willie Jordan"; I. Hashimoto, "Voice as Juice: Some Reservations about Evangelic Composition"; Lester Faigley, "Judging Writing, Judging Selves"; Toby Fulwiler, "Looking and Listening for My Voice"; and Randall Freisinger, "Voicing the Self: Toward a Pedagogy of Resistance in a Postmodern Age."

See: Peter Elbow, *Writing without Teachers* [307].

317   Harris, Jeanette. *Expressive Discourse*. Dallas: SMU Press, 1990.

All discourse can be described as expressive of the writer's ideas and feelings, and virtually no discourse is entirely expressive—that is, devoid of a desire to communicate. Thus, although the category "expressive discourse" is in a sense false, the concept has aided the development of composition pedagogy. Four types of expressive discourse have been promoted. 1) The interior text is the unwritten text in a writer's mind. It serves as the model of the text to be created and may drive the desire to see the text realized. 2) Generative texts include reading journals, summaries, position papers, personal reaction papers, and so on, which help prepare students for more formal writing. 3) Aesthetic discourse forms—poems, stories, and plays—are often taught on the questionable assumption that practicing these forms improves writing generally. 4) Experience-based discourse, or the essay on personal experience, is the type most often assigned in composition classes. There is no evidence that it helps students improve their writing. Moreover, such assignments tend to dichotomize personal writing and information-based writing when a preferable approach is to help students integrate the two.

318   Hollis, Karyn. "Liberating Voices: Autobiographical Writing at the Bryn Mawr Summer School for Women Workers, 1921–1938." *CCC*, 45 (February 1994), 31–60.

The Bryn Mawr Summer School boasted a distinguished faculty, an innovative interdisciplinary curriculum, and an equally innovative pedagogy that included peer collaboration, guided revision, student publication, and links between personal experience and academic disciplines. Writing an autobiography was a key assignment. Today, some critics charge that the autobiographical sensibility is compromised by the masculine belief in a unified self. The Summer School assignments, however, show awareness of the need to be critical of the status quo and not present the themes of bourgeois life as norms. The most popular topic in the autobiographies is work. Most of the autobiographies show a shift from a narrative "I," typical of the unitary bourgeois consciousness, to "we," along with a shift from past to present tense, the "I" being critical and the "we" offering responses to exploitation. This identification with other workers, or with women, or with the family, is the voice of public resistance and empowerment, counteracting the powerless social atom represented by the "I" narrator. Follow-up studies show that many of the students went back to their communities to become civic, church, and union leaders. The "we" of collective subjectivity is rarely seen in student autobiography, but the sense of collective endeavor that supports it might well be encouraged as a way to change consciousness.

319 Macrorie, Ken. *Telling Writing.* Rochelle Park, N.J.: Hayden, 1970.
College students are urged to write dull, impersonal prose: "Engfish." They will write better and learn more if they see writing as a way of telling the truth about their experiences. This textbook contains lessons on telling facts, working through facts to large meanings, using a journal, sharpening word choice, and writing critically. See also *Uptaught* (Rochelle Park: Hayden, 1970), in which Macrorie describes how his dissatisfaction with his own teaching and school standards led him to develop the "telling writing" pedagogy.

See: James Moffett, *Teaching the Universe of Discourse* [291].

320 Spellmeyer, Kurt. "A Common Ground: The Essay in the Academy." *CE*, 51 (March 1989), 262–76.
Proponents of teaching academic discourse depict learning to write as constructing one's knowledge and one's very self through a discourse given by tradition. This approach ignores something universal in all uses of discourse, namely the individual writer's attempts to work out interpretations of experience that make sense to him or her, that allow him or her to retain or reconstruct a feeling of personal coherence. Unity within the writer and within the discourse is best achieved through a form that owes as little as possible to tradition, that contravenes convention for the sake of reproducing the personal viewpoint, yet recognizes stylistic constraints imposed by the attempt to make the personal viewpoint public. The essay best meets this need. Students should be encouraged to write essays in order to learn to put their own stamps on any discourse they employ.

321 Yancey, Kathleen Blake, ed. *Voices on Voice.* Urbana, Ill.: NCTE, 1994.
Voice as a metaphor for style signals a focus on the writer as an individual, on the drive to express oneself, and on the search for personal authenticity, for a distinctive or a natural sound, and for control of various personae that may inhabit a text or speak to a particular discourse community or speak within a particular culture. Eighteen essays explore the range of meanings and pedagogical uses of the idea of voice, including: Peter Elbow, "What Do We Mean When We Talk about Voice in Texts?"; Doug Minnerly, "Affect and Effect in Voice"; Nancy Allen and Deborah Bosley, "Technical Texts/Personal Voice: Intersections and Crossed Purposes"; Carl Klaus, "The Chameleon 'I': On Voice and Personality"; Margaret Woodworth, "Teaching Voice"; John Albertini, Bonnie Meath-Lang, and David Harris, "Voice as Muse, Message, and Medium: The Views of Deaf College Students"; Tom Carr, "Varieties of the 'Other': Voice and Native American Culture"; John Powers and

Gwendolyn Gong, "East Asian Voice and the Expression of Cultural Ethos"; Susan Brown Carlton, "Voice and the Naming of Woman"; Randall Freisinger, "Voicing the Self: Toward a Pedagogy of Resistance in a Postmodern Age"; and Peter Elbow and Kathleen Blake Yancey, "An Annotated and Collective Bibliography of Voice."

Literature and Composition

322   Eldred, Janet Carey, and Peter Mortensen. "Reading Literacy Narratives." *CE*, 54 (September 1992), 512–39.

Sociolinguistic scholarship on literacy provides critical insights into literary works that feature narratives of literacy acquisition. This scholarship has exploded the myth that increased literacy brings social progress and individual advancement, a myth that can be found in literature. Literacy scholarship also calls attention to the ways that literacy acquisition affects the formation of new identities, seen in narratives of socialization. In literature of the contact zone (see Pratt [159]), people struggle with literacy imposed by colonizers. A number of literary works, like Shaw's *Pygmalion,* focus on literacy narratives.

323   Horner, Winifred Bryan, ed. *Composition and Literature: Bridging the Gap.* Chicago: Univ. of Chicago Press, 1983.

This important collection of twelve essays on the theoretical and pedagogical relationships between composition and literature includes J. Hillis Miller, "Composition and Decomposition: Deconstruction and the Teaching of Writing"; Wayne C. Booth, "LITCOMP: Some Rhetoric Addressed to Cryptorhetoricians about a Rhetorical Solution to a Rhetorical Problem"; Nancy R. Comley and Robert Scholes, "Literature, Composition, and the Structure of English"; Elaine P. Maimon, "Maps and Genres: Exploring Connections in the Arts and Sciences" [446]; Walter J. Ong, S.J., "Literacy and Orality in Our Times" [271]; and E. D. Hirsch, Jr., "Reading, Writing, and Cultural Literacy."

324   Lanham, Richard A. *Literacy and the Survival of Humanism.* New Haven: Yale Univ. Press, 1983.

Nine essays on the place of the humanities in the university curriculum. Unless literature and composition are reconciled, not only will the study of literature perish, but our nation will descend into illiteracy and political conflicts among our disparate languages and cultures. Humanities teachers must abandon the notion that language is a neutral medium for exchanging information or expressing oneself. If language were employed only for such rational purposes, humanistic study would be superfluous. A more accurate notion of human motivation is now emerging from interdisciplinary work in the biological and social sciences. This "post-Darwinian synthesis" depicts human beings as motivated by the desire to play games as well as to satisfy appetites. Humanism can offer crucial insight into game-playing motives, particularly as expressed in styles of language use, and into the ways human beings collaboratively construct self and reality. In the final essay, Lanham outlines the UCLA composition program designed to inculcate "post-Darwinian humanism."

325   McQuade, Donald. "Composition and Literary Studies." In *Redrawing the Boundaries: The Transformation of English and American Literary Studies*. Ed. Stephen Greenblatt and Giles Gunn. New York: MLA, 1992.

Composition studies continues to be an academic borderland, a contested territory, seen by outsiders as the site of political struggle over institutional resources and by insiders as a burgeoning area of scholarship and pedagogy dealing with critical issues of power, race, class, gender, and ethnicity at the beginning of every instructional hour. Despite efforts to cast it in a healing role, composition remains a fracture separating literary criticism and rhetoric. In the nineteenth century, as belletristic rhetoric spawned literary studies, composition was placed in a subservient role, a development that was exacerbated by New Criticism and by the general degradation of teaching. The class division persists today. Composition has, in the past two decades, developed and professionalized through vigorous scholarship, while scholars like Wayne Booth, Richard Lanham, and Robert Scholes have shown ways to draw the two fields together by extending our understanding of textuality—all without healing the rift. The work should not be abandoned; however, our students should be taught that there is a continuum from literature to composition on which they can locate their own work.

326   Miller, Susan. "What Does It Mean to Be Able to Write? The Question of Writing in the Discourses of Literature and Composition." *CE*, 45 (March 1983), 219–35.

No theory unites literature and composition. We need to see a written text both as a product, the meaning of which can be analyzed, and as the reflection of a human process. A writing event is both an instance of this process and a unique event. We must acknowledge the history of writings that any new writing enters ("intertextuality"), understand the individual writer's relation to this history and ability to modify it, examine both personally expressive and culturally significant uses of writing, and develop methods to investigate these areas. A unified model of process and product would describe any writing event in terms of its history, its cultural context (language community) and its literary context (textual conventions), its desired outcome, and its immediate or situational context. The context influences the writer's persona as well as her imaginative transformations of setting into "scene" and subject into topic. The model must also account for the genre and organizational structure of the text thus produced; the syntax, diction, and grammar of the text; and its graphic representation. Such a model could be regarded both hierarchically and multivariately in studying or teaching either reading or writing.

327   Petrosky, Anthony R. "From Story to Essay: Reading and Writing." *CCC*, 33 (February 1982), 19–36.

Reading comprehension is not a simple matter of seeing the information in the text but of formulating it through schemata, or culturally determined cognitive frameworks of understanding. Bartholomae's work on basic writers [330] suggests that writing, like reading, is a process of forming through schemata. The literary pedagogy of Louise Rosenblatt,

Norman Holland, and David Bleich provides a way to unite reading and writing instruction productively.

328   Ponsot, Marie, and Rosemary Deen. *Beat Not the Poor Desk*. Upper Montclair, N.J.: Boynton/Cook, 1982.

Writing teachers can facilitate student writing, even under the constraints of time and circumstance, by eliminating class activities that are not writing and by providing opportunities for error-free practice of the elemental skill of writing. Writing should be prolific and guided by the whole structure of the essay. Teachers trained in literature can provide images of the shape of essays: the fable offers a structure for a story with a conclusion, and the parable creates a need for a thesis and clear point of view. Such shapes can be developed inductively and can help make the transition to a sense of other shapes for exposition. The authors describe intermediate steps, many possible shapes for essays, class activities, sample essays, syllabi, ways of teaching grammar, writing about literature, and organizing collaboration. Mina P. Shaughnessy Prize winner.

Basic Writing

329   Anokye, Akua Duku. "Oral Connections to Literacy: The Narrative." *Journal of Basic Writing*, 13 (Fall 1994), 46–60.

Oral narratives can help students appreciate their classmates' cultural and racial diversity and generate a variety of themes for writing. Class discussion of the secrets of storytelling and the ways that tales are told in different cultures is a preliminary to an assignment to tell a familiar folk tale that represents some strongly held value. Folk tales reveal both common themes and cultural differences, oral presentation makes students aware of the need to adapt to the audience, and the stories lead to self-awareness as well as cross-cultural understanding. A second assignment is to tell a family story that goes as far back in history as possible, and a third is to tell a personal life narrative. These assignments generate exciting class discussion about cultures and about composition—anticipating questions and confusion, choosing language both for comprehension and effect, clarifying central ideas, and choosing rhetorical forms. Moving to journal and essay writing, students write the stories themselves, or reflect on cultural difference, stereotypes, customs, or history. Discussions also generate criteria for peer-group response. Such assignments help us fulfill our obligation to open windows on the world for our students.

330   Bartholomae, David. "The Study of Error." *CCC,* 31 (October 1980), 253–69. Rpt. in Tate, Corbett, and Myers [162].

"Basic writing" is not a simplified course for the cognitively or linguistically deficient, but a kind of writing produced by an adult who is, in effect, learning a second language called formal written discourse. While learning the new language, the writer produces a personal version of it, an "interlanguage." More research is needed to discover how students produce their interlanguages. One research technique is to ask students to read their work aloud: students will often orally correct written errors without noticing the difference between written and spoken versions. The researcher can point this out and discuss the reasons for the error. Bartholomae uses error analysis and miscue analysis procedures developed by English as a Second Language (ESL) and reading instructors. Braddock Award winner.

331 Bartholomae, David. "The Tidy House: Basic Writing in the American Curriculum." *Journal of Basic Writing*, 12 (Spring 1993), 4–21.
Basic writing cannot be a course in which students are taught skills preparatory to reading and writing: it must be a course that engages them in the difficult materials the academy regards as its best possessions and should treat their writing seriously as texts in the course. Even a basic writing course that strives for these laudable goals risks patronizing basic writers as recipients of liberal outreach—and worse, ensuring that the category "basic writer" will remain marked and filled—if the course asks students to shape their writing under a single controlling idea, to produce linear arguments, and to exclude the tangential. Such writing makes it impossible to acknowledge the very specifics of race, gender, and class that have contributed to their status as basic writers. Basic writing should adopt the arts of the contact zone (see Pratt [159]), in which unequal cultures struggle and, in so doing, produce texts of uncertain genre. At the same time, we must remember that students need to become more accomplished at controlling their writing to bring in their history and culture; we should not see all nonstandard features as deliberately unconventional. Basic writing, which once served the strategic purpose of making us change the way we talked about students and curriculum, has tended to become fixed. That status must be questioned.

332 Bizzell, Patricia. "What Happens When Basic Writers Come to College?" *CCC*, 37 (October 1986), 294–301. Rpt. in Bizzell [119].
When basic writers begin to learn academic discourse, they are acquiring not only a new dialect (Standard English) and new genres, but also a new worldview. Their difficulties may often stem more from conflicts between this new worldview and their home worldviews than from purely linguistic differences. Therefore, to understand and help them, writing teachers should learn more about both the worldviews basic writers bring to college and the academic worldview. The final position in William Perry's scheme of college-level intellectual development can be taken as a model of the academic worldview. We should be cautious about applying models from orality-literacy theory or European class-based analyses of educational differences to American basic writers; still, we might explore whether the relativism described by Perry is especially off-putting to basic writers from communities that cohere around traditional authorities. Even so, there are some grounds for hope that basic writers can become bicultural in their own and the academic worldviews.

333 Brodkey, Linda. "On the Subjects of Class and Gender in 'The Literacy Letters.'" *CE*, 51 (February 1989), 125–41. Rpt. in Graves [285].
In the postmodern view, the self is constructed in discourse along ideological lines that determine who can create a privileged position and who will be denied such "author-ity." Basic writers' resistance to

academic discourse may be construed as their rejection of the vulnerable subject position this discourse offers them. Academic discourse, therefore, was eschewed for the sake of encouraging fluency in the "Literacy Letters"—personal letters exchanged between six teachers taking a graduate course in teaching composition and six adult students in a basic writing class. The teachers did not correct the letters they received, and the students did not ask for corrections. Still, the teachers asserted their authority to control the discourse by refusing to respond to passages that suggested social-class or gender differences between teacher and student. The teachers maintained the image of classless and sexless academic writing. To author-ize basic writers, class, race, and gender issues that affect them must be acknowledged as classroom realities, even if such acknowledgment threatens the teacher's privileged position.

334   Brooks, Charlotte K., ed. *Tapping Potential: English and Language Arts for the Black Learner.* Urbana, Ill.: NCTE, 1985.
Produced by the NCTE Black Caucus, this collection of forty-three essays on teaching reading, writing, and literature at levels K through 16 includes Clara Alexander, "Black English Dialect and the Classroom Teacher"; Darwin Turner, "Black Students, Language, and Classroom Teachers" and "Black Experience, Black Literature, Black Students, and the English Classroom"; Geneva Smitherman, "'What Go Round Come Round': *King* in Perspective" (see [355]); Miriam Chaplin, "Implications in Personal Construct Theory for Teaching Reading to Black Students"; Robert Fowler, "The Composing Processes of Black Student Writers"; Vivian Davis, "Teachers as Editors: The Student Conference"; William Cook, "The Afro-American Griot"; Mildred Hill-Lubin, "Putting Africa into the Curriculum through African Literature."

335   Cooper, Marilyn M., and Michael Holzman. *Writing as Social Action.* Portsmouth, N.H.: Heinemann, Boynton/Cook, 1989.
Fifteen essays, eight previously published, by the authors separately and collaboratively, focusing on literacy education, include "The Ecology of Writing" [167], "Women's Ways of Writing," and "Why Are We Talking About Discourse Communities? or, Foundationalism Rears Its Ugly Head Once More" (all by Cooper); "A Post-Freirean Model for Adult Literacy Education" [342] and "The Social Context of Literacy Education" (both by Holzman); and "Talking About Protocols" (by Cooper and Holzman).

336   Dean, Terry. "Multicultural Classrooms, Monocultural Teachers." *CCC,* 40 (February 1989), 23–37. Rpt. in Tate, Corbett, and Myers, [162].
The greater the distance between a student's home culture and American academic culture, the greater the likelihood that the student will not succeed in school. This problem can be addressed by including the home culture in the curriculum, involving people from the home culture in the school, allowing students to shape some learning tasks according to their own interests and needs, and encouraging teachers to be advocates who will prevent culture-conflict "problems" from being blamed on the students. If the negotiation between home and school culture is studied sensitively in class, students can become comfortably bicultural.

Students can write about cultural similarities and contrasts that they have observed, about their own cultural identities, and about their experiences in language learning. Monocultural teachers should avoid making assumptions about how students view their cultural identities and the transition to school culture.

See: Sarah D'Eloia, "The Uses—and Limits—of Grammar" [217].

337   Delpit, Lisa D. "The Silenced Dialogue: Power and Pedagogy in Educating Other People's Children." *Harvard Educational Review,* 58 (August 1988), 280–98.
A set of practices or rules for getting, maintaining, and exercising power operates in the classroom as in society at large. Those without power (people of color) benefit from being told what the rules are, but those with power (White people) are often unaware of the existence of the rules or are at least very reluctant to acknowledge them. Indeed, one rule for exercising power is not to acknowledge that you have it. White middle-class teachers must listen to teachers of color who tell them to be more directive and explicit about the rules with students of color, even if doing so violates the Whites' liberal sensibilities. Being more directive may mean being explicit, not only about general rules of conduct in the negotiation of power, but also about specific rules for writing powerfully and correctly.

See: Anne DiPardo, *A Kind of Passport* [419].

338   Enos, Theresa, ed. *A Sourcebook for Basic Writing Teachers.* New York: Random House, 1987.
Forty-two essays and parts of books and three bibliographies, some previously published. Included are Walter J. Ong, S.J., "Literacy and Orality in Our Times" [271]; Mike Rose, "Remedial Writing Courses: A Critique and a Proposal" [351]; E. D. Hirsch, Jr., "Cultural Literacy"; Paulo Freire, "The Adult Literacy Process as Cultural Action for Freedom"; David Bartholomae and Anthony R. Petrosky, "Facts, Artifacts, and Counterfacts: A Basic Reading and Writing Course for the College Curriculum" [280]; Patrick Hartwell, "Grammar, Grammars, and the Teaching of Grammar" [222]; Sarah D'Eloia, "The Uses—and Limits—of Grammar" [217]; Ira Shor, "Reinventing Daily Life: Self-Study and the Theme of 'Work'"; Mina P. Shaughnessy, "Vocabulary" and "Beyond the Sentence" [354]; Nancy Sommers, "Revision Strategies of Student Writers and Experienced Adult Writers" [211]; Ann E. Berthoff, "Recognition, Representation, and Revision"; Kenneth A. Bruffee, "Writing and Reading as Collaborative or Social Acts." This collection is an excellent introduction to the field of composition studies as a whole.

339   Fiore, Kyle, and Nan Elsasser. "'Strangers No More': A Liberatory Literacy Curriculum." *CE,* 44 (February 1982), 115–28. Rpt. in Kintgen, Kroll, and Rose [265].
Paulo Freire's "generative themes" [257] help a college writing class of adult Bahamian women move from personal reflections on their families to social analysis of marriage in the Bahamas, thus developing their critical thinking and writing abilities at the same time.

340   Giannasi, Jenefer M. "Language Varieties and Composition." In *Teaching Composition: Twelve Bibliographic Essays*. Ed. Gary Tate [38].

This bibliographic essay discusses works on dialectal varieties of American English, including Black English; differences between spoken and written dialects; social and cultural factors affecting dialect variation and choice (sociolinguistics); and usage.

341   Gilyard, Keith. *Voices of the Self: A Study of Language Competence*. Detroit: Wayne State Univ. Press, 1991.

Native Black English speakers in an urban public school environment can acquire Standard English language skills and "sociolinguistic competence" if they are encouraged to see their experience according to a transactional model that emphasizes their ability to negotiate and manipulate school language expectations in response to their own belief systems and personal traits. Gilyard surveys research on code-switching, bidialectalism, and the sociopolitical dimensions of schooling, interspersing these scholarly discussions with narratives of his own experience as one such urban Black English speaker making his way through school.

See: Muriel Harris and Katherine E. Rowan, "Explaining Grammatical Concepts" [221].

342   Holzman, Michael. "A Post-Freirean Model for Adult Literacy Education." *CE,* 50 (February 1988), 177–89. Rpt. in Cooper and Holzman [335].

In economically underdeveloped countries, many literacy educators use Paulo Freire's [258] methods with adult students. Here, an "animator" helps students develop literacy materials from their experience that foster insight into the politically oppressive conditions of their lives and the determination to change these conditions. In being so ideologically directive, though, Freirean pedagogy risks appropriating learners' responsibility for their own literacy goals. A post-Freirean model urges the teacher to wait for local initiative and to help student groups organize for whatever educational purposes—including literacy—they feel necessary.

343   Labov, William. *The Study of Nonstandard English*. Urbana, Ill.: NCTE, 1970.

Nonstandard dialects of English, such as Black English, should not be seen as error-ridden deviations from the standard form—but neither should they be seen as separate languages. Comparative studies reveal that nonstandard forms express many of the same logical relations among elements in a sentence that the standard form does, in different yet regular ways. Almost all native speakers of English can use more than one dialect of the language, and almost all have at least some acquaintance with the standard form. Social class tends to determine which dialect a person feels most comfortable using. Nonstandard dialects tend to be socially stigmatized, even by those who feel most comfortable using them. Teachers must be aware of the grammatical structures and conventions governing social use of dialects to mediate between the dialects and Standard English. Some in-class speaking, reading, and writing in the students' dialects may help them to learn the standard form more quickly with less damage to their self-esteem.

344 Lu, Min-Zhan. "Conflict and Struggle: The Enemies or Preconditions of Basic Writing?" *CE*, 54 (December 1992), 887–913.
When students from marginalized cultures enter the academy, they experience the pain of learning to live with multiple, conflicting points of view, but also the exhilarating creativity and insight that their borderland consciousness makes possible. Early work in basic-writing pedagogy sought to alleviate this pain, ignoring the accompanying benefits. Thomas Farrell and Kenneth Bruffee proposed acculturation as the cure, welcoming students into the intellectually superior academic community. This approach calmed colleagues who feared that basic writers would bring destructive change to the academy. Mina Shaughnessy, in contrast, offered accommodation, promising that students could accept the academic worldview without abandoning home allegiances. This approach also spared the academy from change. But the real task of the basic writer is neither to conform to nor abandon a monolithic discourse community, but to find innovative discursive strategies for negotiating the boundaries. Basic writers are complex selves, not to be essentialized as products of a single cultural group. The academy must adjust to these border-crossers' new discursive forms.

345 Lu, Min-Zhan. "From Silence to Words: Writing as Struggle." *CE*, 49 (April 1987), 437–48. Rpt. in Perl [176].
Lu describes her experiences in negotiating among different worlds: her early schooling in Maoist China, her parents' Western education, her graduate work in Pittsburgh. Dealing with the often painful conflicts among these worlds, Lu attests, helped her grow as a thinker and writer. She concludes that writing teachers should avoid making only one kind of discourse acceptable in their classrooms. Students, however, should not be led to believe that they can move freely among the discourses they know and at the same time keep each discourse pure. Instead, the conflict of discourses—in the classroom and in one's head—should be a topic of reflection.

346 Lunsford, Andrea A. "The Content of Basic Writers' Essays." *CCC*, 31 (October 1980), 278–90.
A sample of five hundred entrance exams suggests that basic writers focus on personal experience, using it as conclusive evidence or evaluating abstract questions solely in terms of personal effects; rely on clichéd maxims in place of generalizations; see themselves as passive victims of authority; and use stylistic features (such as personal pronouns) that reflect these content characteristics. All of this suggests that basic writers are arrested in what Piaget and Vygotsky call the "egocentric stage" of cognitive development. A similar study by Susan Miller suggests that they are also stuck in what Kohlberg calls the "conventional" stage of moral development. Basic writers might be helped, therefore, by a curriculum that asks them to solve increasingly abstract cognitive problems.

347   Moran, Michael G., and Martin J. Jacobi, eds. *Research in Basic Writing: A Bibliographic Sourcebook.* Westport, Conn.: Greenwood, 1990.

Ten extensive bibliographic essays: Andrea Lunsford and Particia Sullivan, "Who Are Basic Writers?"; Donn Haisty Winchell, "Developmental Psychology and Basic Writers"; Mariolina Salvatori and Glynda Hull, "Literacy Theory and Basic Writing"; Ronald Lunsford, "Modern Grammar and Basic Writers"; Michael Montgomery, "Dialects and Basic Writers"; Sue Render, "TESL Research and Basic Writing"; Michael Hood, "Basic Writing Courses and Programs"; Stephen Bernhardt and Patricia Wojahn, "Computers and Writing Instruction"; Donna Beth Nelson, "Writing Laboratories and Basic Writing"; and Richard Filloy, "Preparing Teachers of Basic Writing."

See: Marie Nelson, *At the Point of Need* [385].

348   Rose, Mike. "The Language of Exclusion: Writing Instruction at the University." *CE,* 47 (April 1985), 341–59.

The language used to describe and defend writing programs contributes to the attitude that writing is a secondary part of the university curriculum. "Error" was a convenient object of study for behaviorists, who then recommended drilling as a remedy. Their positivistic defense of writing instruction lingers on, despite its limitations and its degrading connotations. The once-effective defense of writing as a "skill" now relegates it to second-class intellectual status. "Remediation" suggests medical deficiency, or that material should have been learned before and is therefore inappropriate to the college curriculum. "Illiteracy" oversimplifies a complex problem and stigmatizes both students and teachers. Finally, the myth that remediation leads to a final cure persists, despite historical evidence, and further marginalizes writing programs and their students as merely temporary phenomena. We must contest the assumptions of such language and offer instead a more cognitively, historically, and culturally accurate description of writing.

349   Rose, Mike. *Lives on the Boundary: The Struggles and Achievements of America's Underprepared.* New York: Free Press, 1989.

"Deprived" and "deficient" elementary school children, "vocational-track" high-school students, and "remedial" college students have all been judged negatively by teachers, by parents, and often by themselves on the basis of their inability to perform a very small set of intellectual activities. But these students possess knowledge and mental capacities fully representative of the richness of human creativity. Their difficulties should be understood in terms of the intellectual and, especially, the affective dissonances evoked by their experiences of crossing boundaries into school from relatively marginalized social positions. Rose offers poignantly detailed anecdotes from his own life as an "underprepared" student and as a teacher of such students, illustrating how teachers, parents, students, and others can sensitively acknowledge the boundary-crossing experience and avoid treating the boundaries as unbreachable walls. Winner of the Mina P. Shaughnessy Prize and the CCCC Outstanding Book Award.

350   Rose, Mike. "Narrowing the Mind and the Page: Remedial Writers and Cognitive Reductionism." *CCC,* 39 (October 1988), 267–302.

The misguided effort to find a single cognitive explanation for complex and varied student problems—cognitive reductionism—has many avatars: studies of cognitive style characterize people as field-dependent or field-independent, brain research uses hemisphericity to account for logical and verbal abilities, the work of Piaget offers stages of cognitive development and logical thinking, and orality-literacy theorists connect literacy to logic and thinking ability. Applying these theories to student writers is problematic because they tend to level differences between individuals, they describe mental processes that can be linked only inferentially to writing, they deflect attention from student writers' immediate social contexts, and they often reproduce cultural stereotypes that should themselves be questioned—as the overrepresentation of socially marginal students at the low end of every scale suggests. Cognition is too complex to be captured in such schemes.

351   Rose, Mike. "Remedial Writing Courses: A Critique and a Proposal." *CE,* 45 (February 1983), 109–28. Rpt. in Enos [338] and in Tate, Corbett, and Myers [162].

The remedial writing course should not assign simple, personal topics so that errors can be more easily isolated. Rather, it should emphasize connections with other college work by challenging students with academic reading and writing and by focusing on strategies for coping with these tasks as part of the composing process.

352   Schwalm, David E. "Degree of Difficulty in Basic Writing Courses: Insights from the Oral Proficiency Interview Testing Program." *CE,* 47 (October 1985), 629–40.

The Foreign Service Institute's Oral Proficiency Interview (OPI) rates adults' conversational competence in a second language according to "function," or ability to interact at an appropriate level of formality; "context/content," or mastery of vocabulary suited to the topic; and "accuracy," or ability to speak correctly and intelligibly. On the six-level OPI scale, movement from level 2 to level 3 is most significant because here the speaker becomes able to explain and argue rather than simply narrate or describe, to employ more abstract and formal vocabulary and demonstrate broad cultural awareness, and to use more complex grammatical structures. The linguistic resources on which basic writers draw in written communication correspond to the characteristics of OPI level 2. Basic writing curricula should be designed specifically to move students into writing tasks requiring the equivalent of OPI level-3 abilities.

353   Shaughnessy, Mina P. "Basic Writing." In *Teaching Composition: Twelve Bibliographic Essays.* Ed. Gary Tate [38].

Little work on college-level basic writing had been done when this bibliographic essay was written in 1976. It cites work on remedial education in general, Black English, social and cultural factors in educational success, Standard English grammar, philosophy of language, and composition pedagogy. All are selected according to Shaughnessy's sense of what might be useful to the basic-writing teacher. The essay thus provides an interesting picture of the development of her thought.

354   Shaughnessy, Mina P. *Errors and Expectations: A Guide for the Teacher of Basic Writing.* New York: Oxford Univ. Press, 1977.
Basic writers' errors in Standard English fall into patterns derived from systematic gaps in students' knowledge of the written form and from students' own idiosyncratic but regular plans for using unfamiliar writing conventions. Chapters 1 to 5 catalog students' problems with handwriting, punctuation, syntax, and spelling. Chapters 6 to 8 show that basic writers are unfamiliar with the concepts and argument forms that are customary in academic writing. To help these students learn Standard English and academic discourse, teachers should not rely on atomized drills. They should instead discuss the grammatical and argumentative principles that inform academic writing. Teachers should remember that basic writers are intelligent adults. This book has had enormous influence on the study of basic writing, not primarily for its ideas on classroom practice, but for its way of understanding the writing that basic writers produce.

355   Smitherman, Geneva. *Talkin' and Testifyin'.* Boston: Houghton Mifflin, 1977.
Black English takes many grammar rules and pronunciation patterns from West African languages. In America, the use of Black English is associated with a culture that values several forms of oral display, such as church oratory, and that holds a worldview different from that associated with Standard English, for example, in its preference for logical structures that are hierarchical or cyclical rather than linear. This book focuses less on Black English than on Black culture, which it describes in detail. Smitherman strongly opposes requiring Standard English forms and culture for Black English speakers. For her comments on a court case mandating bilingual instruction for Black English speakers, see "'What Go Round Come Round': *King* in Perspective," *Harvard Education Review*, 51, no. 1 (February 1981), rpt. in Brooks [334].

356   Williams, Joseph M. "The Phenomenology of Error." *CCC*, 32 (May 1981), 152–68.
When we read student papers, we define "errors" as discrete entities found on the page. But "error" has a more important, social dimension. Our perception of error on the page signals a flawed social transaction between us and the writer, similar to a breach of etiquette. When we read the work of professional writers, we do not expect to find errors because our social relation to these writers is different from our relation to students. Many highly respected essays on writing breach their own rules, but we tend not to see these errors, although we always find errors when we look for them—in student papers. In guiding students away from error, then, we should redefine it not as structurally deviant but as socially inappropriate in writing situations.

Gender and Writing

357 Baron, Dennis E. *Grammar and Gender.* New Haven: Yale Univ. Press, 1986.

Attitudes toward gender have long been reflected in attitudes toward men's and women's uses of language. Two contradictory views prevail: one, that women's language is an inferior subset of men's language; the other, that women's language is grammatically more pure or true to traditional norms than men's language.

358 Bauer, Dale. "The Other 'F' Word: The Feminist in the Classroom." *CE,* 52 (April 1990), 385–96.

Students frequently attack a teacher's feminist perspective as something personal that does not belong in the classroom. Indeed, students do not wish to acknowledge any value contradictions in their academic work. Feminist teachers should recognize that teaching these students will be a form of persuasion, in which they need to adopt an authoritative but not authoritarian position in setting the course's ethical agenda. They should not reject all forms of authority as patriarchal. Moreover, in seeking to persuade students to feminism, teachers should aim to provoke not only resistance to sexism but also identification (in Kenneth Burke's sense) with feminism's egalitarian vision of the social order. In short, feminist teachers should see themselves as rhetors and aim to develop a feminist rhetoric.

359 Brody, Miriam. *Manly Writing: Gender, Rhetoric, and the Rise of Composition.* Carbondale: Southern Illinois Univ. Press, 1993.

To write well in Western culture is to reproduce stylistic virtues considered manly: coherence, clarity, forcefulness, practicality, and truthfulness. Bad writing is often characterized by faults coded as feminine: vagueness, excessive ornamentation, timidity, lack of purpose, and deliberate deceit. These values may be found in Quintilian, but they find their strongest expression after the Royal Society's seventeenth-century pronouncements on the desirability of plain and vigorous style. Standard texts through the eighteenth and nineteen centuries uphold these standards, which are found as well in twentieth-century texts like Strunk and White. Gender-coded valuations of style must be resisted if women and men are to develop richer stylistic capabilities.

See: Linda Brodkey, "On the Subjects of Class and Gender in 'The Literacy Letters'" [333].

360 Catano, James V. "The Rhetoric of Masculinity: Origins, Institutions, and the Myth of the Self-Made Man." *CE,* 52 (April 1990), 421–36.

The myth of self-making is powerful because it provides identities that seem to fit naturally into the requirements of society. The myth errs in equating masculine growth with an escape from origins—sex, race, and class—and from institutions. In the American tradition of individualism, fulfillment comes from applying the virtues of perseverance, loyalty, and so on, virtues that are supposedly not dependent on origins or institutions. The very egalitarianism of this appeal masks social reality, for it is, of course, easier to gain personal fulfillment when supported by the institutions one supposedly spurns. Twentieth-century versions of the myth substitute prowess in corporations for independence from institutions but retain the dichotomy between male identity as self-contained and female identity as interpersonal. In composition pedagogy, the rhetoric of authentic, expressive prose embodies the myth of self-making. Its goal is to free the writer to experience a true self. Ken Macrorie [319], Peter Elbow [134, 307], and William Coles [314], although they reject masculine self-aggression, use traditionally masculine images to define the personae of their self-made teachers and writers, call upon the Emersonian tradition of individualism, and seek freedom from institutions rather than Freirean confrontation with them.

361   Flynn, Elizabeth A. "Composing as a Woman." *CCC,* 39 (December 1988), 423–35. Rpt. in Perl [176].

The work of Nancy Chodorow on differences between male and female children's relations to their mothers, of Carol Gilligan on female moral development, and of Mary Field Belenky and her colleagues on female intellectual development all suggest that women value collaboration and organize knowledge in networks, whereas men value individual achievement and organize knowledge hierarchically. These differences are reflected in the writing of first-year college students. Material on gender should be included in the composition course so that women students will be encouraged to compose in ways congenial to their gender rather than in the male ways traditionally followed in the academy.

362   Frank, Francine Wattman, Paula A. Treichler, et al. *Language, Gender, and Professional Writing: Theoretical Approaches and Guidelines for Nonsexist Usage.* New York: MLA, 1989.

Six essays on language and sexual equality are followed by a set of guidelines with full analysis and explanation of problems and ambiguities. The essays review work on gender and language, give a history of male-chauvinist influences in linguistics, and call for changing sexist language to foster feminist social goals. Essays include Sally McConnell-Ginet, "The Sexual (Re)Production of Meaning: A Discourse-Based Theory"; Paula Treichler, "From Discourse to Dictionary: How Sexist Meanings Are Authorized"; and Susan Wolfe, "The Reconstruction of Word Meanings: A Review of the Scholarship." Extensive bibliography and annotated list of suggestions for further reading.

363   Gannett, Cinthia. *Gender and the Journal.* Albany: SUNY, 1992.

For centuries, women have written journals and diaries to explore their sense of self and to maintain their social networks, although these texts, unlike many men's journals, were never intended for publication. More recently, journal writing has become an accepted part of composition pedagogy because it is seen as fostering pre-writing processes. Social constructionist theory has also supported journal writing through the idea that discourse is constitutive of identity. Expressive writing in journals thus becomes an important way to learn and grow. Feminist theory supports journal writing as a way for women muted by society to come to voice. Research shows that women students are often more comfortable with journal writing and write more than men. Nevertheless, academics remain uneasy with the expressive, personal aspects of journal writing and tend to emphasize its academic function. Journal writing should be treated more seriously as literature and not marginalized.

See: Karyn Hollis, "Liberating Voices" [318].

364   hooks, bell. *Talking Back: Thinking Feminist, Thinking Black.* Boston: South End Press, 1989.
Hooks describes her experiences challenging race, gender, and class barriers to higher education. She analyzes the intersections of race, gender, and class oppressions and articulates a pedagogy to deal with them.

See: Jennifer Horsman, *Something in My Mind besides the Everyday* [264].

365   Kirsch, Gesa. *Women Writing in the Academy: Audience, Authority, and Transformation.* Carbondale: Southern Illinois Univ. Press, 1993.
Interviews with thirty-five women (twenty students and fifteen faculty members) in five academic disciplines suggest that even successful academic writers stuggle to maintain confidence in their own authorial authority. Authority issues can become more salient for women in the higher academic ranks because these women often feel both greater freedom and greater need to challenge disciplinary boundaries and conventional discourse forms. Women should continue to push for more collaborative academic work and more acceptance of a personal dimension in scholarly writing.

366   Kirsch, Gesa E., and Joy S. Ritchie. "Beyond the Personal: Theorizing a Politics of Location in Composition Research." *CCC*, 46 (February 1995), 7–29.
Feminist scholarship has helped to validate personal experience as a source of knowledge in composition research. It is not enough, though, to locate ourselves in our research. To do so risks creating the kind of master narrative that feminism rejects because it silences other views. Rather, the feminist researcher should trace her personal views to their cultural and ideological sources, recognize her multiple and contradictory locations, and use the positions of others to gain critical insight into her own. Specifically, these ends can be served by research practices in which those being studied collaborate with the researcher in designing and interpreting the research. Even so, the researcher, although she cannot avoid being in a position of power, should be sensitive to abuse of power, such as soliciting overly personal information or editing out testimony that supports values different from her own. Ethical issues are critical in such research.

367   Kraemer, Don J., Jr. "Gender and the Autobiographical Essay: A Critical Extension of the Research." *CCC*, 43 (1992), 323–40.
Much research suggests that men write personal narratives in which they are heroic agents struggling for independent achievement. Women's narratives, in contrast, depict the protagonist as one agent among several struggling to forge connections or sort out competing loyalties. Although student writers cannot set aside these gendered discourses, neither are their narratives wholly determined by them. Rather, most personal narratives show authors shaping a complex identity and negotiating among a range of discourses, the events of personal history,

and classroom demands. We should read, and encourage students to read, personal narratives with an eye to the complexities, not just the stereotypes.

368   Lamb, Catherine E. "Beyond Argument in Feminist Composition." *CCC* 42, (February 1991), 11–24.

Monologic argument, in which an author seeks to establish the correctness of his or her view by knocking down all other views, is the dominant form of scholarly writing, a form uncongenial to women, who value relationships and negotiate responsibilities. But monologic argument cannot simply be replaced by autobiography as a preferred form. Women's very concern for others will motivate them to use persuasive power to rectify injustice, although without violence. More collaborative forms of argument are needed, however, in which the parties negotiate a resolution by exploring each other's needs in detail, brainstorming multiple solutions, and discussing alternatives to find a mutually agreeable resolution. Such forms of dealing with conflict, beneficial to both men and women, can be modeled in the composition class.

See: Andrea Lunsford, ed. *Reclaiming Rhetorica* [95].

369   Malinowitz, Harriet. *Textual Orientations: Lesbian and Gay Students and the Making of Discourse Communities.* Portsmouth, N.H.: Heinemann, Boynton/Cook, 1994.

Gay, lesbian, and bisexual students continue to face a deeply homophobic environment in writing classes, making assignments to reflect on the self, narrate personal events, or otherwise reveal the writer's subjectivity highly problematic. The field of composition needs to recognize the existence of lesbian and gay discourses and discourse communities and allow these students to explore the social construction of their identities. Lesbian and gay students in gay-themed writing courses find that sexual identity is a significant epistemological context and social location. They discover the history and thematics of their community, analyze the ways that "gay" and "straight" have been constructed and valued in dominant discourses; excavate social meanings that underlie mainstream attitudes, complicating the very idea of sexual identity; and escape the disenfranchising individualism that confines them in mainstream views of sexual identity. The theories of social construction and critical pedagogy facilitate this understanding and allow further investigation of complex cross-cultural community definitions with similarly disabling mainstream constructions.

370   McCracken, Nancy Mellin, and Bruce Appleby. *Gender Issues in the Teaching of English.* Portsmouth, N.H.: Boynton/Cook, 1992.

Thirteen essays discuss gender along with issues of teaching language, literature, and composition. Aimed primarily at pre-college-level teachers, the book will also be helpful to college writing teachers. Essays include: David Blakesly, "He/Man and the Masters of Discourse"; Cynthia Bowmann, "Gender Differences in Response to Literature"; Duane H. Roen, "Gender and Teacher Response to Student Writing"; Jean Sanborn, "The Academic Essay: A Feminist View in Student

Voices"; Janet Miller, "Gender and Teachers"; and Bruce Appleby, "A Bibliography for Gender Balancing the English Curriculum."

371   Phelps, Louise Wetherbee, and Janet Emig, eds. *Feminine Principles and Women's Experience in American Composition and Rhetoric*. Pittsburgh: Univ. of Pittsburgh Press, 1995.

Fourteen essays explore many aspects of women's work as teachers and writers, including: Patricia Bizzell, "Praising Folly: Constructing a Postmodern Rhetorical Authority as a Woman"; Lillian Bridwell-Bowles, "Discourse and Diversity: Experimental Writing within the Academy"; Robert Connors, "Women's Reclamation of Rhetoric in Nineteenth-Century America"; Mary Kay Crouch, with Son Kim Vo, "The Role of Vietnamese Women in Literacy Processes: An Interview"; Janice Hays, "Intellectual Parenting and a Developmental Feminist Pedagogy of Writing"; Sara Dalmas Jonsberg, with Maria Salgado and the Women of the Next Step, "Composing the Multiple Self: Teen Mothers Rewrite Their Roles"; Louise Wetherbee Phelps, "Becoming a Warrior: Lessons of the Feminist Workplace"; and Nancy Sommers, "Between the Drafts." In addition, six essays comment on the previous fourteen, identifying recurring themes, significant omissions, and directions for further study.

See: Rubin, *Gender Influences* [245]

Advanced Composition

372   Adams, Katherine H. "Bringing Rhetorical Theory into the Advanced Writing Class." *Rhetoric Review*, 3 (1985), 184–89.

Rhetorical theory and research in writing can enhance advanced writing courses. Advanced students are capable of appreciating empirical research. They identify, for example, with the problems attested to by writers in protocol analyses and learn from the research on the effects of revision. Testimony by professional writers can encourage students to see the connection between writing and their own disciplines and careers. Grounding in the history of rhetoric reinforces students' sense of the importance and value of speaking to real audiences. The theories of Plato and others can be effectively applied to current examples of attempted persuasion. Research on heuristics can be an antidote to the current-traditional model that most students learned in freshman composition. This material does not need to become the course, but can be incorporated in workshops and discussions.

373   Adams, Katherine H. *A History of Professional Writing Instruction in American Colleges*. Dallas: SMU Press, 1993.

Professional writing courses began around 1900 as attempts to meet the need for instruction beyond freshman composition and to respond to vocational and professional pressures on the university. At first, instructors were literature faculty, but soon professional writers were brought in. These professionals taught genres and formats particular to their fields—poetry, journalism, business, technology. This training expanded to study of actual rhetorical situations in the field. Soon, as such courses seemed increasingly anomalous in English departments, journalism became a separate program. Creative writing, linked to literature, remained in English. Technical and business writing never gained sufficient support from business and technical departments to become independent programs and so remained peripheral parts of English departments. After World War II, more advanced writing courses and programs appeared, typically following public events: scientific writing grew during the space race, journalism following Watergate. Professional writing courses have always been dogged by the question of whether they are necessary: could practical writing be learned better out in the field? Were theory-based courses worthwhile? Were they good uses of curricular time? Despite such questions, many schools now offer professional-writing minors and majors, a trend that appears likely to continue.

374   Adams, Katherine H., and John L. Adams, eds. *Teaching Advanced Composition: Why and How?* Portsmouth, N.H.: Boynton/Cook, 1991.

Nineteen essays, seven on theory and the problem of distinguishing advanced from freshman courses, and twelve on approaches to teaching. Essays include: Elizabeth Penfield, "Freshman English/Advanced Writing: How Do We Distinguish the Two?"; William Covino, "The Grammar of Advanced Writing"; Michael Carter, "What Is Advanced about Advanced Composition? A Theory of Expertise in Writing"; Michael Keene and Ray Wallace, "Advanced Writing Courses and Programs"; Mary Fuller, "Teaching Style in Advanced Writing Courses"; Sam Watson, "Letters on Writing—A Medium of Exchange with Students of Writing"; Jeanne Fahnestock, "Teaching Argumentation in the Junior-Level Course"; Timothy Donovan and Janet Carr, "'Real World' Research: Writing Beyond the Curriculum"; and Lynn Bloom, "Creative Nonfiction, Is There Any Other Kind?" Includes "Afterword: Needed Scholarship in Advanced Composition" by Gary Olson, and an annotated bibliography of twenty-eight articles on advanced composition.

375   Covino, William A. "Defining Advanced Composition: Contributions from the History of Rhetoric." *Journal of Advanced Composition*, 8 (1988), 113–22.

In their demand for rigor in managing broad and difficult topics and reducing their complexity, advanced composition courses reflect a post-Cartesian notion of advanced knowledge as schematized and well-ordered. Advanced writing students must demonstrate mastery of the conventions of closure, both in composition and, often, in an academic discipline as well. But the post-Cartesian model can be challenged by the older Classical definition of advanced rhetors as more tolerant of ambiguity. Poor rhetors must rely on formulae, whereas better ones probe and search freely. Plato and Cicero depict questioning dialogists as superior to those who seek simple answers or summaries. Montaigne, Vico, and De Quincey criticize Descartes and support the dialogic-dialectical approach to the lost art of rhetoric. As a model for advanced composition, the dialogic approach suggests that research and writing be used to defer judgment, to explore a variety of perspectives on an issue, and to set aside conviction in order to practice rhetoric.

376   Hairston, Maxine. "Working with Advanced Writers." *CCC*, 35 (1984), 196–208.

Advanced writers—honors freshmen and other students taking an elective advanced expository writing course—are reluctant to change writing habits that are earning them good grades, despite felt dissatisfaction with their own writing. Their writing is correct, wordy (repetitive and inflated), heavily nominalized, impersonal, unrealistically ambitious, overly generalized, and without much sense of audience. Their personalities are hidden behind the mask of a bureaucrat or pedantic scholar. They see this style as officially sanctioned; it has earned them rewards, and it is also safe. To persuade them to try anything new, a safe classroom is necessary, where grades are downplayed, risk is rewarded, and a writing community is formed.

377   Snyder, Carol. "Analyzing Classifications: Foucault for Advanced Writers." *CCC*, 35 (1984), 209–16.

Classifications structure discourse in the disciplines, and advanced students are often expected to explain them in their papers. But students typically misunderstand the provisional nature of classification schemes, treating them as permanent and not subject to analysis or change. They can learn much from Foucault, who compares earlier and later classification systems in a field to see changes in the ways that we conceive our subjects. Foucault also analyzes classification schemes as codes with the power to shape social and intellectual reality and to vest that power in certain people and institutions. Students readily add their own examples to Foucault's pictures of the division of people into categories and their distribution into social and physical spaces. Taught to identify the object of classification, the exclusions of the classifying scheme, the people who use the scheme, and the time and space frames of the scheme, students are able to analyze classification systems in their own disciplines, discovering much about the field's history and lines of power.

Teaching English as a Second Language

378   Belcher, Diane, and George Braine, eds. *Academic Writing in a Second Language: Essays on Research and Pedagogy.* Norwood, N.J.: Ablex, 1994.

Sixteen essays exploring the social perspective on ESL writing issues. Included are: Ilona Leki, "Good Writing: I Know It When I See It"; George Braine, "Writing in the Natural Sciences"; Diane Belcher, "Writing Critically across the Curriculum"; Ulla Connor and Melinda Kramer, "Writing from Sources: Case Studies of Graduate Students in Business Management"; Diane Tedick and Maureen Mathison, "Holistic Scoring on ESL Writing Assessment: What Does an Analysis of Rhetorical Features Reveal?"; Ann Johns, "Teaching Classroom and Authentic Genres: Initiating Students into Academic Cultures and Discourses"; and Sally Jacoby, David Leech, and Christine Holten, "A Genre-Based Developmental Writing Course for Undergraduate ESL Science Majors."

379   Carson, Joan G., and Ilona Leki, eds. *Reading in the Composition Classroom: Second Language Perspectives.* Boston: Heinle and Heinle, 1993.

After many years of being taught separately as technical skills, reading and writing are increasingly being taught together in ESL courses that recognize the inextricable links between them. Eighteen essays examine how individual readers process text, how cultural contexts affect understanding, and how reading can be taught in writing classes. Essays include: Ilona Leki, "Reciprocal Themes in ESL Reading and Writing"; Joy Reid, "Historical Perspectives on Writing and Reading in the ESL Classroom"; Barbara Kroll, "Teaching Writing Is Teaching Reading: Training the New Teacher of ESL Composition"; Joan Carson, "Reading for Writing: Cognitive Perspectives"; Douglas Flahive and Nathalie Bailey, "Exploring Reading/Writing Relationships in Adult Second Language Learners"; Ruth Spack, "Student Meets Text, Text Meets Student: Finding a Way into Academic Discourse"; Sarah Benesch, "ESL Authors: Reading and Writing Critical Autobiographies"; and Ann Johns, "Reading and Writing Tasks in English for Academic Purposes Classes: Products, Processes, and Resources."

380   Cummins, Jim. "The Sanitized Curriculum: Educational Disempowerment in a Nation at Risk." In *Richness in Writing: Empowering ESL Students.* Ed. Donna M. Johnson and Duane H. Roen. White Plains: Longman, 1989, pp. 19–38.

The 1983 report "A Nation at Risk" shifted policy emphasis from equity to "excellence." Subsequent reports focus on raising standards and getting tough. This reform movement threatens to disempower students, particularly minority students, by fostering a "transmission" approach to teaching that ignores students' need to develop a sense of efficacy in their relations with educators. Transmission especially harms ESL students by excluding student experience and suppressing the meaningful communication needed to learn language. Moreover, the reforms reflect an autocratic image of society that is counterdemocratic. In addition, the focus on excellence promotes passivity rather than critical thinking. An alternative conception of reform can be based on a more productive interaction between students and teachers, active use of written and oral language for critical thinking, and use of students' cultural resources that will enrich all students. Our children's generation will need critical skills and intercultural understanding in the future and cannot reach the goals set out in "A Nation at Risk" by following the path of "excellence" laid out there.

381   Ferdman, Bernardo M., Rose-Marie Weber, and Arnulfo G. Ramirez, eds. *Literacy across Languages and Cultures.* Albany: SUNY, 1994.

Meeting the English literacy needs of members of linguistic and cultural minorities in the United States requires rethinking many assumptions about literacy itself, especially because most research concentrates on first-language literacy. The eleven essays in this volume probe the meaning of literacy in a multiethnic context, the processes of second-language and second-culture acquisition, and the application of current research to these concerns. Essays include: Stephen Reder, "Practice-Engagement Theory: A Sociocultural Approach to Literacy across Languages and Cultures"; Nancy Hornberger, "Continua of Biliteracy"; Concha Delgado-Gaitan, "Sociocultural Change through Literacy: Toward the Empowerment of Families"; Barbara McCaskill, "Literacy in the Loophole of Retreat: Harriet Jacobs's Nineteenth-Century Narrative"; and Alison d'Anglejan, "Language and Literacy in Quebec."

382   Huckin, Thomas, Margot Haynes, and James Coady. *Second Language Reading and Vocabulary Learning.* Norwood, N.J.: Ablex, 1993.

Fourteen essays report on research into the ways that ESL students learn vocabulary, including analyses of L1 vocabulary learning and the efficacy of contextual guessing, investigation of the assumption that reading improves vocabulary acquisition, and evaluation of pedagogical practices for improving vocabulary. Essays include: Frederika Stoller and William Grabe, "Implication for L2 Vocabulary Acquisition from L1 Research"; Margot Haynes, "Patterns and Perils of Guessing in Second Language Reading"; Chion-Lan Chern, "Chinese Students' Word-Solving Strategies in Reading in English"; Kate Parry, "Too Many Words: Learning the Vocabulary of an Academic Subject"; Mark Stein, "The Healthy Inadequacy of Contextual Definition"; and Cheryl Brown, "Factors Affecting the Acquisition of Vocabulary: Frequency and Saliency of Words."

383   Kutz, Eleanor, Suzy Q. Groden, and Vivian Zamel. *The Discovery of Competence: Teaching and Learning with Diverse Student Writers.* Portsmouth, N.H.: Boynton/Cook, 1993.

Teachers of writing, especially to ESL students, should begin with students' competences and not focus on correcting their deficits. Understanding the complexities of language acquisition allows teachers to help students acquire new competencies in academic discourse. The academy is a culture with a discourse and mindsets that are alien to many students, particularly to ESL students. Teachers can, however, make the transition to the new culture less frustrating and alienating by designing courses that allow students to discover and build on existing abilities and knowledge as they investigate new conditions and expectations. Language learning comes from the desire to make meaning, not from building up incremental linguistic units; so, too, with a second language or dialect. Moreover, intellectual development and cognitive orientations to learning that characterize extant competencies need to be respected and not forced into academic molds. Teachers can use the classroom as a research site for discovering students' abilities and examining their own teaching methods, taking a critical view of their curricular frameworks. The authors include many excerpts from student papers reflecting on their language-learning experiences, describe classroom research practices, suggest ways to assess student competences, and offer advice about creating multicultural frameworks for curriculum development.

384   Leki, Ilona. *Understanding ESL Writers: A Guide for Teachers.* Portsmouth, N.H.: Boynton/Cook, 1992.

Although teaching writing to ESL students is not radically different from teaching writing to native speakers, it helps to understand the difficulties of learning to write in an L2. Native speakers must orchestrate many skills and strategies to write: ESL writers face, in addition, limited vocabulary, cultural and idiomatic complexities, unfamiliar style and audience expectations, and the frustration of not being able to express their real thoughts or knowledge. Only slowly has ESL teaching shifted from structure-based language instruction to process-based instruction. Research confirms that the desire to communicate aids language acquisition, whereas knowledge of rules and error-correction does not. Immersion in language, especially reading, is vital for writing. At the same time, social comfort increases the desire to communicate. Leki sensitively discusses the characteristics of ESL students and ways to distinguish ESL students from basic writers in classes where they are mixed, recommends classroom practices for teachers in ESL and mixed classes, analyzes ESL-student writing behavior (concerning personal writing, plagiarism, sophistication, and so on), describes L2 writing processes, surveys findings of contrastive rhetoric for several cultures, discusses sentence-level correction, and offers advice about responding. Includes an extensive, unannotated bibliography.

385 Nelson, Marie W. *At the Point of Need: Teaching Basic and ESL Writers.* Portsmouth, N.H.: Boynton/Cook, 1991.
Beginning with the premise that attending closely to students' own descriptions of the writing help they needed would improve their pedagogy, teams of writing-center tutors over five years carefully recorded their interactions with basic-writing and ESL students—and with each other—as they sought to discover how best to teach writing. The teams discovered significant similarities between ESL and basic writers in writing behaviors, assumptions, and development. Students also had unrecognized skills of invention and language production that could be tapped once they were given permission to use them. Allowing students to be independent of the teacher produced the best results in the long term, a condition accomplished by establishing a safe atmosphere, modeling successful writing behaviors, unteaching misperceptions about how to write, pointing out strengths in student writing, rewarding critical attitudes and risk taking, and so on. The tutors refined the process of working with students and the steps that might be taken to help writers become independent and fluent. Many case studies illustrate the development of students—basic writers and ESL students from many cultures—and of the tutors. Chapters examine longitudinal studies of writers, types of writing assigment, the organization of the writing center, the training of tutors, and research design.

386 Raimes, Ann. "Out of the Woods: Emerging Traditions in the Teaching of Writing." *TESOL Quarterly*, 25 (1991), 407–30.
Four approaches characterize ESL teaching since the mid-1960s. At the beginning of this period, the audiolingual method made writing subservient to oral learning. Students wrote only to practice grammatical or rhetorical forms. In the late 1970s, influenced by L1 scholars' research on composing processes, L2 teachers began to think about writers, meaning-making, multiple drafts, and journals, downplaying linguistic

accuracy—at least in early drafts. In the late 1980s, some reacted against process, arguing that academic writing was what students would need to do, resulting in the adjunct course model to provide academic content. At the same time, a focus on academic readers' expectations generated English for academic purposes and a concern for socializing students into the academic discourse community. These methods all continue to stir controversy. Should students do personal writing or practice "real" academic writing? When we teach to the academic discourse community, mustn't we beware of simply enforcing submission to a set of rules (as L1 researchers warn)? In this same period, contrastive rhetoric has developed. Although it offers no pedagogical suggestions, contrastive rhetoric raises consciousness about composing conventions in different cultures. This consciousness makes us aware not only of English forms, but of alternate rhetorics from many cultures. The field of ESL teaching must continue to recognize the complexity of composing, the diversity of students and their composing processes, the politics of pedagogy, and the need for classroom-based research.

See: Alice Roy, "ESL Concerns for Writing Program Administrators" [413].

387   Tucker, Amy. *Decoding ESL: International Students in the American College Classroom.* Portsmouth, N.H.: Boynton/Cook, 1995.
Teaching writing to international students is not training in an isolated skill, but in a way of experiencing the world. Contrastive rhetoric shows that the errors of ESL writers can be read not as random mistakes, but as patterns that are inevitable in cultural transformation. In our readings of other cultures, we must be students of cultural difference, conscious of the rhetorical limitations placed on both writer and reader (the teacher) by limitations of language, the clash of conventions, deep ideological differences, and current political situations. These are not incapacitating differences, but challenges that ultimately deepen cross-cultural understanding. Tucker illustrates with case studies of students from Afghanistan, Russia, Greece, China, and Japan, examining their experience in writing and literature courses.

388   Valdes, Guadalupe. "Bilingual Minorities and Language Issues in Writing." *Written Communication,* 9 (January 1992), 85–136.
The teaching of English is divided into segments, with mainstream and basic writers in one group and ESL students in the other. This division fails to take into account the complexity of bilingualism in America. A bilingual individual's ability to function in a second language depends on a large number of social factors such as age, previous language learning, and degree of contact with fluent speakers of the second language. These factors also affect the time it takes to pass through the incipient (nonfluent) bilingual stage. The difficulty of identifying these factors causes confusion about some students' instructional needs in our simple bipartite system. The very same nonnativelike features in their writing can be variously interpreted. Some nonidiomatic forms persist, for example, in the writing of fluent bilinguals who don't need ESL instruction. ESL research has focused on some groups of bilinguals, but the profession as a whole must deal with the entire range of bilinguals.

To do so, we must do more research on the kinds of writing bilingual minorities are exposed to, the ways that mainstream teachers respond to the writing of these students, and the linguistic and social factors that affect their writing. To address these pressing issues, we must break out of our current compartmentalization.

389   Zamel, Vivian. "Writing One's Way into Reading." *TESOL Quarterly*, 26 (1992), 463–85.

Both reading and writing are acts of meaning-making, yet reading continues to be taught by a transmission or information-retrieval model. Reading ought not to be passive, but a transaction between the text and the reader's knowledge and experience. Writing can reveal and enhance this transaction by enabling students to engage the text through their responses. Reading journals or logs are effective for this purpose, as research attests. Sequencing assignments around readings is another way of allowing students to approach a text from different perspectives, avoiding the sense that there is a single meaning to extract. Students can become better readers by becoming better writers.

Writing in the Workplace

390   Anderson, Paul V., R. John Brockmann, and Carolyn R. Miller, eds. *New Essays in Technical and Scientific Communication: Research, Theory, Practice*. Farmingdale, N.Y.: Baywood, 1983.

Twelve essays take a serious scholarly approach to empirical research, theory, pedagogy, and historical study in the field of technical communication. Essays include: Lee Odell, Dixie Goswami, Anne Herrington, and Doris Quick, "Studying Writing in Non-Academic Settings"; Linda Flower, John Hayes, and Heidi Swarts, "Revising Functional Documents: The Scenario Principle"; Lester Faigley and Stephen Witte, "Topical Focus in Technical Writing"; Jack Selzer, "What Constitutes a 'Readable' Technical Style?"; James Zappen, "A Rhetoric for Research in Sciences and Technologies"; Charles Bazerman, "Scientific Writing as a Social Act: A Review of the Literature of the Sociology of Science"; and David Dobrin, "What's Technical about Technical Writing?" Winner of the NCTE Award in Technical and Scientific Communication.

391   Bazerman, Charles, and James Paradis, eds. *Textual Dynamics of the Professions: Historical and Contemporary Studies of Writing in Professional Communities*. Madison: Univ. of Wisconsin Press, 1990.

In the workplace, "textual dynamics are a central agency in the social construction of objects, concepts, and institutions" (4). Fifteen essays examine the textual construction of professions, the dynamics of professional discourse communities, and the operational force of texts. Essays include: Charles Bazerman, "How Natural Philosophers Can Cooperate: The Literary Technology of Coordinated Investigation in Joseph Priestley's *History and Present State of Electricity* (1767)"; Greg Myers, "Stories and Styles in Two Molecular Biology Review Articles"; James Zappen, "Scientific Rhetoric in the Nineteenth and

Early Twentieth Centuries: Herbert Spencer, Thomas N. Huxley, and John Dewey"; Robert Schwegler and Linda Shamoon, "Meaning Attribution in Ambiguous Texts in Sociology"; Carl Herndl, Barbara Fennell, and Carolyn Miller, "Understanding Failures in Organizational Discourse: The Accident at Three Mile Island and the Shuttle Challenger Disaster"; and Amy Devitt, "Intertextuality in Tax Accounting: Generic, Referential, and Functional."

392   Blyler, Nancy Roundy. "Theory and Curriculum: Reexamining the Curricular Separation of Business and Technical Communication." *Journal of Business and Technical Communication*, 7 (1993), 218–45.

Business and technical communication have conventionally been separated in academe, a separation supported by institutional practices and by a formalist rhetoric that posits business communication as chiefly persuasive and technical writing as chiefly informative. Social-epistemic rhetoric, which links language with knowledge and centers on the social context of discourse rather than taxonomies of finished products, posits that discourse does not reflect reality but presents visions of reality that have been accepted as true. Social-epistemic rhetoric treats both business and technical writing as thoroughly rhetorical, a view confirmed by studies of workplace writing. The curricular division has thus lost its rationale. Teaching that emphasizes the ways that social context influences content and form decisions is superior to labeling and dividing typical forms. Students are better served when they learn about the social construction of knowledge and the ways it illuminates the production and reception of workplace communication.

393   Blyler, Nancy Roundy, and Charlotte Thralls, eds. *Professional Communication: The Social Perspective.* Newbury Park, Calif.: Sage, 1993.

Fourteen essays examine the ways that the social paradigm in the study of writing and rhetoric can contribute to an understanding of professional communication. Essays include: Charlotte Thralls and Nancy Roundy Blyler, "The Social Perspective and Professional Communication: Diversity and Directions in Research"; Bruce Herzberg, "Rhetoric Unbound: Discourse, Community, and Knowledge"; Ben Barton and Marthalee Barton, "Ideology and the Map: Toward a Postmodern Visual Design Practice"; Thomas Kent, "Formalism, Social Construction, and the Problem of Interpretive Authority"; Joseph Comprone, "Generic Constraints and Expressive Motives: Rhetorical Perspectives on Textual Dialogues"; James Porter, "The Role of Law, Policy, and Ethics in Corporate Composing: Toward a Practical Ethics for Professional Writing"; Janice Lauer and Patricia Sullivan, "Validity and Reliability as Social Constructions"; and Mary Lay, "Gender Studies: Implications for the Professional Communication Classroom." Winner of the NCTE Award in Technical and Scientific Communication.

394   Brockmann, R. John, ed. *The Case Method in Technical Communication: Theory and Models.* St. Paul, Minn.: Association of Teachers of Technical Writing, 1984.

The case method holds that writing is best learned by performing in situations that specify data, characters, politics, and a writer's role. This collection offers seven essays on using and generating cases, an annotated bibliography on the case method in communication, eight cases for writing, and two cases for graphics. Includes: John Brockmann, "What Is a Case"; Marcus Green, "How to Use Case Studies in the Classroom"; and Charles Sides, "Comparing the Case Approach to Five Traditional Approaches to Teaching Technical Communication."

395   Brown, Robert L., Jr., and Carl G. Herndl. "An Ethnographic Study of Corporate Writing: Job Status as Reflected in Written Text." In *Functional Approaches to Writing: Research Perspectives.* Ed. Barbara Couture. London: Francis Pinter, 1986, pp. 11–28.

Despite convincing research, commonsense observation, and direct instruction, some professionals continue to use ineffective techniques such as excessive nominalization and long project narratives in their writing. These features appear to be signs of status and anxiety rather than decisions about effective writing. In a study, nominalization was greater for those whose job position had changed or seemed vulnerable. It was also greater in writing for the eyes of upper management and greater generally for those who worked in a corporation undergoing internal reorganization. Nominalization appears to be an attempt to be hypercorrect and to show sophistication. Inappropriate narration seems to come most from young technical professionals who are maintaining a distance from decision making (which depends on interpretation, not narration) and mirroring scientific method. These and perhaps other instances of less-effective writing choices reflect social circumstances in the workplace. Stress tends to reduce fluency; nominalization and narration tend to preserve anonymity; hypercorrection reflects insecurity about status. These forces are more powerful than conscious knowledge about preferred writing conventions.

396   Connors, Robert J. "The Rise of Technical Writing Instruction in America." *Journal of Technical Writing and Communication,* 12 (1982), 329–52.

The need for technical writing instruction grew in the latter part of the nineteenth century in the United States as engineering education grew and classical education shrank. However, no courses in technical writing were offered before 1900, reflecting the hope that freshman composition would suffice. It did not, as complaints in professional journals about nearly illiterate engineers attest. The first technical writing textbook, in 1908, concerned usage for professionals. The 1911 textbook by Samuel Chandler Earle is the first genuine attempt to address the needs of an advanced undergraduate technical-writing course. It condemned the "two cultures" split, chastising English teachers for regarding engineers as philistines. Earle used the modes of discourse as his pedagogical model. By 1920, though, books using technical-writing formats began to appear, along with a wave of books that attempted to humanize the engineering student by combining literature with writing instruction. World War II dramatically increased the need for technical-writing instruction: technical writing became a distinct job description, and teaching technical writing began to have more professional status, a trend particularly strong since the 1970s, with the appearance of professional societies and journals.

397   Couture, Barbara. "Categorizing Professional Discourse: Engineering, Administrative, and Technical/Professional Writing." *Journal of Business and Technical Communication*, 6 (1992), 5–37.

Because knowledge depends on interpretation that is constrained by communal values (see Winsor, "The Construction of Knowledge in Organizations" [408]), scholars of professional writing need to develop an understanding of how discourse is framed and interpreted in organizations. Rhetorical categories can help reveal both textual and contextual elements in interpretive frames. Such categories are not technical labels, but indicators of situations, disciplines, and forms that operate in particular contexts. Three rhetorical categories that identify group values and their effect on interpretation appear to have theoretical and empirical validity. The first, engineering writing, responds to the professional values of scientific objectivity, professional judgment, and corporate interests. The second, administrative writing, reflects decision-making authority and promotes institutional identity. The third, technical/professional writing, aims to accommodate the audience by meeting professional readability standards. Defining the characteristics of these types more precisely can help describe writing in ways that are more telling and more usable for those who teach professional writing.

398   Harris, John S. *Teaching Technical Writing: A Pragmatic Approach.* St. Paul, Minn.: Association of Teachers of Technical Writing, 1992.

Beginning teachers of technical writing (and more experienced teachers looking for new ideas) can learn much from a book that not only presents materials and methods for teaching the course but also speaks frankly about the career path of such teachers in the academy. In twenty-one chapters, Harris defines technical writing, describes programs and textbooks, and tells how to work within an indifferent English department, design a course, teach special forms (proposals, correspondence, term papers, graphics), grade papers, and get promoted.

399   Kogen, Myra, ed. *Writing in the Business Professions.* Urbana, Ill.: NCTE, 1989.

Fourteen essays investigate professional and pedagogical concerns in the development of business communication as an academic discipline. Essays include: Linda Flower, "Rhetorical Problem Solving: Cognition and Professional Writing"; Jack Selzer, "Arranging Business Prose"; Edward P. J. Corbett, "What Classical Rhetoric Has to Offer the Teacher of Business and Professional Writing"; Janice Redish, "Writing in Organizations"; George Gopen, "The State of Legal Writing: Res Ipsa Loquitur"; John DiGaetani, "Use of the Case Method in Teaching Business Communication"; David Lauerman, "Building Ethos: Field Research in a Business Communication Course"; C. H. Knoblauch, "The Teaching and Practice of 'Professional Writing'"; and John Brereton, "The Professional Writing Program and the English Department."

400   Lay, Mary M., and William M. Karis, eds. *Collaborative Writing in Industry: Investigations in Theory and Practice.* Amityville, N.Y.: Baywood, 1991.

The theory and practice of collaborative writing as it applies to workplace writing, along with studies of the implications of this research for the classroom are the subjects of twelve essays, including: David K. Farkas, "Collaborative Writing, Software Development, and the Universe of Collaborative Activity"; Timothy Weiss, "Bruffee, the Bakhtin Circle, and the Concept of Collaboration"; Barbara Couture and Jone Rymer, "Discourse Interaction between Writer and Supervisor: A Primary Collaboration in Workplace Writing"; William Van Pelt and Alice Gillam, "Peer Collaboration and the Computer-Assisted Classroom: Bridging the Gap between Academia and the Workplace"; Dixie Elise Hickman, "Neuro-Linguistic Programming Tools for Collaborative Writers"; and Roger Grice, "Verifying Technical Information: Issues in Information-Development Collaboration." Winner of the NCTE Award in Technical and Scientific Communication.

401   Locker, Kitty O. "What Do Writers in Industry Write?" *Technical Writing Teacher*, 9 (1982), 122–27.

Students in technical writing classes are often surprised to hear that people in business and industry routinely write more than ten pages a week and often much more. Writing is invaluable because it provides a permanent record, it is often more effective than other means of communicating, it is often less expensive than other forms of communicating, it is taken more seriously than oral communication, and so on. Thus, a huge amount of writing goes on in the workplace—far more than could ever be handled by a corps of professional writers. There are innumerable genres of reports, proposals, and letters, external and internal, to be produced regularly. Technical writing teachers should be aware of these forms and include business communication, logic, and audience analysis in their courses.

402   Matalene, Carolyn B., ed. *Worlds of Writing: Teaching and Learning in Discourse Communities of Work.* New York: Random House, 1989.

Adequate understanding of writing in the workplace cannot be provided by traditional academic analyses of texts and processes. The special concerns of collaborative writing, audience constraints, and the conventions of workplace writing must become part of the undergraduate writing curriculum. Twenty-three essays analyze discourse communities of work, including: Kristin Woolever, "Coming to Terms with Different Standards for Excellence for Written Communication"; Stephen Doheny-Farina, "A Case Study of One Adult Writing in Academic and Nonacademic Discourse Communities"; Janette Lewis, "Adaptation: Business Writing as Catalyst in a Liberal Arts Curriculum"; Theresa Enos, "Rhetoric and the Discourse of Technology"; Nancy Wilds, "Writing in the Military: A Different Mission"; Janis Forman, "The Discourse Communities and Group Writing Practices of Management Students"; Carolyn Matalene, "A Writing Teacher in the Newsroom"; Aletha Hendrickson, "How to Appear Reliable without Being Liable: C.P.A. Writing in Its Rhetorical Context"; Philip Rubens, "Writing for an On Line Age: The Influence of Electronic Text on Writing"; John Warnock, "To English Professors: On What to Do with a Lawyer"; and James Raymond, "Rhetoric and Bricolage: Theory and Its Limits in Legal and Other Sorts of Discourse."

403 Miller, Carolyn R. "A Humanistic Rationale for Technical Writing." *CE*, 40 (1979), 610–17.

A pervasive positivist view of science is the source of the erroneous belief that technical writing is a skills course. Believing truth to be a function of perceiving material reality, positivists wish scientific and technical rhetoric to subdue language and transmit bare technical knowledge. Technical-writing textbooks endorse this antirhetorical belief. The shortcomings of the positivist view are evident in the confused definitions of technical writing it produces ("clarity" neither defines nor characterizes technical writing), in its emphasis on form at the expense of invention, and in its tendency to analyze audience in terms of "levels" (which reduces to vocabulary choice). Yet scientists themselves no longer hold a positivist view, but understand that knowledge is inseparable from the knower: Communal discussion and argument determines knowledge. From this perspective, teaching technical writing is a form of enculturation, not a set of forms and techniques, but an understanding of how to participate in a community, a thoroughly humanistic endeavor.

404 Miller, Carolyn R. "What's Practical About Technical Writing?" In *Technical Writing: Theory and Practice*. Ed. Bertie E. Fearing and W. Keats Sparrow. New York: MLA, 1989, pp. 14–24.

Technical writing has long been regarded as practical in the "low" sense of being mundane and untheoretical. This view gives rise to a contradiction in technical writing instruction: that workplace writing is at once imperfect (requiring improvement through instruction) and authoritative (the goal of instruction). This contradiction mirrors the larger conflict between practical and humanistic studies in the recent history of education. Professional education tends to acquiesce in treating common industry or professional practice as useful and therefore good. There is a "high" sense of practicality, though, that can be applied to technical writing and other professional education. Aristotle characterizes rhetoric as techne or art, a middle term between theory and practice, "a productive state that is truly reasoned." To this should be added Aristotle's sense of phronesis or prudence: rhetoric in this sense is a form of conduct, like ethics, drawing upon observation of human affairs in order to take socially responsible action. Practical rhetoric of this sort must allow for criticism and judgment, and take responsibility not only for the corporation but for the larger community in which it operates.

405 Odell, Lee, and Dixie Goswami, eds. *Writing in Nonacademic Settings*. New York and London: Guilford Press, 1985.

Fourteen essays describe how to conduct research on writing in the workplace; what such research has found concerning the structure of professional discourse, the use of electronic media, and the social/institutional influences on nonacademic writing; and how such research can influence academic and nonacademic writing instruction. Essays include Stephen Doheny-Farina and Lee Odell, "Ethnographic Research on Writing: Assumptions and Methodology"; Carolyn R. Miller and Jack Selzer, "Special Topics of Argument in Engineering Reports"; Lester Faigley, "Nonacademic Writing: The Social Perspective"; David A. Lauerman, Melvin W. Schroeder, Kenneth Sroka, and E. Roger Stephenson, "Workplace and Classroom: Principles for Designing Writing Courses."

406   Spilka, Rachel, ed. *Writing in the Workplace: New Research Perspectives.* Carbondale: Southern Illinois Univ. Press, 1993.
Nineteen essays report on research in workplace communication based on the social-perspective model and examine implications of recent research for teaching and future research. Includes: Barbara Couture and Jone Rymer, "Situational Exigence: Composing Processes on the Job by Writer's Role and Task Value"; Jamie MacKinnon, "Becoming a Rhetor: Developing Writing Ability in a Mature, Writing-Intensive Organization"; Judy Segal, "Writing and Medicine: Text and Context"; Jennie Dautermann, "Negotiating Meaning in a Hospital Discourse Community"; Graham Smart, "Genre as Community Invention: A Central Bank's Response to Its Executives' Expectations as Readers"; Rachel Spilka, "Influencing Workplace Practice: A Challenge for Professional

Writing Specialists in Academia"; and Stephen Doheny-Farina, "Research as Rhetoric: Confronting the Methodological and Ethical Problems of Research on Writing in Nonacademic Settings."

407   Winsor, Dorothy. "Engineering Writing/Writing Engineering." *CCC,* 41 (1990), 58–70.
We accept the idea that knowledge is shaped by language, but engineers tend to see knowledge as coming from physical reality without textual mediation. Textbooks often reinforce the view of language as merely a means of transmitting information. A study of a veteran mechanical engineer's writing showed, though, that most source documents and his own writing were based on other documents rather than direct observation. Writing about a new engine, the engineer referred not to the engine but to documents reporting the results and interpretations of tests, to technical summaries, and to handouts used in oral reports. Moreover, many of the reports were written in such a way as to suggest that decisions were consistently made in an orderly way on the basis of prior information, rather than on hunches or instinct. These reports reflect the engineers as they imagine themselves to be. Engineering writing, like all writing, constructs the world that the writer can bear to inhabit.

408   Winsor, D. "The Construction of Knowledge in Organizations: Asking the Right Questions about the Challenger." *Journal of Business and Technical Communication,* 4 (1990), 7–20.
Research on communication failures that led to the Challenger explosion asked why those who knew about the faulty O-rings failed to pass the information to decision makers. This question betrays a simplistic notion of knowledge and a conduit model of communication. Knowledge is, in fact, socially conditioned and does not come about, as is usually imagined, by contemplating evidence. The engineers and managers of the Challenger project were using different ideas of what counted as evidence, influenced by factors other than evidence, chiefly by membership in task groups with particular views of the project. Knowledge is not certain. Thus, information—such as that the O-rings were faulty—cannot simply be passed on. Reception of a report does not signify reception of information because information does not con-

vey its own interpretation. The questions to ask in this case concern the rhetorical power to affect communal knowledge, which is the crucial factor. See also Couture [397].

Writing Programs

Writing Program Administration

409 Bishop, Wendy. *Something Old, Something New: College Writing Teachers and Classroom Change.* Carbondale: Southern Illinois Univ. Press, 1990.
Ethnographic study of five writing teachers' responses to a graduate seminar in basic writing pedagogy shows that each assimilated the recommended collaborative method in a different way, as a function of his or her developing identity. Writing program administrators and teacher trainers seeking to implement curricula with a diverse staff need to be aware of the factors that may lead to change and resistance.

410 Connolly, Paul, and Teresa Vilardi, eds. *New Methods in College Writing Programs: Theories in Practice.* New York: MLA, 1986.
Twenty-eight model writing programs are described briefly by their directors. Each entry explains staffing, class and program size, theoretical model, course description, faculty-preparation method, related programs, and strengths and weaknesses. Connolly observes that these programs show a trend toward improvement in teacher training, expansion of cross-curricular responsibility for writing instruction, writing instead of reading as the basis for freshman English courses, school-college collaboration, increased use of proficiency tests, and more writing centers.

411 Hartzog, Carol P. *Composition and the Academy: A Study of Writing Program Administration.* New York: MLA, 1986.
A report on the results of a survey of forty-four writing programs at a variety of colleges and universities, as well as extensive descriptions of the programs at Chapel Hill, University of Pennsylvania, and Harvard. The survey data cover administrative structures, program design, staffing, and campus attitudes toward writing. No single model for success is apparent, but good programs seem to be aided to some degree by writing program alliances within the university, the pedagogical skill and scholarly visibility of the director and staff, and a campus commitment to liberal education. Includes extensive bibliography.

See: Harvey Kail and John Trimbur, "The Politics of Peer Tutoring" [424].

412 Raines, Helon Howell. "Teaching Writing in the Two-Year College." *WPA: Writing Program Administration,* 12 (Winter 1988), 29–37.
A survey of 230 two-year colleges shows that most of their English departments concentrate on teaching writing rather than literature. Writing

courses are not in separate programs, there are few program administrators, and course planning is often done by committee, with individual teachers retaining much classroom autonomy. Writing courses often concentrate on basic skills, academic discourse, and technical or business writing. Most teachers have five courses per semester, three of them in composition, and see themselves primarily as teachers, not researchers. Their lack of familiarity with current professional discourse can make them feel excluded, but university-level writing program administrators would do well to bring them into collaborative projects to draw on their rich stores of pedagogical knowledge.

413   Roy, Alice. "ESL Concerns for Writing Program Administrators: Problems and Policies." *WPA: Writing Program Administration,* 11 (Spring 1988), 17–26.
ESL students may be foreign students planning to return home after college, recent immigrants, or bilingual native students. Current theories of second-language acquisition are similar to current theories of composition for native English speakers, namely, that ESL students need practice in writing to make meaning and to develop strategies for construing meaning rather than grammar drill or audio-lingual work. Linguists tend not to be the best writing teachers for ESL students because they are likely to use a grammar-based approach. Specialists in ESL are better because they bring knowledge of cultural diversity and contrastive rhetoric, but often their training has concentrated on oral communication. ESL students may be best served by composition specialists familiar with college-level reading and writing. Mainstreaming ESL students instead of offering a separate ESL course may offer students more sophisticated instruction and oral practice while benefiting native English speakers by providing cultural diversity. Schools should provide support programs for mainstreamed ESL students rather than track them into courses where English competency may not be needed.

See: Robert C. Small, Jr., and Joseph E. Strzepek, *A Casebook for English Teachers: Dilemmas and Decisions* [298].

414   White, Edward M. *Developing Successful College Writing Programs.* San Francisco: Jossey-Bass, 1989.
Writing program directors seeking to design or redesign a program can plan for organic development by taking a comprehensive view of the many separate activities that constitute a good program. Ten concise chapters examine the campus climate for writing programs (the roles of the English department, the writing program administrator, and the administration), research on existing programs, prevalent teaching methods, course designs, assessment issues and practices, instructor evaluation, administration (setting policies on placement and credit for remedial courses, setting up ESL and writing-across-the-curriculum programs), training and support of faculty, and evaluation of the program.

415   Witte, Stephen P., and Lester Faigley. *Evaluating College Writing Programs.* Carbondale and Edwardsville: Southern Illinois Univ. Press, 1983.

Two models dominate writing program evaluation. The qualitative "expert-opinion approach," used by teams from the Council for Writing Program Administrators, confuses description with evaluation. Moreover, team members sometimes differ greatly in the quality of their "expert" credentials and use disparate evaluation methods. The quantitative approach, used in many pre- and posttest studies (four of which are analyzed here), rests on faulty assumptions about the writing process, does not assess either a program's goals or its administrative structure, and tends to produce data with only local applicability. An adequate theory of program evaluation would allow for both qualitative and quantitative measures in assessing a program's cultural and social context, institutional context, administrative structure, curriculum, and pedagogy. See also Faigley et al. [238].

416 WPA Board of Consultant Evaluators. "Writing Program Evaluation: An Outline for Self-Study." *WPA: Writing Program Administration*, 4 (Winter 1980), 23–28.
A list of seventy-six questions based on the guidelines for WPA Consultant Evaluators covers curriculum (subdivided into courses and goals, syllabus, methods, testing, grading), program administration (institutional and program structure, the writing program administrator's job description), faculty development (current conditions, support), and support services (organization, personnel, administration).

417 *Wyoming Resolution*
Robertson, Linda R., Sharon Crowley, and Frank Lentricchia. "The Wyoming Conference Resolution Opposing Unfair Salaries and Working Conditions for Post-Secondary Teachers of Writing." *CE*, 49 (March 1987), 274–80.

CCCC Committee on Professional Standards for Quality Education. "CCCC Initiatives on the Wyoming Conference Resolution: A Draft Report." *CCC*, 40 (February 1989), 61–72.

MLA Commission on Writing and Literature. "Report of the Commission on Writing and Literature." *Profession 88* (1988), 70–76.
At the 1986 University of Wyoming summer conference on composition and literature, a protest was raised against the generally low professional status of composition scholars and the economic exploitation of many writing teachers. The resolution resulting from this protest calls on the CCCC to formulate standards for the working conditions of postsecondary writing teachers and to prescribe grievance and sanction procedures where these standards are not met. The resolution was unanimously endorsed at the Business Meeting of the 1987 CCCC Convention, and, in response, the CCCC Executive Committee created the Committee on Professional Standards for Quality Education, charged with delineating such standards and developing ways for the CCCC to support efforts at reform. The committee's draft report concludes with appendices on professional organizations and accrediting bodies to which teachers might appeal. At the 1989 CCCC Convention, the Executive Committee promulgated an official statement on profes-

sional standards. This statement offers guidelines on optimal teaching conditions as well as on the placement and evaluation of writing teachers who are tenure-line faculty, graduate students, part-time faculty, and full-time temporary faculty members. This statement also refers positively to the report of the MLA Commission on Writing and Literature, which provides guidelines for evaluating scholarship and professional activities in composition studies.

Writing Centers

418   Brooks, Jeff. "Minimalist Tutoring: Making the Student Do All the Work." *Writing Lab Newsletter*, 15 (February 1991), 1–4.
The tutor's job is not to improve papers (tempting though that is) but to improve writers. To avoid the temptation to edit, the tutor should follow simple rules: sit beside the student, keep the paper close to the student, don't hold a pen or pencil, and have the student read the paper aloud at the start of the conference to reinforce the student's authority and engagement. In addition, be sure to praise something in the paper, ask questions rather than giving suggestions, and, if possible, have students do some writing. Don't allow students to force you to edit: they will ultimately appreciate your refusal to do so.

419   DiPardo, Anne. *A Kind of Passport: A Basic Writing Adjunct Program and the Challenge of Student Diversity.* Urbana, Ill.: NCTE, 1993.
Case studies focus on four basic writers—a Mexican American woman, a Native American woman, an African American man, and a recently arrived Salvadoran man—and on the adjuncts assigned to them for tutorial support—two more accomplished undergraduate writers, an African American woman and a European American woman. Their struggles and successes suggest that the tensions aroused by campus diversity and educational-opportunity programs should be discussed openly by faculty and students, that basic writers need help finding personal meaning in the academic work in a cultural environment that is often unfamiliar or hostile, and that peer tutors need to extablish their role as facilitators without being undermined by student resistance or riding roughshod over it.

420   Harris, Muriel. "Talking in the Middle: Why Writers Need Writing Tutors." *CE*, 57 (1995), 27–42.
Tutoring should not be seen as an extension of other forms of instruction. In the one-to-one experience of working with a tutor, student writers gain knowledge that does not arise in other settings. The tutor is a middleperson mediating between the teacher and the student, a role teachers cannot truly take. The tutorial relationship is, moreover, flexible and conversational and therefore more personal than classroom interaction. Students feel helped rather than instructed by the tutor. Writing-center evaluations show that students prefer to do their own work, to reach their own conclusions—again, a situation not usually available in a class setting. Talking to a teacher, students feel pressured to perform rather than to think freely, as they can with a tutor. In the

tutoring experience, students actually write, reread, and revise, gaining practical knowledge in collaboration with the tutor. Students can also express anxiety with a tutor, rarely if at all with a teacher. In their intermediate position, tutors are able to interpret academic language and ease the transition to a new discourse community. In short, writing instruction without a writing center would lack activities essential for students to mature as writers.

See: Muriel Harris, *Teaching One-to-One: The Writing Conference* [242].

421 Harris, Jeannette, and Joyce Kinkead, eds. *Writing Centers in Context: Twelve Case Studies.* Urbana, Ill.: NCTE, 1993.
Twelve circumstantial descriptions of working writing centers provide concrete details about how centers work. Each description follows the same outline: history, physical description (including a floor plan), chronology of a typical day, clientele, selection and training of tutors, types of services (including tutoring, testing, computers, WAC, etc.), administration (management, staff, budget), evaluation, research, and plans for the future. Centers described are at Purdue, Medgar Evers College, University of Toledo, Lehigh University, University of Southern California, Harvard, University of Puget Sound, Johnson County Community College, University of Washington, Utah State, and Colorado State. A concluding essay by Kinkead examines themes raised in the text. Includes bibliography and index.

422 Healy, Dave. "Countering the Myth on (In)dependence: Developing Life-Long Clients." *Writing Lab Newsletter*, 18 (1994), 1–3.
Metaphors of writing centers as clinics and clients as diseased cast the center as a place that should cure and discharge the client. One who returns is not fully cured. Although these metaphors have been thoroughly criticized, we still assume that the goal of the center is to make the client independent, to leave the center and not return. Those who do return signal the center's failure. But this view misrepresents the center's mission. Centers are not storehouses dispensing knowledge, but Burkean parlors where writers can discuss writing and get feedback. Writing, we know, is ongoing collaboration. The image of the solitary writer is a throwback. Why stigmatize those who seek the presence of others? A place where talk about writing occurs should hardly be seen as a place where there is an impoverished understanding of writing.

423 Hult, Christine, and Joyce Kinkead, eds. Writing Centers Online, a special issue of *Computers and Composition*, 12.2 (1995).
Twelve essays comprise this special issue, including: Jane Nelson and Cynthia Wambeam, "Moving Computers into the Writing Center: The Path to Least Resistance"; Muriel Harris and Michael Pemberton, "Online Writing Labs (OWLS): A Taxonomy of Options and Issues"; David Coogan, "E-Mail Tutoring, a New Way to Do New Work"; Irene Clark, "Information Literacy and the Writing Center"; Gail Wood, "Making the Transition from ASL [American Sign Language] to English: Deaf Students, Computers, and the Writing Center"; and Cindy Johanek and Rebecca Rickly, "Online Tutor Training: Synchronous Conferencing in a Professional Community."

424   Kail, Harvey, and John Trimbur. "The Politics of Peer Tutoring."
       WPA: Writing Program Administration, 11 (Fall 1987), 5–12.
       Peer tutoring may be based in the writing center or in the curriculum.
       The writing-center model makes tutoring voluntary and open with re-
       gard to the stage of writing or questions addressed. Its success depends
       on publicity and image. In the curriculum-based model, tutoring is re-
       quired of writing students. More students see tutors this way, and the
       program is easier to administer. But in the curriculum-based model, tu-
       tors are part of the institution and share its authority, and this situation
       inhibits collaboration. The writing-center model is superior in this re-
       gard. Writing-center collaboration also challenges institutional authority
       and may demystify the institution's ideology of knowledge delivery.

425   Konstant, Shoshana Beth. "Multi-Sensory Tutoring for Multi-
       Sensory Learners." *Writing Lab Newsletter,* 16 (May–June 1992),
       6–8.
       Learning disabled students—who are of average intelligence but have
       perceptual or processing problems—require a bit more creativity from
       tutors. First, find the student's strongest perceptual channel—visual,
       auditory, or kinesthetic. Many LD students know their best learning
       style or channel, so ask first. For visual learners, use charts, diagrams,
       colors, and gestures; for auditory learners, read aloud, use the tape re-
       corder, and encourage the student to record classes and assignments; for
       kinesthetic learners, use physical objects and act out ideas. But don't be
       formulaic. Try a variety of approaches, use whatever works, and be pa-
       tient.

426   Lunsford, Andrea. "Collaboration, Control, and the Idea of a
       Writing Center." *Writing Center Journal,* 12 (1991), 3–10.
       The idea of collaboration is based on a view of knowledge as socially
       constructed. Collaboration threatens the idea of the writing center as a
       storehouse of knowledge that prescribes skills and strategies to individ-
       ual learners, given that the storehouse approach incorporates the
       assumption that knowledge is external and accessible. Collaboration
       also threatens the idea of the center as a writer's garret because that ap-
       proach incorporates the assumption that knowledge is interior, within
       the student. Both kinds of center do good work, but we must acknowl-
       edge the superiority of collaboration as a model of real-world writing,
       as an aid in problem solving and to critical thinking, and as a route to
       excellence. Collaborative centers are difficult to create because they re-
       quire appropriate tasks and group cooperation. But the need to help
       students learn to work with others is paramount. Collaborative centers
       engage students not only in solving problems set by teachers, but in
       identifying problems for themselves, negotiating issues of control, and
       valuing diversity.

427   Maxwell, Martha, ed. *When Tutor Meets Student.* 2nd ed. Ann
       Arbor: Univ. of Michigan Press, 1994.
       Fifty-four stories of tutoring encounters by student writing tutors at UC Ber-
       keley. The tutors describe tutoring sessions and the process of defining their
       roles, dealing with cultural diversity and gender difference, and learning
       from their experiences. The stories, addressed to new tutors, reveal successes

and failures, insights, techniques, personal dilemmas, and awkward situations (plagiarism, unwanted advances, problems with a teacher, tutor dependency). Includes, in appendices, descriptions of and paperwork for the UC Berkeley peer-tutoring center.

428 Meyer, Emily, and Louise Z. Smith. *The Practical Tutor.* New York: Oxford Univ. Press, 1987.

Experienced writers who serve as tutors may take for granted the very skills most difficult for inexperienced writers to attain. The fourteen chapters of this textbook lead tutors through sets of problems and strategies for dealing with them: establishing a tutorial dialogue that maintains trust; dealing with anger and frustration; avoiding evaluation; using open-ended questions; promoting fluency through heuristics; deepening critical analysis and concept formation; using teachers' comments productively during revision; reclaiming the writer's authority over the text; addressing sentence-level errors, punctuation, spelling, vocabulary, and dialect-based errors; helping writers to develop reading strategies; and tutoring with computers. Writing assignments, suggestions for class activities, and a bibliography end each chapter.

429 Mullin, Joan, and Ray Wallace, eds. *Intersections: Theory-Practice in the Writing Center.* Urbana, Ill.: NCTE, 1994.

Fifteen essays explore and critique composition theories, particularly those concerning collaboration, as they have been and might be applied to writing-center practices. Included are: Eric Hobson, "Writing Center Practice Often Counters Its Theory. So What?"; Sallyanne Fitzgerald, "Collaborative Learning and Whole Language Theory"; Christina Murphy, "The Writing Center and Social Constructionist Theory"; Alice Gillan, "Collaborative Learning Theory and Peer Tutoring Practice"; Julie Neff, "Learning Disabilities and the Writing Center"; Muriel Harris, "Individualized Instruction in Writing Centers: Attending to Cross-Cultural Differences"; Jay Jacoby, "'The Use of Force': Medical Ethics and Center Practice"; and Mary Abascal-Hildegrand, "Tutor and Student Relations: Applying Gadamer's Notions of Translation."

430 Murphy, Christina, and Joe Law, eds. *Landmark Essays on Writing Centers.* Davis, Calif.: Hermagoras Press, 1995.

Writing centers have had a place in American universities since the 1930s, and their methods have generally followed the theoretical directions of the profession as a whole. Twenty-one previously published essays examine the history, theory, and praxis of writing centers, including: Lou Kelly, "One-on-One, Iowa City Style: Fifty Years of Individualized Writing Instruction"; Muriel Harris, "What's Up and What's In: Trends and Traditions in Writing Centers"; Gary Olson and Evelyn Ashton-Jones, "Writing Center Directors: The Search for Professional Status"; Judith Summerfield, "Writing Centers: A Long View"; Stephen North, "The Idea of a Writing Center"; Kenneth Bruffee, "Peer Tutoring and the 'Conversation of Mankind'" (see [126]); Lisa Ede, "Writing as a Social Process: A Theoretical Foundation for Writing Centers?"; Andrea Lunsford, "Collaboration, Control, and the Idea of a Writing Center"; Marilyn Cooper, "Really Useful Knowledge: A Cultural Studies Agenda for Writing Centers"; Harvey Kail and John

Trimbur, "The Politics of Peer Tutoring"; and Meg Woolbright, "The Politics of Tutoring: Feminism within the Patriarchy."

See: Marie Nelson, *At the Point of Need* [385].

431   North, Stephen M. "The Idea of a Writing Center." *CE,* 46 (September 1984), 433–46. Rpt. in Graves [285].
English-department faculty have a false sense of what goes on in the writing center. This makes it difficult to dispel their notion of the center as a fix-it shop that deals with "special problems" in composition, corrects mechanical errors, and serves only poor writers. Such ideas created the skill-and-drill model that most writing centers have battled to escape. Writing centers attempt to produce better writers, not better writing, through a student-centered, process-oriented approach, which chiefly means talking to writers about writing. Teachers should not send students to the center—students must come when they are ready to talk about writing. Writing centers are gaining recognition, but institutional and faculty support leave much room for improvement.

432   Olson, Gary A., ed. *Writing Centers: Theory and Administration.* Urbana, Ill.: NCTE, 1984.
Nineteen essays on theory, administration, and special concerns include Kenneth A. Bruffee, "Peer Tutoring and the 'Conversation of Mankind'" (see [126]); Stephen M. North, "Writing Center Research: Testing Our Assumptions"; Patrick Hartwell, "The Writing Center and the Paradoxes of Written-Down Speech"; Linda Bannister-Wills, "Developing a Peer Tutor Program"; and Alexander Friedlander, "Meeting the Needs of Foreign Students in the Writing Center."

433   Simpson, Jeanne. "The Challenge of Innovation: Putting New Approaches into Practice." *Writing Lab Newsletter*, 18 (September 1993), 1–3.
Writing centers face, like the rest of the academy, threats of budget cuts and calls for accountability. It would be a mistake to be defensive in this situation. Rather, we should see opportunities here. It is important to participate in the processes of institutional change. The growth of writing centers so far has come from steady work and innovation, not from revolution, a process to be continued in the new era. We must tell our stories better to all academic constituencies, connecting with institutional governance in ways that are presently not typical. Institutional service has not been seen as part of the career path for center directors, but it is the path of change.

434   Wolff, William C. "Annotated Bibliography of Scholarship on Writing Centers and Related Topics." *Focuses,* annually.
Comprehensive listing of items, all briefly annotated, on writing-center issues as well as a wide range of theoretical and pedagogical concerns. Published annually.

Writing across the Curriculum

435   Anderson, Worth, Cynthia Best, Alycia Black, John Hurst, Brandt Miller, and Susan Miller. "Cross-Curricular Underlife: A Collabo-

rative Report on Ways with Academic Words." *CCC,* 41 (February 1990), 11–36.

Five students and their teacher observed language use in several courses, discovering how it differed from the freshman-composition image of academic discourse. Teachers and students did not seem to form discourse communities but maintained separate views of their roles and of appropriate language use. The writing course did prepare students to analyze and imitate writing in other courses, but its model of collaborative knowledge making did not match the practice in other courses. Recording their motives for taking courses, enrollment and attendance, and types of writing assigned for each of sixteen courses, the students describe teachers', students', and their own uses of language for learning—or, rather, for succeeding in each class. There were few formal assignments; the audience approach taught in the writing course did help students decide what was called for in each class in all language interactions. Note taking was the writing skill most needed in all courses.

436   Anson, Chris M., John E. Schwiebert, and Michael M. Williamson. *Writing across the Curriculum: An Annotated Bibliography.* Westport, Conn.: Greenwood, 1993.

A bibliography of 1067 items, with annotations of about 50 words each, in eleven categories. Part One, on scholarship, is subdivided into bibliographies, collections, history and implementation, research studies, and theory. Part Two, on pedagogy, is subdivided into general, arts and humanities, math and science, social science, business and economics, and textbooks.

437   Bazerman, Charles, and David R. Russell, eds. *Landmark Essays on Writing across the Curriculum.* Davis, Calif.: Hermagoras Press, 1994.

Thirteen essays on history, programs, pedagogy, and writing in disciplines, including: Bazerman and Russell, "The Rhetorical Tradition and Specialized Discourses"; David Russell, "American Origins of the Writing-across-the-Curriculum Movement"; Toby Fulwiler, "How Well Does Writing across the Curriculum Work?" [440]; James Kinneavy, "Writing across the Curriculum" [444]; Susan McLeod, "Writing across the Curriculum: The Second Stage, and Beyond"; Jane Emig, "Writing as a Mode of Learning" [184]; Charles Bazerman, "What Written Knowledge Does" [111]; and Greg Myers, "The Social Construction of Two Biologists' Proposals."

438   Blair, Catherine Pastore. "Only One of the Voices: Dialogic Writing across the Curriculum." *CE,* 50 (April 1988), 383–89.

The social theory of knowledge that informs the writing-across-the-curriculum movement suggests that each academic discipline has its own way of using language, which makes sense only in the disciplinary context. The discipline of English studies knows only its own discourse, not all the others, and not some generic academic discourse. There is, therefore, no reason to entrust all writing instruction to the English department. A better writing-across-the-curriculum program would be taught by professors from all disciplines, whose dialogues over the common writing curriculum would reveal the discursive properties of each discipline in contrast to the others. Composition specialists could serve as consultants to such programs. See Smith [450].

439   Fulwiler, Toby. "The Argument for Writing across the Curriculum." In *Writing across the Disciplines: Research into Practice*. Ed. Art Young and Toby Fulwiler. Upper Montclair, N.J.: Boynton/Cook, 1986.

Three principles that underlie writing across the curriculum should be elaborated in faculty workshops: that composing is a complex intellectual process of making choices and making meaning; that writing is a mode of learning that calls for expressive as well as transactional composing; and that writing problems arise from a variety of sources, including attitude, skills, and knowledge. Two pedagogical issues are also at issue in workshops: making good assignments and evaluating or responding to student writing. Good assignment design includes setting up a context, allowing time for the composing process, varying the audience, and giving clear directions. Evaluation should, among other things, be positive and specific and focus on content.

440   Fulwiler, Toby. "How Well Does Writing across the Curriculum Work?" *CE*, 46 (February 1984), 113–25. Rpt. in Art Young and Toby Fulwiler, eds., *Writing across the Disciplines*. Upper Montclair, N.J.: Boynton/Cook, 1986.

The interdisciplinary writing workshops at Michigan Technological University introduced the idea that writing can promote learning in all areas. After six years, the program seems to have enjoyed uneven success. Problems have included misunderstanding of special terminology (chiefly "expressive writing"); resistance by suspicious faculty members; conflicts with some members of the English and philosophy departments about language theory; inability to apply the ideas generated in the workshops to some classes, especially large ones; distrust of the peer-review technique and lack of commitment to methods that require it; and lack of reinforcement by the administration. But benefits have included the growth of a community of scholars, a general sense that the program has helped improve students' ability to communicate, more writing by faculty members in the program, greater sensitivity to pedagogy, development of collaborative projects among participants in the program, and more cohesion in the writing department itself.

441   Fulwiler, Toby, and Art Young, eds. *Language Connections: Writing and Reading across the Curriculum*. Urbana, Ill.: NCTE, 1982.

Twelve essays describe the writing-across-the-curriculum program at Michigan Technological University. Essays include Toby Fulwiler, "The Personal Connection: Journal Writing across the Curriculum"; Toby Fulwiler and Robert Jones, "Assigning and Evaluating Transactional Writing"; Peter Schiff, "Responding to Writing: Peer Critiques, Teacher-Student Conferences, and Essay Evaluation"; Diana Freisinger and Jill Burkland, "Talking about Writing: The Role of the Writing Lab"; and Bruce Petersen, "A Select Bibliography" (annotated).

442   Griffin, C. Williams, ed. *Teaching Writing in All Disciplines*. San Francisco: Jossey-Bass, 1982.

Ten essays on writing-across-the-curriculum programs, teaching writing in disciplines other than English, and teaching techniques for using writing as learning include Toby Fulwiler, "Writing: An Act of Cognition"; Barbara King, "Using Writing in the Mathematics Class: Theory and Practice"; Dean Drenk, "Teaching Finance Through Writing"; and Elaine P. Maimon, "Writing across the Curriculum: Past, Present, and Future" [447].

443   Herrington, Anne, and Charles Moran, eds. *Writing, Teaching, and Learning in the Disciplines.* New York: MLA, 1992.

Fourteen essays examine the history, theoretical coherence, and pedagogical practices of writing across the curriculum, including: Nancy Martin, "Language across the Curriculum: Where It Began and What It Promises"; David Russell, "American Origins of the Writing-across-the-Curriculum Movement"; James Britton, "Theories of the Disciplines and a Learning Theory"; Charles Bazerman, "From Cultural Criticism to Disciplinary Participation: Living with Powerful Words"; Jacqueline Jones Royster, "From Practice to Theory: Writing across the Disciplines at Spelman College"; Toby Fulwiler, "Writing and Learning American Literature"; Joy Marsella, Thomas Hilgers, and Clemence McLaren, "How Students Handle Writing Assignments: A Study of Eighteen Responses in Six Disciplines"; Louise Dunlap, "Advocacy and Neutrality: A Contradiction in the Discourse of Urban Planners"; and Anne Herrington and Charles Moran, "Writing in the Disciplines: A Prospect."

444   Kinneavy, James L. "Writing across the Curriculum." *ADE Bulletin,* 76 (Winter 1983), 14–21.

Writing across the curriculum responds to concerns about declining literacy and reasserts the importance of rhetoric in the liberal arts curriculum. Writing across the curriculum takes two forms: writing-intensive courses in all departments, and courses in writing for other disciplines offered by the English or writing department. In the first kind of program, the teacher is an expert in the discipline and knows its vocabulary and genres. Students can thus use highly technical language and discipline-specific forms of writing. But such programs reinforce disciplinary isolation and create a heavy burden of writing instruction for teachers untrained in composition. In the second kind of program, esoteric material, technical vocabulary, subtle methodology, and distinctiveness may be sacrificed, but with gains in writing expertise and an opportunity to open a large academic conversation and perhaps, ultimately, an educated public discourse. A well-designed program benefits from both approaches by offering different kinds of writing courses "vertically" throughout the college experience.

445   Kirscht, Judy, Rhonda Levine, and John Reiff. "Evolving Paradigms: WAC and the Rhetoric of Inquiry." *CCC,* 45 (October 1994), 369–80.

The WAC movement continues to be divided between the writing-to-learn model—in which writing is seen as an integral part of the learning process in all disciplines—and the writing-in-the-disciplines model—which studies the discourse communities of the disciplines and brings that knowledge to the writing class. WAC proponents are deeply divided along these lines. The social-constructionist view of disciplines as rhetorically negotiated territory resolves the conflict by treating writing-to-learn as an inquiry into the ways that knowledge is produced in the disciplines. Disciplinary forms and conventions are not separated from the writing process but are presented as communally accepted ways of looking at a particular subject matter, forms that can then be analyzed to determine how they shape the knowledge they produce.

446   Maimon, Elaine P. "Maps and Genres: Exploring Connections in the Arts and Sciences." In *Composition and Literature: Bridging the Gap.* Ed. Winifred Bryan Horner [323].

We need to know the forms and traditions of writing in all disciplines in order to fill in the largely uncharted territory we label "nonfiction prose" on our maps of the genres of writing. Trained in literary criticism, we are well suited to exploring the relation of discipline-specific genres to modes of thought in the discipline. Just as the lyric poet writes within and against the structure of his genre, so too the scientist works through the conventions, rituals, and assumptions of lab reports and other genres. Writing students should understand the concept of genre and practice several academic genres. The "modes of discourse" and "composing process" approaches may obscure questions of audience, purpose, and disciplinary method—questions that concern writing as it is used in the academic community—but these approaches can lead to writing that does enter the academic conversation.

447   Maimon, Elaine P. "Writing across the Curriculum: Past, Present, and Future." In *Teaching Writing in All Disciplines.* Ed. C. Williams Griffin [442].

The development of writing-across-the-curriculum programs has been an effort to make writing an integral part of the learning process in all courses. This effort reinforced the shift in composition pedagogy from a product to a process orientation because the learning process and the writing process work together. Writing across the curriculum has also promoted collaborative-learning techniques. Process pedagogy requires many drafts and much feedback, and small groups of students can provide each other with audience feedback that may be even more valuable than the teacher's responses. Writing-across-the-curriculum programs are helping students find "an authentic voice in the community of educated people."

448   Martin, Nancy, ed. *Writing across the Curriculum Pamphlets: A Selection from the Schools Council and London University Institute of Education Joint Project: Writing across the Curriculum.* 1973, 1974, 1975. Rpt. Upper Montclair, N.J.: Boynton/Cook, 1983.

James Britton's colleagues, who worked with British schoolchildren of elementary- and high-school age, offer assignment suggestions and samples of student writing. Included are Nancy Martin, Peter Medway, and Harold Smith, "From Information to Understanding: What Children Do with New Ideas"; Nancy Martin, Peter Medway, Harold Smith, and Pat D'Arcy, "Why Write?"; Peter Medway, "From Talking to Writing"; Pat D'Arcy, "Keeping Options Open: Writing in the Humanities"; and selections from *Writing in Science* (essays by Sue Watts and Jeff

Shapland) and *Language and Learning in the Humanities* (essays by
Bryan Newton, and Peter Medway and Ivor Goodson).

449   McLeod, Susan, and Margot Soven, eds. *Writing across the
Curriculum: A Guide to Developing Programs.* Newbury Park,
Calif.: Sage, 1992.
Twelve essays on the practical elements of setting up and developing
WAC programs, including: Barbara Walvoord, "Getting Started"; Joyce
Neff Magnetto and Barbara Stout, "Faculty Workshops"; Linda Peter-
son, "Writing across the Curriculum and/in the Freshman English
Program"; Christine Farris and Raymond Smith, "Writing-Intensive
Courses: Tools for Curricular Change"; Christopher Thaiss, "WAC and
General Education Courses"; Muriel Harris, "The Writing Center and
Tutoring in WAC Programs"; and Tori Haring-Smith, "Changing Stu-
dents' Attitudes: Writing Fellows Programs."

See: David Russell, *Writing in the Academic Disciplines, 1870–1990* [105].

450   Smith, Louise Z. "Why English Departments Should 'House'
Writing across the Curriculum" *CE,* 50 (April 1988), 390–95.
Catherine Blair's account [438] of writing-across-the-curriculum theory
is correct. She errs, however, in asserting that English departments can
know only their own discipline-specific discourse. Postmodern literary
theory blurs disciplinary boundaries by analyzing the influence of canonical cultural artifacts on the supposedly value-neutral discourse of
other academic disciplines and by denying the distinction between literary and nonliterary language. Thus, English departments contain many
scholars, including composition specialists, who have expertise in examining the relationship between language and knowledge and how
these relationships might be taught. The authoritative influence of compositionists may be necessary to prevent mere editing across the
curriculum even as we learn about disciplinary discourses from novice
writing teachers from other departments.

Computers and Composition

451   Bolter, Jay David. *Writing Space: The Computer, Hypertext, and the
History of Writing.* Hillside, N.J.: Lawrence Erlbaum, 1991.
Writing is a technology inseparable from the materials and techniques
of writing. Forms of text—scroll, codex book, electronic text—
determine the organization and presentation of knowledge. Print books
make text seem permanent and widen the gap between text and author.
Electronic text does the opposite: the reader organizes, shapes, and adds
to text, calls up other texts from databases, and creates a unique text in
the process of reading. Print text must impose a hierarchy on ideas, reducing the typically associative writing process to linear form.
Hypertext restores associative composing and requires associative
reading through the layering of text. It comprises a network of verbal
ideas. Electronic text recalls older forms of literacy, using picture writing in its icons, and restoring the formulaic, associative, and dynamic
qualities of oral literature. Electronic texts dissolve into parts to be re-

combined and merge into larger textual structures, disrupting the traditional notion of authorship. Electronic fiction takes advantage of these qualities, offering a multitude of paths for the reader to travel. The plurality of the text and the disappearance of the author, imagined by innovative authors and critical theorists, are realized in electronic texts.

452 Handa, Carolyn, ed. *Computers and Community: Teaching Composition in the Twenty-First Century.* Portsmouth, N.H.: Boynton/Cook, 1990.

Nine essays, five on teaching and four on theory, describe and explore the changes to pedagogy and classroom structure wrought by computerized classrooms: enhanced collaboration, a stonger sense of community and audience, less focus on the teacher as reader, more fun with writing. Essays include: Thomas Barker and Fred Kemp, "Network Theory: A Postmodern Pedagogy for the Writing Classroom"; Carolyn Boiarsky, "Computers in the Classroom: The Instruction, the Mess, the Noise, the Writing"; Kathleen Skubikowski and John Elder, "Computers and the Social Contexts of Writing"; Mary Flores, "Computer Conferencing: Composing a Feminist Community of Writers"; and Carolyn Handa, "Politics, Ideology, and Strange, Slow Death of the Isolated Composer or Why We Need Community in the Writing Classroom."

453 Holdstein, Deborah, and Cynthia L. Selfe, eds. *Computers and Writing: Theory, Research, Practice.* New York: MLA, 1990.

Ten essays address problems associated with computers and writing, such as software selection, staffing, control of equipment and facilities, and courseware development. Helen Schwartz argues in "Ethical Considerations of Educational Computer Use" that the inflexibility of software affects teacher-student interactions, that teachers are responsible for training as well as using software, that student ownership of texts in networks must be protected, that program limitations may cause miseducation, that software piracy must be prevented, and that access to technology must be spread as widely as possible. In "A Limitation on the Use of Computers in Composition," David N. Dobrin maintains that text processors are reliable and make no claims to give advice or analyze meaning, but that style analyzers, idea processors, and invention programs do not live up to their claims and are of little use. Michael Spitzer, in "Local and Global Networking: Implications for the Future," discusses how recognition of the capabilities of different kinds of networks facilitates selection of a variety of opportunities for collaborative writing, such as coauthorship, text swapping, conferencing, teacher coaching, and research.

454 Selfe, Cynthia L., and Susan Hilligoss, eds. *Literacy and Computers: The Complications of Teaching and Learning with Technology.* New York: MLA, 1994.

The twenty essays here "foreground the political, social, and economic character of literacy education; the roles of authors and of readers; the nature of interpretation and subjectivity" (2) and discuss the effects of technology on literacy within those contexts. Included are: Billie Wahlstrom, "Communication and Technology: Defining a Feminist Presence in Research and Practice"; Johndan Johnson-Eilola, "Reading and Writing in Hypertext: Vertigo and Euphoria"; Davida Charney, "The Effect of Hypertext on Processes of Reading and Writing"; L. M. Dryden, "Literature, Student-Centered Classrooms, and Hypermedia"; and David Dobrin, "Hype and Hypertext."

455 Tuman, Myron C., ed. *Literacy Online: The Promise (and Peril) of Reading and Writing with Computers.* Pittsburgh: Univ. of Pittsburgh Press, 1992.

Ten essays in five sections on computers and new forms of texts, teaching, critical thought, administrative control, and knowledge. Includes: Jay David Bolter, "Literature in the Electronic Writing Space"; Helen Schwartz, "'Dominion Everywhere': Computers as Cultural Artifacts"; Stanley Aronowitz, "Looking Out: The Impact of Computers on the Lives of Professionals"; Eugene Provenzo, Jr., "The Electronic Panopticon: Censorship Control, and Indoctrination in a Post-Typographic Culture"; and Richard Lanham, "Digital Rhetoric: Theory, Practice, and Property."

Index of Authors Cited